Innovative Business Management Using TRIZ

Also available from ASQ Quality Press:

Navigating the Minefield: A Practical KM Companion
Patricia Lee Eng and Paul J. Corney

We Move Our Own Cheese!: A Business Fable About Championing Change
Victor E. Sower and Frank K. Fair

Musings on Internal Quality Audits: Having a Greater Impact
Duke Okes

The Magic of ISO 9001: How to Make It Fully Materialize
John F. Graham

The Quality Toolbox, Second Edition
Nancy R. Tague

Root Cause Analysis: Simplified Tools and Techniques, Second Edition
Bjørn Andersen and Tom Fagerhaug

The Certified Six Sigma Green Belt Handbook, Second Edition
Roderick A. Munro, Govindarajan Ramu, and Daniel J. Zrymiak

The Certified Manager of Quality/Organizational Excellence Handbook, Fourth Edition
Russell T. Westcott, editor

The Certified Six Sigma Black Belt Handbook, Third Edition
T. M. Kubiak and Donald W. Benbow

The ASQ Auditing Handbook, Fourth Edition
J.P. Russell, editor

The ASQ Quality Improvement Pocket Guide: Basic History, Concepts, Tools, and Relationships
Grace L. Duffy, editor

Innovative Business Management Using TRIZ

Sunil Kumar V. Kaushik

ASQ Quality Press
Milwaukee • Wisconsin

American Society for Quality, Quality Press, Milwaukee 53203
 Published 2017
Printed in the United States of America
23 22 21 20 19 18 17 5 4 3 2 1

Library of Congress Cataloging-in-Publication Data

Names: Kaushik, Sunil Kumar V., 1983– author.
Title: Innovative business management using TRIZ / Sunil Kumar V. Kaushik.
Description: Milwaukee, Wisconsin : ASQ Quality Press, [2018] | Includes bibliographical references and index.
Identifiers: LCCN 2017050122 | ISBN 9780873899642 (soft cover : alk. paper)
Subjects: LCSH: Problem solving. | Decision making. | Product management. | Industrial management.
Classification: LCC HD30.29 .K385 2018 | DDC 658.4/03—dc23
LC record available at https://lccn.loc.gov/2017050122

ISBN: 978-0-87389-964-2

Ray Zielke: Director, Quality Press and Programs
Paul Daniel O'Mara: Managing Editor
Randall L. Benson: Sr. Creative Services Specialist

ASQ Mission: The American Society for Quality advances individual, organizational, and community excellence worldwide through learning, quality improvement, and knowledge exchange.

Printed on acid-free paper

Quality Press
600 N. Plankinton Ave.
Milwaukee, WI 53203-2914
E-mail: authors@asq.org
The Global Voice of Quality®

I dedicate this book to those wonderful human beings who welcomed us with open arms into their homes during our 500 days on the road, with no money, in 21 countries where this book was written.

I dedicate this book to my mother, brother, family, and friends, who all provided moral support while we were on the road.

I dedicate this book to my lovely wife Yuka Yokozawa, who made sure I did not lose focus throughout this project, and took on the responsibility of making sure I had shelter and food and provided the small comforts that I craved during our 500 days on the road creating this book.

Table of Contents

List of Figures and Tables

Acknowledgments

Throughout my career I have worked with many and have made many friends who have directly or indirectly contributed to this book. This book would be incomplete if I do not mention them

Georgios Zampetas—While in Turkey I got in touch with George who at that time held a senior position at ASQ and hosted several TRIZ workshops in Greece. From then on he has been a student, mentor, friend, guide and everything. We are now collaborating and writing our next book on TRIZ.

Dr. Annabelle Palladas—She is another active member of ASQ who invited me to conduct a workshop at her company and made sure I enjoyed my stay in Greece. From then on we have been very close friends and well-wishers. We are discussing to collaborate and publish our book on Lean.

Dr. Danut Iorga—Dan invited me to give a talk in Bucharest institute of Economic studies for the PhD students on TRIZ. He is a Master Black Belt and an expert in statistics. I have learnt a lot from him and he is another author along with George in our book about TRIZ.

Prof George Bohoris—I met George Bohoris when he invited me to conduct a workshop at the University of Piraeus and in that six-hour workshop the students came up with an innovation which got published as a white paper which has been included in this book.

Baba Varanasi and Mandeep Attri—Baba is Deputy General Manager and Mandeep is a Associate Director in Innovation and Quality for Fortune 500 company. We worked together and they have been inspiring me with their creative entrepreneurial ideas and thoughts, which helped in me staying focused and think beyond my limits.

Gloria Graves—When she read one of my papers on running Six Sigma projects 100 times faster, she got in touch with me to conduct a workshop for her steel company. That was one of my short and interesting remote consulting assignments and a huge learning. She also was a generous donor for my trip.

George Assimacopoulos—He was a participant in my workshop and during a session when I explained the TRIZ contradiction matrix he immediately said it would be a very useful tool in creating QFD, which I had not thought till then and I included it as a chapter in this book.

Adam Wise—I worked closely with Adam for more than three years where he edited all my published articles for ASQ, many of which are included in this book.

Paul O'Mara—I wouldn't be lying if I say 50% of the effort in releasing this book was from Paul, the editor and project manager for this book. He never missed a schedule (though I did many times) and did a tremendous turnover in correcting all the grammar, punctuation, and so on and gave life.

Paulo Sampaio—I contacted Paulo before coming to Portugal to conduct a workshop on TRIZ. Though he was unavailable, between his busy schedule he organized a workshop through APQ. Now I am offering a 40-hour course on TRIZ at his university MINHO.

Costas Papaikonomou—Costas is the founder of happen.com and one of the most innovative individuals I have come across. We met in a conference at Athens and he helped in providing many examples for this book.

Valeri Souchkov—Valeri is a TRIZ master himself and when I connected on Linkedin to use some of his material for this book, he did not think twice and gave more than I needed.

Cesar Remartinez Martinez—Cesar is a ASQ country councilor for Spain and organized a workshop for me in Barcelona in a very short notice.

Preface

In 2015 my wife and I set out on a round-the-world bicycle tour, cycling through 21 countries, including Thailand, Laos, Vietnam, China, Kyrgyzstan, Uzbekistan, Turkmenistan, Iran, Turkey, Georgia, Armenia, Greece, Italy, France, Spain, and Portugal, on a budget of less than five dollars a day. We received generous donations, places to crash in the evening, and food to keep us moving most of the time. This book was written during this journey, on the road, inside tents in the wild, and in the houses of generous unknown families who welcomed us with open arms, irrespective of class, economic status, race, and so on. I got an opportunity to train and consult for private- and public-sector organizations, universities, and startups in all the 21 countries. I conducted close to 50 workshops and training sessions and trained more than 1000 professionals on TRIZ without any remuneration. It was a huge learning experience for me, cutting across different geographies, cultures, practices, and thought processes. I designed the trip using the TRIZ principles, which helped in innovating a method of traveling the world with almost no money and with an Indian passport that has a lot of visa restrictions, finding sponsors, and creating value for our future through this journey.

THE PLANNING

We wanted to go everywhere. Initially, we thought of going to Myanmar so that we didn't need to fly, but some other issues cropped up and we decided to fly to Bangkok. Africa was on our itinerary, but due to the current situation we dropped the idea for the time being. We decided to go with the flow and chart our future course when we reached Portugal. We wanted our plan to be flexible so that we could have more fun on the road. More importantly, we made sure that we would be in our dream country, Iran, in its best season, May.

LAST-MINUTE CHANGE OF PLAN

A month before our trip, we hosted two Malaysian boys traveling on folding bikes. They convinced us that folding bikes were better. We were convinced, but we had already invested our money in touring bicycles and had been using them for a year. Eventually, Sunil also bought into the idea and started thinking of ways of buying folding bikes, as we didn't have any extra money.

Sunil then started sending e-mails and PowerPoint presentations to bicycle manufacturers asking if they would sponsor our cycles. To our surprise, Brompton offered us a huge discount. Two Brompton bikes arrived the day before our trip!

THE PRAYER

I was always fascinated by Indians offering prayer for new vehicles and wanted to do the same. Sunil thought I was crazy (he is not religious), but his mother was happy to help me. I got some lemons, and Sunil's mother arranged for the flowers and the rest. The lemons were crushed under the wheels of the cycle. Three dogs were our witnesses. Sunil folded the bikes and we were ready to hit the road. After taking a flight to Bangkok, of course.

1

Introduction to TRIZ

TRIZ is the Russian acronym for *theory of inventive problem solving.* TRIZ was developed by Russian engineers in the middle of the 20th century in the former Soviet Union to provide a method that would support a process of generating inventive ideas and breakthrough solutions in a systematic way. Until the early 1990s, TRIZ was little known outside the Soviet Union. Once the Soviet Union broke apart, it started to become more and more popular among technology and engineering groups within companies like General Electric, Samsung, and so forth. The basic assumption behind this theory is "Someone somewhere has already solved your problem or a very similar problem, and all we need to do is apply the same principle to the current problem and solve it similarly." This approach saves a lot of time and energy. For example, look at Figure 1.1. You need to identify which thread, A, B or C, leads to the arrow as quickly as possible.

There are many ways to solve this problem. If this problem is given to a kid, they will first start from one of the ends, for example, A, and identify where it leads. If it doesn't lead to the arrow, they will choose B or C, and then if it still doesn't lead to the arrow, they will choose the final thread. This is called the *trial-and-error* method. There is a simpler way to solve this problem: begin from the arrow and the line will lead you to B; problem solved, and the time and effort taken in the process of going through B and C is completely eliminated (see Figure 1.2).

Now the kid has learned a new way of solving a problem. Suppose you give the next puzzle to the same kid, for example, the one shown in Figure 1.3 where the path has to be identified from the key to the main door. Where do you think the kid would start from, the key or the house?

You are correct; for any similar problem from now on, the kid will use the same approach. In TRIZ, we call this principle *inversion.* There are millions of inventions and problems that have been solved in the past,

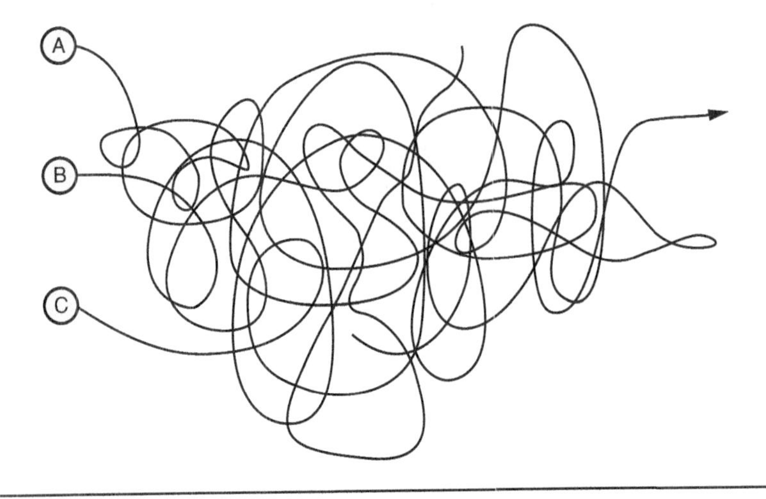

Figure 1.1 Puzzle—connect the thread to the arrow.

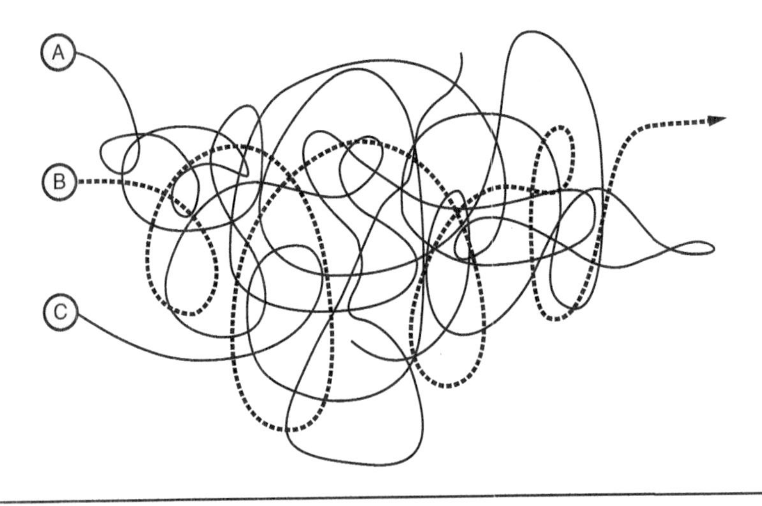

Figure 1.2 Puzzle solution.

but, like the kid, we make the same mistake of going through the trial-and-error method until we finally find the right path, and in the process we lose a lot of time and money. The reason for this is that we do not have visibility to the techniques that were used for similar problems that were solved in the past. This leads to the next problem: among the millions of inventions,

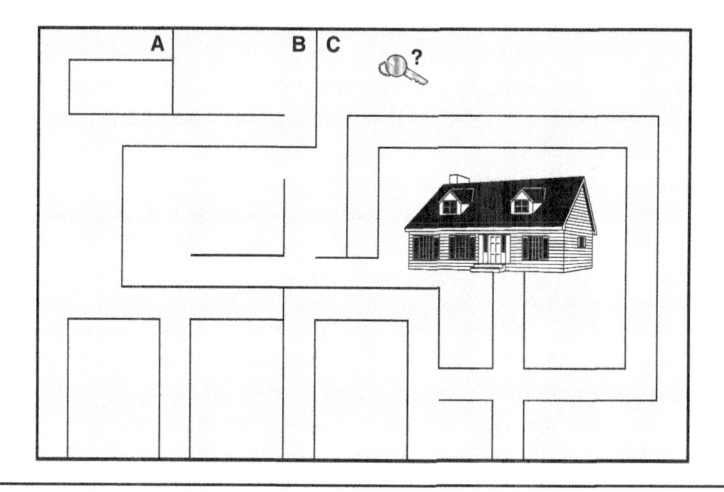

Figure 1.3 Puzzle—trace the path to the house.

how would I know which invention is similar to the problem I am trying to solve?

Like Einstein, Genrich Altshuller (founder of TRIZ) was working as a clerk in a patent office in Russia. He studied 200,000 inventions and identified patterns or common solutions between inventions. TRIZ broke with the traditional convention of creativity and helped create a systematic approach that could make anyone an inventor. He and his peers (mostly engineers) studied more and more technological solutions and invented the TRIZ contradiction matrix. Altshuller was soon imprisoned for political reasons and made to work in harsh labor camps. One of the reasons for his imprisonment is assumed to be that when Joseph Stalin was selling the Germans the invention database for a very low price (assumed to be in exchange for food), Altshuller wrote a letter to Stalin asking him not to sell it. He explained his ideas and TRIZ, and that he knew the Germans had developed a lot inventions, and thus this database was a gold mine. He also told Stalin that Russian engineers had been wasting a lot of time and money in the process of inventing, which hurt Stalin's ego. He sent Altshuller to work in the coal mines. In the labor camp he continued his research further and contributed more to TRIZ.

Every time I conduct a training or workshop, or even start a discussion related to TRIZ, there are common questions. I am sure some of these might be in your head at the moment, and you might be asked these questions in future. Hence, I decided to put them in a question-and-answer format.

1. *Can TRIZ provide a solution to any problem?* Yes and no. TRIZ does not always provide a solution; it provides a few principles that can be used to solve a problem. For example, if you want to reduce project cost without cutting down on resources, TRIZ will not provide you with a set of activities to be done to achieve your cost and resource objectives, but it will provide you with some principles that were used to solve a similar problem so you can then apply them to solve your problem.

2. *So why do I need to use TRIZ?* It guides you to think in a specific direction rather than getting lost. Suppose you have misplaced your house key and you need to search the entire house: four bedrooms, lawn, garage, kitchen, living room, dining room, and bathroom. Would you enjoy it? It's miserable. How would you feel if your son said he saw it in a particular room some time back? Would it not be a big relief? You have narrowed down the problem from the entire house to just one room. But let me also caution you so that you have the right expectation: TRIZ is a tool that helps in the thinking process, but is not a replacement for the thinking process itself.

3. *Can I be an innovator and patent my ideas after reading this book?* Yes and no. Every time I begin a workshop or training or consult, the goal is to have at least one innovation per attendee. You can innovate, and you will definitely be a better problem solver after reading this book. I guarantee it. But what I cannot guarantee is the patenting part, as this is not within our control. There is always a good probability that either someone else before you patented the same innovation, or the innovation does not have commercial value. But still I want you to cherish and celebrate, because you did innovate. Though you are unable to claim the rights, you independently thought the same way as the previous inventor.

4. *Why is TRIZ not as popular as lean or Six Sigma?* The reason is that it was kept a secret in Russia until the Soviet Union broke up in the early 1990s. Then, from the late '90s onward, it did start becoming popular outside Russia. Modern TRIZ is a large body of knowledge combining a theory of solving inventive problems and systems evolution, analytical tools and methods for problem solving and analysis, collections of patterns of solutions, databases of specific effects and technologies, and techniques for creative imagination development.

5. *If TRIZ can solve all problems, do I still need Six Sigma or lean if I am a quality professional?* Yes. While TRIZ can help you execute Six Sigma projects 10 to 50 times faster, Six Sigma has its own benefits. For example, TRIZ can say what principle you need to apply to improve the performance of a process, but to measure it we fall back to Six Sigma. Similarly, lean is a subset of TRIZ principles, as both are thinking methods. But lean comes with ready-to-use tools that work very well with TRIZ. I have executed some Green Belt and Black Belt projects within a few days to several weeks. Normally, a value stream mapping workout takes at least a month: a few weeks for prework, 2–3 days for workout, and a few weeks for implementing the solutions. With the help of TRIZ the entire value stream mapping was done in a couple of days with less effort and time. You will be able to appreciate TRIZ, Six Sigma, and lean and see the differences as we move forward.

6. *Have you invented and patented ideas?* Yes and no. I have invented the TRIZ virtual reality (VR) application called Ideality, which helps organizations to move toward ideality in a fun way. I have invented an idea generation process where hundreds to thousands of ideas for improving a product or service can be generated in minutes through a systematic approach. I have had an opportunity to solve many problems. But I do not patent my ideas as it is not cost-effective as a freelancer with different priorities leading a nomadic life on the road.

7. *Why is TRIZ more popular among engineering professionals and less popular among business and management professionals?* The reason is that TRIZ was created by engineers for engineers. One of the key challenges is that most of the available TRIZ literature uses terminology that is very specific to engineering professionals. In this book, my goal is to take some of these wonderful concepts to nonengineering, specifically management, professionals.

8. *What is the goal of this book?* The goal while penning this book was not to make you a TRIZ master. If that is your expectation, I am sorry, but you will be disappointed, as I am not a TRIZ master myself. My goal is to use some of the simple TRIZ tools to help you immediately solve problems, innovate, be creative, think, and discover the joy of experiencing the thinking process in new dimensions that you might not have previously. I have also tried to limit my scope to help nonengineering and management

professionals to apply the concepts of TRIZ immediately and reap benefits, rather than trying to cover different theories and concepts of TRIZ.

9. *We have DMAIC, DFSS, and other frameworks in Lean Six Sigma; are there any frameworks for TRIZ projects?* Yes. In Six Sigma we convert a practical problem into a statistical problem, look for statistical solutions, convert them into practical solutions, deploy the solutions, and reap the results. Similarly, in TRIZ we define a specific problem and convert it into a generic TRIZ problem, then find a generic TRIZ solution, and lastly convert it into a specific solution and deploy.

10. *Is there a way to derive TRIZ principles using mathematics, logic, or other theories?* No. TRIZ emerged through empirical studies, that is, through observation and experience, and hence so far we do not have any theories that help us derive and explain how TRIZ works the way it works. It is a mystery of the human creative mind.

11. *Where can I use TRIZ?* Let me reemphasize: TRIZ is domain independent, and it's a way of thinking. It can be used across industries and domains like sales, marketing, software development, and so on. It will be of significant help in personal life in staying creative. My wife and I gave a humorous TEDx talk, and the entire speech was designed using TRIZ principles. A stand-up comedian can use it, or if you want to reinvent yourself as a stand-up comedian, for example, you can use TRIZ to do so.

12. *What is the TRIZ for business model?* A major contribution of TRIZ came from engineers who studied the development of technologies by resolving contradictions. Through these studies the 40 inventive principles were derived. But in a broader sense, if you ask me what these 40 principles are, I would say they are creative thinking approaches to solving a problem. So, engineers used these creative thinking approaches to study and solve technological problems. But these principles and approaches are true for any domain, including business, medicine, politics, and so on. As a matter of fact, studies show that even nature uses the principles of TRIZ to resolve contradictions. Most of the principles are straightforward and can be understood and applied by nonengineers. In the fast-paced global market, businesses need to be extremely creative with models and fast in solving

problems effectively. I am not aware of a better tool than TRIZ for deriving a solution or taking us closer to the solution at a faster pace. The problem of a heavy truck unable to go fast is similar to a complex process with a huge team unable to implement quick improvements, and in both situations, we can use the same principles of TRIZ.

13. *What is a good TRIZ problem?* Before I answer this question, I want you to close this book and write your own definition of a problem. Hint: Take a problem that you have come across in the past. It does not matter whether you have solved it or not. Write it down on a piece of paper and write down what is stopping you from solving the problem.

JOURNEY THROUGH THAILAND

The bustling streets proved too much for us the moment we stepped out of our French friend's flat in the heart of Bangkok. It was the first day of our cycling trip, and we soon realized that we had not practiced enough on our Brompton foldable bicycles. On top of that, all the luggage made the handling even more difficult. We were headed for Ayutaya, some 90 km away from Bangkok, but the traffic was terrible.

AYUTAYA

"Hello! Welcome to my house," said Pui Chan. He is half Thai, half Japanese, and we found him through couch surfing. He lived in a big family house on his own, with many framed photos of the king and queens. We slept soundly in one of the rooms. "I need to leave for Bangkok to see my family, but you can stay if you want," Pui Chan said. Before he left we dressed him up in a lungi *as a token of our gratitude. We visited temples and saw the world-famous reclining Buddha. After a day spent cycling and walking down the street, we rested for dinner. "Thank you, Pui Chan, we love you," we cheered as we dug into the slow-cooked char-grilled fish and Thai red curry.*

UNDER THE MANGO TREE

"Sawadee kha, sawadee kha," we shouted. A middle-aged lady came out, and we explained to her that we were cyclists and wanted to pitch our tent under her mango tree. "Yes. And you can eat as many mangos as you want from the bucket," she replied. When we woke up to hit the road the lady gave us a small bag. It had a small pendant with a photo of a Thai monk. "It will keep you safe," she said.

NEW UMBRELLAS

We arrived in a small town on our way to Laos and it started drizzling. We took shelter under the roof of a restaurant and the owner came up to us. "Around the world by bike? Wow!" he said and returned with chocolate brownies. "Please try them. It will give you good energy."

A restaurant customer and her son joined in the conversation as we were munching on the brownies. The two left after a while, but then the boy came back with two brand-new umbrellas and four boxes of dried fruits and nuts.

"Please keep them with you," the boy said. We were moved by their generosity and had to explain to the boy that we could not ride with the umbrellas.

After some time, we were sitting on a bench near the street food market next to the train station. "We thought you might be around here," someone said suddenly.

It was the boy and his mother. They had brought a big box full of steamed sweet pumpkin, carrot, and boiled eggs, and so forth, and they gave us two big nylon sheets to shield our luggage from the rain.

We were speechless.

2
Problem

Irrespective of the problem you thought about, there will be two components to it. The first one is the parameter that you want to improve, and the second one is the parameter that is stopping you by causing some undesirable result when you try to improve the first one. For example, one of the biggest problems in the food industry is the shelf life of products, and hence it is good to maintain low inventory. But when we try to reduce the inventory, there are a few undesirable results. For example, there is a very high risk of going out of stock, transportation costs increase as the store has to reorder more frequently, and since the ordering quantity is low, the procurement cost increases, to name a few potential undesirable results. The dictionary definition of a *problem* is "a matter or situation regarded as unwelcome or harmful and needing to be dealt with and overcome." So, what we have been assuming to be a problem for centuries is often an illusion and in reality is just a contradiction wherein you try to improve something and along with it you get an undesirable effect. If you look at the dictionary definition for *contradiction*, it states "a combination of statements, ideas, or features of a situation that are opposed to one another." So, for many years we have been confusing a contradiction with a problem. I can give more examples from daily life that we think are problems but in reality are simply contradictions:

1. *It is hard to reduce project cost.* Reducing the project costs leads to decrease in scope or quality.
2. *Long project durations have led to customer dissatisfaction.* Completing the project on time demands an increase in resources.

3. *Scope changes affect the project schedule.* Accepting scope changes leads to an increase in project duration.

4. *Procurement cost of a commodity is very high.* Reduction in procurement cost increases the inventory holding cost.

So, now we are clear that every problem relating to a particular subject, art, or craft, or its technique, is a *contradiction*, and the goal of TRIZ is to eliminate such contradictions. I will not be surprised if you are thinking that you have solved many problems with conflicts in the past and used *optimization* techniques to resolve such contradictions. Optimization is a good solution but definitely not the best, as it compromises the end goal and settles for something less. For example, to balance inventory level and service level, optimization technique will recommend choosing an optimum level where there is a very small trade-off in service level and inventory levels. TRIZ considers optimization or trade-off as the biggest enemy; TRIZ believes you can resolve the contradictions without any compromise. You can have the cake and eat it too, according to TRIZ! Breakthrough solutions require breakthrough thinking, something that can overcome *psychological inertia*. During my workshops, whenever I am asked what psychological inertia is, I present this puzzle. There is a plank inclined at a 45-degree angle, and a horizontal pipe is sitting still at the top of the plank. Can anyone tell me why the pipe doesn't roll down? I get different answers, such as the pipe has been glued, the pipe is heavy, it is a metallic pipe, magnetic fields are acting against gravity, and so on. This is psychological inertia, where we start assuming things based on our past experiences, and this is a huge hurdle for innovation. Why should a pipe always have a circular cross-section? The pipe will not roll down if it has a rectangular cross-section. As kids have fewer experiences relative to adults, kids are often more innovative as they have less psychological inertia. For example, when I ask an adult to visualize and draw a big cup, they draw the biggest cup they have seen in their life, but when I went to a primary school and asked the kids to draw a big cup, they were extremely creative and innovative. One kid drew a huge stadium and a big cup inside the stadium almost touching the sky! TRIZ principles help in breaking psychological inertia and helping us to narrow down our thinking toward the solution.

LEAVING THAILAND

The next stop was a revelation. As we came cross a big gate, I said "sawadee kha" to the man inside. As soon as he realized Yuka was Japanese, he said, "The owner lived in Japan for 13 years." Kate and her husband started talking to her in fluent Japanese. After coffee, they prepared barbecue dinner and we washed it down with beer. They had many funny stories from Japan (let's keep those for some other time). The next morning, Kate had packed a big breakfast for us. I had tears in my eyes by the time we left.

BROMPTONS IN THAILAND

"What are you doing on a Brompton?" asked Charlie. "I am a big fan of Brompton for 10 years, and I have some collections." Charlie is a German and comes to Thailand every winter to spend some time with his Thai girlfriend. He told us we could pitch our tent in front of his girlfriend's flat, which was right in front of the Mekong River. Charlie offered us a glass of good, old Scotch and swore at the music coming from the other side of the river.

The next morning, Charlie came with a pot of yellowish green tea. He had bloodshot eyes, as he couldn't sleep due to the music from Laos. We had fresh oolong tea from Charlie's tea collection while looking at the "friendship bridge" that connects Thailand and Laos across the Mekong River.

Charlie and his girlfriend accompanied us to the border and gave us a small tin with tasty oolong tea leaves inside. "Remember us whenever you drink this," said Charlie.

When we finished immigration formalities, we looked behind us to see Charlie and his girlfriend waving at us. We were in Laos.

"Kob khun ka, Thailand," we said. Thank you for bringing so much sunshine into our lives.

3

Separation Principle

A physical contradiction occurs when there is a conflict between two mutually exclusive physical requirements to the same parameter, or simply when different values are required for a given parameter. The popular example of a physical contradiction in the TRIZ world is the bulletproof jacket of a police officer. The requirement is that the jacket has to be strong enough to take the momentum of the bullet, that is, it should be heavy, but at the same time it has to be light enough that the officer can run faster and longer. In short, the bulletproof jacket has to be heavy and light at the same time. Do you see the conflict? There are many such conflicts, for example:

- Investments should have higher and lower risk exposure at the same time.
- Transactions should be performed faster to increase throughput, but slowly to be more accurate.
- A business should be large for profits and resources and small for flexibility.

So how do we resolve them? One of most significant of all the many problem-solving principles and tools within the broad category of TRIZ is that of the *separation principles*. These principles are used extensively in analyzing and solving technical problems that involve major contradictions in technical and physical performance issues.

There are four separation principles:

1. *Separation in space*. This concept is based on the definition of *operational space*, that is, where exactly do we need the system to perform the opposite requirements? To perform contradictory

functions, try to break the systems into subsystems and assign each contradictory function to a different subsystem in such a way that the operation that has a conflict takes effect at different times, or simply *separate opposite requirements in space.* For example, making a team work during a single shift will increase team bonding but also increase the infrastructure cost. Hence, separate the team in space by providing them the option of working from home and connecting virtually instead of separating them in time through different shifts.

2. *Separation in time.* This concept is based on the definition of *operational time*, that is, when exactly do we need the system to perform the opposite requirements? To perform contradictory functions, try to schedule in such a way that the operation that has a conflict takes effect at different times, or simply *separate opposite requirements in time.* For example, aircraft wings are longer for takeoff, and then pivot back for high-speed flight. Another example would be to reduce operating cost by having more resources during the execution phase of the project and fewer resources during the planning phase.

3. *Separation by condition.* A characteristic is high under one condition and low under another condition. For example, a kitchen sieve is porous with regard to water and solid with regard to food. Another example would be having a communication filter in an organization provide access only based on need to ensure that information flows to relevant stakeholders.

4. *Separation between parts and the whole.* This principle is applied when a characteristic has one value at the system level and the opposite value at the component level, or a characteristic exists at the system level but not at the component level (or vice versa). For example, a bicycle chain is rigid at the micro level (subsystem or component) for strength, and flexible at the macro level (system). For another example, to make a business large and small at the same time, we can separate its parts or functions in space by forming a conglomerate of small independent organizations under one umbrella.

So, how do we use these principles? *Nine windows* is a visual management tool that helps in breaking psychological inertia and systematically using the separation principles. It helps in resolving the problem at a system level by separating the product/service/result in space, in time, by condition, and between parts and the whole.

Table 3.1 TRIZ nine windows.

	Past	Present	Future
Supersystem	–SS	SS	+SS
System	–S	**S**	+S
Subsystem (Components)	–C	C	+C

NINE WINDOWS

Table 3.1 shows the nine windows. Always begin from the present system (S), which represents how the product/service/process looks at present. So, what is the present system? The present system is where the focus lies, where the problem is seen. This is where the problem or the product that needs improvement will be entered. –S will represent how the previous state of the system looks before performing the function in the present, and +S is how the system looks in the future state after performing the function. Subsystem, or components, are the inputs, components, and segments of the system. –C, C, and +C represent the components of the system in the past, present, and future. Supersystem (SS) is the big picture, which represents how the system interacts with the external environment. –SS and +SS represent the big picture of the system in the past and future (see Table 3.2).

Nine windows is an excellent tool for innovative problem solving as it helps in separating the problem in space and time. Once you have separated the problem, it helps in changing the parameters of the objects based on condition, time, or environment, or all three. Let us look at an example where a purchasing team creates a lot of purchase orders (POs) in a day. The team has to do a lot of analysis before placing the PO manually. There have been numerous instances where there was an error in the PO that resulted in the supplier shipping either the wrong material, wrong quantity, or to the wrong address, or the PO was sent to the wrong supplier and the product was not delivered on time. The conflict was that the process required the team to prepare POs faster, while at the same time the POs should be prepared slowly to manage accuracy. This has affected the company's revenue and needs an immediate fix. The purchasing team decides to start with nine windows to solve this problem.

The first step is to define the system. In this problem the system is the POs with errors, and is entered in the Present/System window (see Table 3.3).

Table 3.2 Components of nine windows.

	Past	Present	Future
Supersystem	Changes to supersystem to prevent the appearance of the problem in order to achieve the objective	Changes to supersystem to make the system deliver the objective without any harm	Changes to supersystem in order to make the system achieve the objective
System	Changes to system to prevent the presence of the problem in order to achieve the objective	Changes to system to deliver the objective without harmful side effects	Changes to system in order to make the system achieve the objective
Subsystem (Components)	Changes to subsystems to prevent the appearance of the problem in order to achieve the objective	Changes to subsystems to deliver the objective without harmful side effects	Changes to subsystems to deliver the objective

Table 3.3 Nine windows for POs.

	Past	Present	Future
Supersystem			
System		*Too many errors in the purchase order*	
Subsystem (Components)			

The subsystem will contain all the components of the PO, and the supersystem will contain how the PO interacts with the external environment, that is, outside the purchasing department. Now let us fill all the nine boxes:

- *Present/System.* Always start with this box by writing the problem.
- *Present/Subsystem.* Include all the components of the system here, for example, PO, quantity, price, supplier information, and so on.
- *Present/Supersystem.* How does the PO interact with the external environment? It is sent to the supplier, and the supplier starts procuring the raw material, allocating the budget and manpower, and so on.
- *Past/System.* Before the process of placing the PO, the previous step was to analyze and confirm the need.
- *Past/Subsystem.* How is the need analyzed and the information collated? What process is used to analyze the need, and so on?
- *Past/Supersystem.* Where is the need coming from? Is there a forecast, and how accurate is the forecast? Do we foresee any demand changes in the near future?
- *Future/System.* The incorrect PO is executed and incorrect products, or quantity, are delivered on the wrong date to the wrong shipping address.
- *Future/Supersystem.* Unable to meet the customer's requirement, revenue loss, stakeholder dissatisfaction, and so on.
- *Future/Subsystem.* Excess quantity, unusable product, canceled PO, excess inventory, revenue loss, and so on.

We have now separated the problem in space and time as shown in Table 3.4. We can see the problem at different time frames (past, present, and future) and spaces (system, subsystem, supersystem) and have the liberty to fix it at one or more places. This table will let you see a different picture of the same problem and help you come up with numerous innovative solutions:

1. Looking at Past/Subsystem, can we automate the process of placing the PO and analysis? *(Separation in space and time)*
2. Looking at the Past/System, can we implement mistake-proofing and auditing processes to validate the accuracy of the need and information at critical process steps? *(Separation by condition)*
3. Looking at Past/Supersystem, can we forecast and implement one blanket purchase order to eliminate the process of creating multiple PO's? *(Separation in time)*

Table 3.4 Nine windows for POs.

	Past	**Present**	**Future**
Supersystem	Demand or reason for need to procure	Suppliers start procuring raw material and manufacturing *Can the supplier generate the PO draft himself, and the buyer just reviews and approves? Blanket PO?*	*Incorrect product delivered. Pay the fee*
System	Analyze the need and gather information *How to avoid the errors before preparing the PO*	**Too many errors in the purchase order**	How to correct the errors once the products are delivered or PO is closed
Subsystem (Components)	Demand, process, supplier list, product type, price *Can we auto-populate the information rather than manual entry?*	Enter the quantity, price, clause, supplier information, buyer, knowledge, lead time, product type	Closed purchase order, inventory, product, PO status, shipment

4. Looking at the Present/Supersystem, can we have an agreement in the contract that allows changes or corrections to the PO, with a clause specifying that neither the supplier nor the buyer takes the loss? *(Separation by condition)*
5. Looking at the Present/Subsystem, can we improve the existing process using Lean Six Sigma? *(All)*

6. Looking at the Future/Supersystem, can we anticipate such risks and have a mitigation plan in place to meet the customer's demand? *(Separation in space and time)*
7. Looking at the Future/System, can we try to negotiate with the supplier to return the products to the supplier in exchange for extending the contract or doing a favor to the supplier? *(Separation between parts and the whole)*

The above solutions are not limited to each window. We can invent a solution by taking an action from one box and putting it in another box. For example, the demand or need can be made visible to the supplier, and the entire process of analyzing the need and placing the PO can be outsourced to the supplier, making them accountable for the accuracy. For another example, once the incorrect material is delivered, can we perform reverse engineering to check whether we can create a need that can be seen as an opportunity to release a new product into the market?

> ***Idea:*** *Design a tool or an application that integrates all the boxes to detect errors and make the problem instantly visible to all the stakeholders and initiate corrective actions. Think of guided workflow.*

Here is another example. An organization has a huge problem with attrition of resources from projects, and the human resources (HR) director would like to fix this problem as soon as possible. They decide to start with nine windows. As the system clearly states that the problem is related to Project, the Supersystem could be Project, Program, or Portfolio. You are free to go to much higher System levels, for example, Super-Supersystem can have Program. When there is attrition, the bigger picture at the immediate present at a Project/Program/Portfolio level is entered at the present Supersystem level. At the present Component level we include all the parameters, activities, and factors related to attrition. Similarly, we fill blocks for all three levels in the past and future as shown in Table 3.5.

Now there are many aspects that help in managing the attrition problem better. For example, the organization can anticipate attrition in advance and include buffer resources at Supersystem/Present level, or change the management style and work environment at Present/Component level, or anticipate attrition and include the anticipated loss in the contract at Supersystem/Future level. It can separate the problem in time; for example, work environment dissatisfaction under Present/Component can be moved to Past/Component where HR can look at the gap between the work culture in the current organization and the previous organization of a potential

Table 3.5 Nine windows for the attrition problem.

	Past	Present	Future
Supersystem	Hiring cost, knowledge and skill pool, capacity, and so on	Project reschedule, skill availability, stakeholder dissatisfaction	Loss of revenue, losing customer, project delay, employee satisfaction rating
System	Project members interviewed and hired into the team	**Project team members moving out of the organization**	Project resources released from the project. Hire and train new project team members
Subsystem (Components)	Interview process, employee expectation, trainings, project requirements	Team members' stress, employee motivation, compensation, work environment, management style, attitude, training, and so on	Employee feedback, unhappy stakeholder, hiring lead time

hire and decide whether to hire or not. Similarly, a solution can also be found by moving the problem in space and time by letting the end customer and stakeholders at Supersystem level know about the training needs or employee dissatisfaction at Component/Present level to avoid risk and panic.

It is very helpful to use visualization and imagination skills while developing nine windows. Here is a step-by-step guide with a simple exercise that will help you strengthen your visualization skills:

1. Pick your favorite movie.
2. In the Present/System box enter your favorite scene in the movie.

3. In the Present/Subsystem box enter all the objects, emotions, and characters that you observed in your favorite scene.
4. In the Present/Supersystem box, enter how this scene helped the plot.
5. In the Past/System box, enter a summary of the first five to 10 minutes of the movie.
6. In the Past/Subsystem box enter all the characters, emotions, objects, and so on, that you observed during the first 10 minutes.
7. In the Past/Supersystem box enter how this scene helped the plot.
8. In the Future/System box, describe the climax of the movie.
9. In the Future/Subsystem box enter all the objects, characters, and emotions in the climax scene.
10. In the Future/Supersystem box enter how the climax helped the plot.

Now you see the entire movie in a different perspective. Try to change or replace the characters, scenes, plot, emotions, and so on, from one box to another and see if you can improve the movie. You will be surprised to see a creative screenplay writer hidden inside you coming out. Now do the same with your process or project.

FIRST NIGHT IN LAOS

Just like we had done in Thailand, we were looking for a place to pitch our tent. We saw a house with a big, open garage and went up to the man sitting in a chair. We put on as big a smile as we could, but he just waved his hand. "Go to the temple," he said, pointing to the one opposite his house. He was a friendly man and started talking to me in Japanese—he used to be the driver for the Japanese ambassador. He offered us some biscuits and coffee, and I was hoping that he would eventually say "you can stay." He asked us to come back the next morning to have a cup of coffee. We went to the temple and spoke to some young monks. They suggested we speak to the head monk, who was out. We decided to sit on the long bench in the temple and saw a young monk take a break from collecting leaves and light a cigarette. "Wow! The monks in Laos smoke and have tattoos," I said when I saw that he had a big, beautiful tattoo on his shoulder. When the head monk arrived, he readily agreed to let us stay in the main hall. We saw three Buddha statues there and felt a bit odd. "You need to promise us that you won't kiss in front of the Buddha. It will be disgraceful," the head monk said. We nodded like two obedient children.

FIRST TEACHING EXPERIENCE ON THE ROAD

Since I used to be a teacher, I asked one of the teachers if I could teach origami to the children. They agreed and returned to their chit-chat. I sat in the middle of the room and started folding a paper. I was soon surrounded by small, curious faces. I had only one A4 sheet with me, so I asked the teachers if they had any. But since they didn't, I improvised. I asked the children to sit around me and I started to tell them a story using paper. The children needed to guess the name of the shape I was making. When I made a cat or a dog and said "meow" or "bow wow," they laughed and told me the corresponding word in Lao. By the time I finished, they had learned to say hello, mountain, cats, dogs, hat, fish, thank you, and goodbye in English. I wondered about the iPads, smartphones, and computers that today's children use in classrooms and whether I would fit in. I hope I do.

LET'S TRY THE SHORTEST ROUTE TO VIETNAM

"Look! They have a route map to the Laos border," Sunil told me at the Vietnamese consulate in Luang Prabang. The map showed three ways of going to the Vietnamese border. We examined the map and decided to take the route that was the shortest. After we got our visa to Vietnam, we said goodbye to beautiful Luang Prabang and headed to Pak Xiang.

After some hours, we found ourselves in a remote area and hardly saw anybody. After a while, as luck would have it, I saw a man who looked like an Indian. I started chatting with him. He was a second generation Indian; his parents had a small shop in this remote area. I asked him if we were headed in the right direction; he nodded but said we still had a long way to go.

The road was getting worse, and we soon realized that we were in the hills. They were getting steep, and we had to get off and push our bikes. We were exhausted.

4

TRIZ Principles and the Contradiction Matrix

During the late '50s Genrich S. Altshuller came up with an approach to developing inventive principles. As a patent examiner Altshuller refused to accept the fact that innovators and creative people were born with their skills. He wanted to develop a standard process for successful innovation. While studying 200,000 patents he recognized that the development of technological systems follows predictable patterns that cut across all areas of technology. He also recognized that problem-solving principles are predictable and repeatable. These principles are the known solutions that were used to solve similar problems in the past and guide us to think in a particular direction. This is how he discovered that 95% of patented innovations were based on an already known 40 principles, that is, every innovation that he studied traced back to one or more of the 40 principles. Hence, anyone can invent if they understand these 40 principles!

Here I present the 40 principles. I have taken all the principles and definitions from the book *The Innovation Algorithm* written by Genrich Altshuller himself, and translated by Lev Shulyak and Steven Rodman, and have tried to give a nonmanufacturing example for each principle. Every time you see the word *object* in the principle definition, it could also mean *process, project, function, product, service, people, methodology, idea, program, portfolio*, and so on.

After each principle there is a number within parentheses that represents the frequency of usage in the contradiction matrix or the usefulness of the principle. The ranking is from 1 to 40, with 1 being the highest and 40 the least. For example, TRIZ principle 35, "Parameter change" is ranked #1 as it resolves 413 contradictions, and TRIZ principle 20, "Continuity of useful action," is ranked #40 as it resolves just 20 contradictions.

1. *Segmentation* (3). The core of this principle is to break the process, product, function, project, or business parameter into

segments to solve a business problem. A large project scope can be managed by breaking it into smaller deliverables (work breakdown structures). Some of the ways to apply it are:

a. Divide an object into independent parts.

Example: Divide an organization into different business units; divide a product into strength, weakness, opportunity, and threat; break deliverables into activities.

b. Make an object sectional—easy to assemble or disassemble.

Example: Use contract employees, customized services, flexible investment plans.

c. Increase the degree of fragmentation or segmentation.

Example: Build process improvement and the lean thinking mind-set into every individual in the organization; push feedback mechanisms down to the lowest level of the organization.

2. *Taking out or Separation or Extraction* (5). The goal of this principle with respect to business management is to remove or separate a disturbing process, process step, or its components and also extract or retain just the necessary process, process step, or its components in the business and solve the problem. Some of the ways to apply it are:

a. Extract the disturbing part or property from an object.

Example: Eliminate fear; remove waste from the process; nonsmoking areas at airports; children-only areas in public places; eliminate performance reviews.

b. Extract the only necessary part (or property) of an object.

Example: Outcome-based pricing instead of activity-based pricing model; provide only highest value-added services and products; use barking dog alarm for security if you are not a dog lover.

3. *Local quality* (12). This principle is partially the opposite of standardization and recommends that a process, process step, business environment, business decision, and so on, move toward nonuniformity from uniformity, and solve the problem by making

sure that each process step performs a unique complementary activity in the best-suited environment. Some of the ways to apply it are:

a. Change an object's structure from uniform to nonuniform.

   Example: Put more effort into high-value customers; casual dress code for employees who do not face the customer.

b. Change an action or an external environment (or external influence) from uniform to nonuniform.

   Example: Take account of market conditions when designing processes; create goals and objectives for the team members depending on employees' strengths and weaknesses.

c. Make each part of an object function under conditions most suitable for its operation.

   Example: Move operations to business-friendly regions; move management offices close to manufacturing floors; flexible work hours for employees; allow the employee to choose the salary structure; freezer in the refrigerator.

d. Make each part of an object fulfill a different and/or complementary useful function.

   Example: Make sure every process step delivers a measurable value addition to the end product; use experts with specialized skills rather than generalists; organize the department by process rather than product; rehire retired employees for a few hours to use their expertise.

4. *Asymmetry* (24). The asymmetry principle solves the business problem by designing the process, process step, and components with dissimilar parts or components either in appearance, character, or quantity. Some of the ways to apply it are:

   a. Change the shape or properties of an object from symmetrical to asymmetrical.

      Example: Build a team where the team members fail to correspond to one another in skill, experience and knowledge, background, and so on.

   b. Change the shape of an object to suit external asymmetries.

Example: Add more resources to critical process steps; change the incentive structure depending on the seasonal demand; change the marketing strategy for each client; keys.

c. If an object is asymmetrical, increase its degree of asymmetry.

Example: Increase the interaction between different levels of the organization; move from the waterfall model to agile methodology.

5. *Merging* (33). This is an extremely simple and powerful principle that solves a business problem by bringing two processes together in space or time or both. Some of the ways to apply it are:

a. Bring closer together (or merge) identical or similar objects or operations in space.

Example: Move the supply chain department to the manufacturing shop floor; identify suppliers closer to the organization; multi-blade razors.

b. Make objects or operations contiguous or parallel; bring them together in time.

Example: On-the-job training; lunchtime meeting; involve the customer in product or solution design.

6. *Universality* (20). The core of this principle is to solve the business problem by making one process or resource perform multiple functions. Some of the ways to apply it are:

a. Make an object perform multiple functions; eliminate the need for other parts.

Example: Cross-training resources; hiring resources with multiple skills; make one department perform multiple functions; Swiss Army knife.

7. *Nested doll* (34). The best examples for this principle are the Russian nested doll or a telescope, where space is optimized by placing one component inside another. This principle helps in solving a business problem by placing one process or process step inside another (like a Gantt chart with closely packed *finished to start* dependencies). Some of the ways to apply it are:

a. Place one object inside another.

Example: Every process must have a supplier sending the input and a customer receiving an output. If this condition is not met, then the process can be eliminated.

b. Place multiple objects inside others.

Example: Activities inside the work breakdown structure (WBS), WBS inside deliverable, deliverable inside scope, and scope inside the project; telescope; brush attached to inside of cap of nail polish.

c. Make one part pass (dynamically) through a cavity in the other.

Example: Move niche skilled resources to process steps based on need.

8. *Anti-weight or counterweight* (32). To counterbalance the force or pressure acting on the business process or project, try to add processes to counterbalance the effect and keep business moving smoothly. Some of the ways to apply it are:

    a. To compensate for the weight of an object, merge it with other objects that provide lift.

    Example: Invest in sales and marketing when the market is down; acquire companies that are stronger in the weaker areas of the acquiring company; hot air or helium balloon.

    b. To compensate for the weight of an object, make it interact with the environment.

    Example: Post trending topics to attract more traffic into the social media channel; attach product or service to a cause; make use of centrifugal forces in rotating systems.

9. *Prior counteraction or preliminary anti-action* (39). You can solve the business problem by using this principle, in which you take all necessary actions to mitigate the harmful effects in advance. Some of the ways to apply it are:

    a. When it is necessary to perform an action with both harmful and useful effects, this should be replaced with counteractions to control the harmful effects.

    Example: Perform risk assessment and have a mitigation strategy; make clay pigeons out of ice or dung—they just melt away; what-if analysis.

b. Create beforehand stresses in an object that will oppose known undesirable working stresses later on.

Example: Include risk avoidance clauses in the agreement; standard procedures to rectify issues in the process; clear guidelines to handle noncompliance.

10. *Prior action or preliminary action* (2). Simply solve the problem by performing process steps ahead of when they are required or currently done. In any of my consulting assignments, my default question to the client would be, when was the last time they performed a 5S? Some of the ways to apply this principle are:

    a. Perform the required change of an object in advance.

    Example: Perform part of the process beforehand; fetch all the customer information before meeting the customer.

    b. Prearrange objects such that they can be put into action from the most convenient place and without losing time for their delivery.

    Example: Get all the inputs in order before initiating the process; publish the agenda before the meeting; perform 5S workout.

11. *Cushion in advance, or beforehand cushioning, or previously placed pillow* (29). This principle helps in risk-related business problems by asking the consultant to use a buffer to the processes. In all the projects that I handle, I do not feel comfortable if I do not add at least 10% buffer to the schedule and cost irrespective of how sure I am. Some of the ways to apply this principle are:

    a. Prepare emergency means beforehand to compensate for the relatively low reliability of an object.

    Example: Battery back-up/back-up parachute; contingency planning; plan for the worst-case scenario; include a penalty clause in the contract.

12. *Equipotentiality* (37). The essence of this principle is to solve the problem by eliminating or minimizing the motion between processes through process design. To simplify and explain this principle in lean terminology, I would say avoid unnecessary motion between the process steps. It could be going to multiple screens multiple times to get data, or even scrolling the screens

back and forth multiple times to fill out an application. Some of the ways to apply this principle are:

a. If an object has to be raised or lowered, redesign the object's environment so the need to raise or lower it is eliminated or performed by the environment.

Example: Remove authority during brainstorming meetings across levels; move to a flat organization with not more than three or four levels; create horizontal career movement instead of vertical growth.

13. *The other way round, or inversion* (10). This principle recommends to do the exact opposite of the process that is currently being done. This principle is very simple and effective in boosting creativity. During my consulting assignments many clients have felt and even expressed that I sound creative and I have won their trust. The simple secret lies in this principle. Every time they explain a problem, I apply this principle and sometimes arrive at a solution and sometimes not, but the clients are happy that I am thinking in an altogether different direction, when all I do is think the opposite way they had been before. Some of the ways to apply this principle are:

a. Invert the action used to solve the problem.

Example: Make use of recession to hire skilled employees rather than laying off employees; invest in customer service instead of marketing to improve sales; make to order to assemble to order; to loosen stuck parts, cool the inner part instead of heating the outer part.

b. Make movable parts (or the external environment) fixed, and fixed parts movable.

Example: Escalator; build the product at the customer's location; work from home; hire qualified customers into the organization.

c. Turn the object (or process) "upside down."

Example: A renowned automobile company provided the highest salary to the maintenance employee who worked the least to motivate the team to work on preventing problems rather than temporarily fixing them.

14. *Spheroidality or curvature* (21). The U-shaped cells in a factory are more efficient as they let the operators at different process steps communicate and pass materials between noncontiguous process steps more effectively and quickly. This is one example of how a business problem can be solved by making processes that are straight into curves. Some of the ways to apply it are:

    a. Move from flat surfaces to spherical ones, and from parts shaped as a cube (parallelepiped) to ball-shaped structures.

       Example: Make the team work in a U-shaped cubicle to have easy interaction with other processes; spoke-and-wheel system; ergonomic chair.

    b. Use rollers, balls, spirals.

       Example: Ballpoint pen for smooth flow of ink; attaching wheels to products like books and food leads to new service delivery models like mobile libraries and doorstep deliveries; spiral model risk-driven process generator.

    c. Go from linear to rotary motion (or vice versa).

       Example: Rotate job roles; complete the supply chain model by introducing a reverse supply chain; create another link from customer to supplier; quality circles; develop a circle of influence; use a mouse ball to produce linear motion of the cursor through rotatory motion.

15. *Dynamics or dynamacity* (6). It's all about dynamics. Solve the business problem by making the static process steps movable. Some of the ways to apply this principle are:

    a. Change the object (or outside environment) for optimal performance at every stage of the operation.

       Example: Continuous improvement; skill-based routing in call centers.

    b. Divide an object into parts capable of movement relative to each other.

       Example: Virtual teams working with colocated teams; investments diversified with respect to sector or company; folding chair.

    c. Change from immobile to mobile.

Example: Change roles and responsibilities of the employees depending on organizational requirements; restaurant where the customer can cook his/her meal with a standard procedure.

16. *Partial or excessive action* (16). This principle is about doing things more or less than required to solve the business problem. I have been a project manager for some time, and as a project manager, 90% of my effort goes into communication. Providing a little bit more relevant information than requested by every e-mail I respond to resulted in reducing e-mail traffic drastically in my mailbox, and stakeholders were very happy. Try to think of two additional pieces of information that you can provide or ask every time you write an e-mail, and experience the magic. Some of the ways to apply this principle are:

    a. If you can't achieve 100 percent of a desired effect—then go for more or less.

    Example: Overspray when painting, then remove the excess; overcommunicate; when beginning a venture, "bootstrap," that is, start small and grow from internal funding; when unclear about a requirement, provide more information and later remove the excess information.

17. *Another dimension or new dimension* (19). This principle is all about thinking out of the box to resolve the business problem. The good news is that it clearly guides you as to which side of the box you can open and explore. Some of the ways to apply it are:

    a. Move into an additional dimension: from one to two, from two to three.

    Example: Spiral staircase uses less floor area; 360-degree appraisal; penetrate new markets with existing capabilities.

    b. Go from single story or layer to multistory or multilayered.

    Example: Multistory office blocks or parking ramps; increase or decrease organizational hierarchy.

    c. Incline an object, lay it on its side.

    Example: Switch from vertical to horizontal career path.

    d. Use the other side.

Example: See the product from other angles (customer, supplier, competitor); luncheon meetings; produce in low-cost countries and sell in high-cost countries; hire retired employees and contractors.

18. *Mechanical vibration* (8). Speed, speed, and speed—the current mantra for any efficient process. This principle can be applied to increase the execution speed of the process step to solve the business problem. Remember, a human being is also a mechanical system. Some of the ways to apply this principle are:

    a. Cause an object to oscillate or vibrate.

    Example: Electric carving knife with vibrating blades; catchball process of hoshin planning to get the whole organization "vibrating"; create roles in the organization with dual reporting structure.

    b. Increase its frequency (even up to the ultrasonic).

    Example: Overcommunicate; more performance reviews; nondestructive crack detection using ultrasound; have 15 minutes of training each day rather than full-day classroom training.

    c. Use an object's resonant frequency.

    Example: Ultrasonic resonance to destroy kidney stones; use different communication techniques for different levels; use of kansei engineering, a Japanese technique for improving products based on customers' feelings; use of just-in-time principle.

19. *Periodic action* (7). The core of this principle is to move from executing the processes with larger lead time to process steps with smaller lead time to solve the problem. While having lunch with a Chinese tea master, he gave me a useful tip for staying focused and enjoying every single bite of the noodle dish that was served. He asked me to break the process of eating every single bite into three steps: first, to observe the bowl for two seconds, then pick the noodle and wait for two seconds, and lastly eat the noodle and wait for five seconds before going on to the next bite. I was following the same process steps, but by adding a small gap, I could focus more on each and every process step. Some of the ways to apply this principle are:

a. Instead of continuous action, use periodic or pulsating actions.

Example: Reschedule the project resource capacity based on seasonal demand rather than keeping it fixed; replace a continuous siren with a pulsed sound; replace micro management by macro management; periodically change the work times or work location, or roles and responsibilities.

b. If an action is already periodic, change the periodic magnitude or frequency.

Example: Use of AM, FM, PWM to transmit information; smoothe the spike in demand by introducing discounts and campaigns periodically; increase the review frequency for critical deliverables.

c. Use pauses between actions to perform a different action.

Example: Get work done between meetings; inkjet printer cleans heads between passes; give pauses while multiple conversations are taking place along the same telephone transmission line; invest in training of employees during low-demand season.

20. *Continuity of useful action* (40). This is the opposite of the previous principle, where processes have to be accomplished without any gap in between: keep doing the good work without any break. Some of the ways to apply this principle are:

a. Carry on work without a break. All parts of an object operating constantly at full capacity.

Example: Heart pacemaker; continuous improvement programs; 24/7 customer service.

b. Eliminate all idle or intermittent motion.

Example: Conduct training during pauses in work; eliminate customer wait time or engage the customer with other products during the waiting period.

21. *Rushing through or skipping* (35). This is very similar to the previous principle with the small addition that the business problem can be solved by rushing through the processes without a break. How would it be if you had to fire an employee, tell her she

is going to be fired, and then take a month for the firing process to be complete? Some of the ways to apply this principle are:

a. Conduct a process, or certain stages of it (for example, destructive, harmful, or hazardous operations) at high speed.

Example: Zero waiting time in hotels; fail fast, learn fast; make the process of firing someone quick; burn the excess inventory faster.

22. *Blessing in disguise or harm to benefit* (22). Look for positive risks, convert threats into opportunities, transform weaknesses into strengths are some of the mantras of this principle that can be applied to an unstoppable harmful effect to convert it into a useful effect. Some of the ways to apply it are:

a. Use harmful factors (particularly, harmful effects of the environment or surroundings) to achieve a positive effect.

Example: Use customer complaints for process improvement; recycle waste (scrap) material from one process into raw materials for another; use employee errors for lessons learned meetings.

b. Eliminate the primary harmful action by adding it to another harmful action to resolve the problem.

Example: Add a buffering material to a corrosive solution (for example, an alkali to an acid, or vice versa); eliminate fear of change by introducing fear of competition; put a "problem" person on an assignment in another area where he/she can do well and not be a disruption to the original group.

c. Amplify a harmful factor to such a degree that it is no longer harmful.

Example: Try to convert the bugs in the software into a feature; reduce the capacity to an extremely low level to identify new ways of performing the job; use a backfire to eliminate the fuel from a forest fire.

23. *Feedback* (36). By using this principle a business problem can be solved by introducing one or more feedback loops between processes, resources, projects, external environments, and so on. Some of the ways to apply it are:

a. Introduce feedback to improve a process or action.

Example: Introduce cross-functional feedback mechanisms into the organization; introduce feedback mechanisms at all levels; statistical process control.

b. If feedback is already used, change its magnitude or influence in accordance with operating conditions.

Example: Increase the feedback depth for resources handling critical processes; increase the frequency of collecting feedback from high-value customers; instead of waiting for customer feedback, some companies proactively use computerized information systems; change a management measure from budget variance to customer satisfaction.

24. *Intermediary or mediator* (18). The essence of this principle is that a business problem can be solved by introducing a new process, technology, resource, and so on, into the system to solve the business problem. Some of the ways to apply it are:

a. Use an intermediary carrier article or intermediary process.

Example: Using a mediator or a neutral external person during negotiations; using external consultants; technical writers; wholesaler; using a Black Belt to drive process improvement.

b. Merge one object temporarily with another (that can be easily removed).

Example: Temporary project manager from the customer's company works on the project; subcontracting housekeeping services.

25. *Self-service* (28). The primary goal of this principle is to make the process solve the problem itself. Some of the ways to apply it are:

a. An object must service itself by performing auxiliary helpful functions.

Example: Self-help groups; customer's search history for marketing campaigns; brand image circularity; auto-deleting cookie.

b. Use waste resources, energy, or substances.

Example: Use animal waste as fertilizer; study process wastes to design the process; rehire retired workers as consultants.

26. *Copying* (11). Using inexpensive copies instead of the originals will open up a lot of opportunities for innovation and improvement. The copies could be photographic images, videos, data, soft copy of documents, servers, scientific models, process maps, and so on, that can be used in a process to resolve the problem. Some of the ways to apply this principle are:

    a. Replace unavailable, expensive, or fragile objects with available or inexpensive copies.

       Example: Virtual reality instead of physical prototype; online training videos; record customer complaints for quality and training purposes; imitation jewelry.

    b. Replace an object or process with optical copies.

       Example: Measure an object by scaling measurements from a photograph; videoconference instead of physical travel; use electronic copies of invoices and payment details rather than physical copies.

27. *Cheap short-living objects or cheap disposables* (13). This is very similar to the previous principle, but instead of using a copy of the original, we will use a cheap or inexpensive object that can be disposed of after the purpose is served. Some of the ways to apply this principle are:

    a. Replace an expensive object with multiple inexpensive objects comprising certain qualities, such as service life.

       Example: Use short-term resources on contract during high-demand periods; disposable diapers/paper cups/plates/cameras/lighters/and so on; free download of a trial version of software.

28. *Replace mechanical system* (4). Replacing a mechanical system with sensors and fields will increase the efficiency and effectiveness of the process. A business problem can be solved by replacing mechanical systems involving human actions, intuitions, and judgments with fields like information, methodology, data, and so on, in conjunction with controlled fields like desktop process automation applications, artificial intelligence software, big data applications, and so on. Some of the ways to apply this principle are:

    a. Replace a mechanical system with a sensory one.

Example: Automation software that mimics human intelligence; videotapes of lectures, and CD recordings; electronic voting; using smells from bakery to attract customers.

b. Use electric, magnetic, and electromagnetic fields to interact with the object.

Example: Employee magnetic badges allow entrance to a facility; using GPS sensors to help insurance auditors; electronic tagging.

c. Replace stationary fields with moving fields; replace unstructured fields with structure.

Example: Mind-mapping techniques give a structure to random ideas; organizing random improvement ideas; organizing cross-functional workshops in product design.

d. Use fields in conjunction with field-activated (for example, ferromagnetic) particles.

Example: Set performance goals by exposing employees to performance data; value stream mapping using software tools.

29. *Pneumatics and hydraulics* (14). The core idea of this principle with respect to business problem solving is to make things that are discrete and rigid more continuous and flexible. Some of the ways to apply it are:

a. Use gas and liquid parts for an object instead of solid parts (for example, inflatable, filled with liquid, air cushion, hydrostatic, hydro-reactive).

Example: Have frozen, liquid, and free zones within which customers can modify placed orders; fixed and liquid assets; use influence, or pressure, from the environment as trigger activities; inclusion of "breathing spaces" into contracts.

30. *Flexible membranes/thin films* (25). This principle helps in isolating the process from harmful effects, the external environment, another process, resources, customers, and so on, using a thin structure. Some of the ways to apply it are:

a. Use flexible shells and thin films instead of three-dimensional structures.

Example: Measuring the performance of a process with a single metric that is a function of many metrics.

b. Isolate the object from its external environment using flexible membranes.

Example: "Umbrella" organizations; isolating project in-scope and out-of-scope by drawing boundaries on a process map and giving some conditional flexibility through clauses; well-defined roles and responsibilities.

31. *Porous materials* (30). The essence of this principle is to solve the business problem by opening up the process and process steps, which will allow the flow of communication, information, and material through. Some of the ways to apply it are:

a. Make an object porous or add porous elements (inserts, coatings, and so on).

Example: Special lanes in the supermarket for customers who buy less to reduce queue time; communications are filtered between the layers of an organization; an open communication channel between top management and the lowest-level employees to help understand problems related to high-value customers.

b. If an object is already porous, use the pores to introduce a useful substance or function.

Example: Empower employees in a customer-facing role with necessary training; fill holes in the organization structure with expanded capabilities.

32. *Color or optical change* (9). By changing the way things look, a problem can be solved. A simple red or green dot next to a process step in an excel spreadsheet gives a lot of information on its status. Visual boards can also be used to solve business problems. Some of the ways to apply this principle are:

a. Change the color of an object or its external environment.

Example: Changing the color of a logo to change the brand image; changing the color combination of the templates used; changing lighting in the work area; highlighting important points with colors.

b. Change the transparency of an object or its external environment.

Example: Use bold to highlight important points; blur confidential information; increase the transparency of the information based on the role; smoke screen.

c. In order to improve observability of things that are difficult to see, use colored additives or luminescent elements.

Example: Use opposing colors to increase visibility; use red/green/yellow in status reports; kanban; change the color of the applications depending on the criticality.

33. *Homogeneity* (38). This principle solves the business problem by making similar items interact with each other. Many business problems can be solved by making similar processes interact with each other, sharing the best practices, or bringing the knowledge level of the whole team to the same standard, and so on. In Japan, the top leaders stripped their designations and came to the shop floor and sat with the operators to understand the problem. Some of the ways to apply this principle are:

    a. Objects interacting with the main object should be of the same material (or material with identical properties).

    Example: Colocated project teams; team members provide feedback to another team member rather than a supervisor.

34. *Discarding and recovering* (15). A business problem can be solved by removing a process, along with all its supporting components, once it has delivered the output, or by adding a process in between the process or operation. Some of the ways to apply this principle are:

    a. After completing their function (or becoming useless) reject objects, make them go away (discard them by dissolving, evaporating, and so on), or modify them during the process.

    Example: Variable project team size; level loading capacity using contract labor.

    b. Restore consumable/used-up parts of an object during operation.

    Example: Continuous refresher training; reusable templates; using old project plan, data, estimates, and lessons learned.

35. *Parameter change or change property* (1). This is the most used principle, where we try to change the property of a process or its components to solve the business problem. Changing the property could be replacing a resource, training, changing the color of a document, moving from physical to electronic format, changing the attitude or personality of an employee, and so on. Some of the ways to apply this principle are:

    a. Change the physical state of the object.

    Example: Traditional banking replaced by e-banking and telephone banking; simulation software; paper voting replaced by electronic voting.

    b. Change the concentration or density.

    Example: Increase the concentration of experienced resources in critical projects and less-experienced resources in less-critical projects.

    c. Change the degree of flexibility.

    Example: Increase the degree of customization in the product or service.

    d. Change the temperature or volume.

    Example: Excite the employees by giving them new responsibilities; change the tone in which the news is conveyed.

    e. Change the pressure.

    Example: Create a sense of urgency in the team; increase communication frequency to reduce stakeholder pressure.

36. *Phase transition* (27). The goal of this principle is to take advantage of an existing trend to solve a problem. We can use different processes to take advantage of changes in the economy, clients, culture, technology, teams, motivation levels, and so on. This principle can also be used to change the environment to improve the performance of the process. Some of the ways to apply it are:

    a. Use the phenomena of phase transitions (for example, volume changes, loss or absorption of heat).

Example: Have different marketing strategies for different geographies.

37. *Thermal expansion* (26). This principle uses the sensitivity and reaction of the process and its components to its advantage to solve the business problem. Some of the ways to apply it are:

    a. Use thermal expansion, or contraction, of materials.

    Example: Make use of "hot" trending topics to increase social media reach; deploy highly enthusiastic resources in challenging, complex activities.

    b. Use multiple materials with different coefficients of thermal expansion.

    Example: Have a team with mixed skill sets, and employees with different stress tolerance levels.

38. *Accelerated oxidation or strong oxidants* (31). The goal of this principle is to nourish the process with the useful necessary input in larger quantities to get a better output. Some of the ways to apply it are:

    a. Replace common air with oxygen-enriched air.

    Example: Provide incentives, rewards, and recognition; bring in life coaches.

    b. Replace enriched air with pure oxygen.

    Example: Remove mundane activities from skilled resources' deliverables; tie employee pay levels directly to company performance; for critical roles, do not compromise on any skill requirement.

    c. Expose air or oxygen to ionizing radiation.

    Example: Empower top performers with niche training; provide loyal customers with top-notch service levels.

    d. Use ionized oxygen.

    Example: Hire resources with technical, leadership, and interpersonal skills.

39. *Inert atmosphere* (23). This principle is the opposite of thermal expansion, where we solve the problem by making the process

and its components less reactive to the external environment. Some of the ways to apply it are:

a. Replace a normal environment with an inert one.

Example: Make sure the project team works in an environment with zero distraction or interference from external stakeholders.

b. Add neutral parts, or inert additives, to an object.

Example: Having a third person during negotiations; creating customer relationship roles to bridge the concerns between organization and customer.

40. *Composite materials* (17). This principle is the opposite of standardization, where the problem is solved by making the process and it components more amalgamated. Some of the ways to apply it are:

a. Change from uniform to composite (multiple) materials.

Example: Use activities with music and video to increase audience engagement in training; multidisciplinary project teams; combined high-risk/low-risk investment strategy.

(Altshuller 1999) (Scanlan n.d.)

The combination of nine windows and the 40 TRIZ principles becomes a wonderful tool for breaking psychological inertia and generating hundreds of ideas in a short time. When I visit universities or my clients on consulting assignments, I use this method to generate thousands of ideas in a very short time, and by the end of my workshop every participant has a patentable idea or white paper to be published.

1. I ask them to create a nine windows for the problem/product/service that needs improvement.
2. I pick one principle and explain the principle.
3. I then take them through each window in the nine windows and ask them if they can apply the principle for each of the components in the nine windows.
4. I then pick the next principle, explain it, and repeat step 3.

I do this for all the 40 principles, and by the end of the workout the participants have thought in 40 × 9 × Average number of parameters in the nine windows ways. So at the minimum, they would have thought in 360 ways, and in my experience, on an average there would be at least three parameters per window, and hence they would have thought in 1080 ways. On average it takes 120 minutes with a 10-minute coffee break in between to complete this workout. Isn't it amazing!

Post completion of a project and before kick-starting the next project it is always a good practice to do a brainstorming, mind mapping, or other group creativity or nominal group technique workout with relevant stakeholders to recollect the lessons learned in the previous project and improve the performance of the next project. But the problem is, during these workout sessions, past experiences, lessons learned from previous projects, expertise, knowledge, and skill are some of the inputs that are used to come up with improvement ideas for the upcoming project. These input factors are extremely valuable, but they become a disadvantage when they start to act as psychological inertia. Let us take one principle at a time and try to apply it to the nine windows, where the goal is to identify ideas to improve project execution (see Table 4.1).

Table 4.1 Nine windows for a project.

	Past (1)	**Present (2)**	**Future (3)**
Supersystem (A)	Resource availability, stakeholder inputs, budget, infrastructure, risks, out of scope	External risk, external stakeholders, customer, change requests, funding	Customer satisfaction, external stakeholders, open issues and risks, contract, lessons learned
System (B)	Project scope	**Project**	Deliverables and results
Subsystem (C)	Requirements, scope, feasibility, milestones, assumptions	Project team, process, skill, internal risk, cost, leadership, schedule, templates, documents, contract	Output quality, cost/schedule variance, project baselines

Segmentation:

A. Divide an object into independent parts.

B. Make an object sectional—easy to assemble or disassemble.

C. Increase the degree of fragmentation or segmentation.

1. Break the project into independent phases and manage the baselines (cost, schedule) for the deliverables rather than the entire project to simplify the process of estimating baselines and implementing change. (B2)
2. Make the project team sectional by hiring resources based on skill requirements just when the skill is required, and release immediately. (C2)
3. Fragment or break down the project activities to a more granular level to improve the cost estimation accuracy. (C2)
4. Break large deliverables into smaller usable segments to add value to the customer and reduce waiting time. (B3)
5. Deliver the standard requirements and create multiple nonstandard requirements received from different stakeholders that can be assembled or disassembled into the standard requirements. (B3)
6. Measure and report the baseline performance for each deliverable rather than the entire project. (C3)
7. Capture customer satisfaction for each deliverable rather than the entire project. (A3)
8. Go through each activity and list all the risks and assumptions in the contract. (A3)
9. Increase the level of communication to the customer on project progress, issues, and concerns. (A2)
10. Prepare and keep project management templates ready for each deliverable in advance. (C3)

Taking out or separation or extraction:

A. Extract the disturbing part or property from an object.

B. Extract the only necessary part (or property) of an object.

1. Remove all the governance processes and procedures that do not add value to the project. (B2)
2. Monitor activities to make sure there is no scope creep. (B2)
3. Include only the requirements that have a significant return on investment as part of the scope statement. (C1)
4. Remove the requirements that disturb other requirements, or push them to the end of the execution phase once the other requirements are delivered. (C1)
5. Remove or isolate resources who cause inconvenience to the team members. (C2)
6. Plan and prioritize the funding. (A2)
7. Discuss the deliverables with issues and concerns in a separate meeting rather than combining them with other deliverables. (B3)
8. Communicate only relevant information to the stakeholders. (A2)
9. Separate the action plans for satisfied and dissatisfied customers. (A3)
10. Separate/isolate all the deliverables that did not meet the quality requirements and come up with preventive actions. (C3)

As you can see, I have not gone through each parameter in the nine windows for two reasons: the economy of space of this book, or because the principle might not be practically applicable to a particular parameter.

> ***Activity:*** *Complete this exercise by applying all the 40 principles to the nine windows, and keep a note of the time and the number of ideas you generate. By practicing this for different products/services you will enhance your creativity and thinking power.*

So what do we do with all those ideas? No idea is a bad idea, but it is impossible to implement hundreds of ideas into a project. The best method is to categorize the ideas into need-based categories, for example, based on urgency, benefit, future requirements, productivity, compliance, cost savings, speed, customer satisfaction, defect reduction, implementation cost and duration, and so on, and use them as and when required. But there is a limitation to this method. If we are given a specific problem—for example, to increase the productivity of the hiring team—it is practically not the best option to create a nine windows and go through all the 40 principles and select the most feasible ideas from hundreds or even thousands of options. The effort and time consumed to find a solution in this process becomes more painful than the problem itself. But not to worry, the TRIZ contradiction matrix comes to the rescue.

SLEEPING IN THE VILLAGE MEETING HALL

We eventually arrived at a small village and saw a group of ladies sitting and chatting in front of a small shop. It wasn't 4 p.m. yet, so it was the perfect time to find a place to sleep in. We asked the ladies through gesturing if there was a place where we could pitch our tent. One lady called out to the man inside the shop because he spoke a smattering of English. "Hello! How are you?" he asked. He seemed to be the head of the village and showed us to an old building in the middle of the village.

The building was very dirty and dusty, but we could see that it was the meeting place for this small village. Long chairs were arranged side by side. There was no lock, and children kept banging on the door and poking their faces through the broken windows, looking at the two strangers who had arrived on bicycles. The village head wanted to show us the village, so we walked down to the river where we could see mangroves; children were playing with a bicycle wheel and started shouting.

LACKING MOTIVATION

We needed a lot of motivation to continue the ride. Sunil pushed me, saying, we'll cycle for an hour and then break for snacks or biscuits, or by encouraging me to snap a selfie when we reached the mountaintop. But it was very difficult getting to the top; just as we thought the top was around the corner, there were more twists and turns. It was endless, but it made us laugh each time. Occasionally, we found the road going downhill and we would freak out. "Wheeeeeereeeeeeee! Woo hoo!" We screamed like children since there was nobody else on the road.

A VERY COLD NIGHT

When we asked the villagers if we could pitch our tent somewhere in the village, a man showed us a shed, which was the village meeting room (again!). The hall was by the road, and it was in the middle of the village. We were not sure if it was a safe village to sleep in but we didn't have any other options. We put down our luggage and went out again to sit by the fire. Sunil tried to a talk to a man through gestures, which made him laugh a lot. Later, we realized that we didn't have proper clothes. We wore everything we could to keep ourselves warm. Can you imagine how we slept? My head was next to Sunil's feet and Sunil was holding my feet. We tried to warm each other through our breath, and eventually we fell asleep.

5

The Contradiction Matrix

Genrich Alsthuller has made huge contributions to the field of innovative problem solving, but one thing that he will always be remembered for is the *contradiction matrix*. After studying 200,000 patents he discovered that there are many things in common between innovations, and they follow a pattern. He found that 95% of the innovations used the 40 basic principles that we have already presented. A *problem* is a *contradiction* where we try to improve a parameter but an undesired result occurs by changing another parameter along with it. For example, if I want to increase the volume of a water bottle to hold more water, the area of the bottle increases as well, which is an undesirable result. There are 39 parameters in the TRIZ contradiction matrix, as shown in Figure 5.1.

There are two kinds of contradictions, physical contradictions and technical contradictions. A *physical* contradiction occurs when a system has opposite requirements at the same time, for example, a bulletproof vest should be heavy enough to be strong and yet extremely light to help the officer run faster. So, at the same time the vest needs to be heavy and light.

A *technical* contradiction occurs when the system tries to meet an objective and an undesired factor pops up, for example, when we increase the speed of an automobile and the fuel consumption increases.

If you observe the parameters in Figure 5.1, it is quite simple to discover that these parameters were created by engineers for engineers. I have been providing an analogy and translating these parameters for project managers, operations managers, supply chain professionals, insurance professionals, business executives and more, the reason being that most of these parameters will assume different meanings depending on the problem, environment, and situation, though there are a few parameters where the meaning remains the same.

Before understanding the parameters, we need to understand moving and stationary objects with respect to business:

- *Moving objects.* Objects that can change position in space and time. For example, planned activities change in space in the planning document while getting executed, so activities in the execution phase are moving objects.
- *Stationary objects.* Objects that do not change position in space or time. Activities in the initial phase of the project are static, as the project has not yet begun. Hence, they are stationary objects. The same is applicable to the requirements that are not part of the project scope.

1. Weight of moving object	14. Strength	27. Reliability
2. Weight of stationary object	15. Duration of action of moving object	28. Measurement accuracy
3. Length of moving object	16. Duration of action of stationary object	29. Manufacturing precision
4. Length of stationary object	17. Temperature	30. Object-affected harmful factors
5. Area of moving object	18. Illumination intensity	31. Object-generated harmful factors
6. Area of stationary object	19. Use of energy by moving object	32. Ease of manufacture
7. Volume of moving object	20. Use of energy by stationary object	33. Ease of operation
8. Volume of stationary object	21. Power	34. Ease of repair
9. Speed	22. Loss of energy	35. Adaptability or versatility
10. Force (intensity)	23. Loss of substance	36. Device complexity
11. Stress or pressure	24. Loss of information	37. Difficulty of detecting and measuring
12. Shape	25. Loss of time	38. Extent of automation
13. Stability of the object's composition	26. Quantity of substance/ matter	39. Productivity

Figure 5.1 List of engineering parameters.

I will ignore the first eight parameters for the time being and talk about them at the end as they need a bit of analogy.

- *Speed.* Speed is the rate of progress over time. If the critical to quality (CTQ) parameter in your problem has something to do with the rate at which someone or something moves or operates or is able to move or operate, rapidity of movement or action, rapidity, swiftness, speediness, alacrity, quickness, fastness, celerity, velocity, dispatch, promptness, immediacy, expeditiousness, expedition, or briskness, we will be using this as the improving or worsening parameter. *Example: Cycle time; throughput time; TAT time.*
- *Force.* Force is an interaction intended to change an object's condition. Management is the force that is often applied in the form of decisions to change a process, person, or behavior. *Example: Few processes or people require constant monitoring and control, while few can perform with minimal interaction with the managers. This parameter will be used if you intend to change the amount of interaction between the manager, process, and people.*
- *Stress or pressure.* Defined as force per unit area, also called *tension.* Do these two words ring a bell? How would you feel if your manager were asking for a status update every five minutes in spite of you making it clear that you will deliver the results in eight hours? You would be tense and feel the pressure, as no one likes to be micromanaged. For another example, if a customer is given a defective product and the customer service team is putting more force on the customer by not picking up his calls, this will create tension and pressure on the customer.
- *Shape.* Defined as the external contours and appearance of the system. This parameter will be considered if the improving or worsening parameter is related to shapes like organization structure or project schedule where internal and external dependencies play a key role.
- *Stability of the object's composition.* Defined as the wholeness or integrity of the system; the relationship of the system's constituent elements. Increase in disorder within the system leads to increase in instability. If the increasing or worsening parameter is something related to instability within the business, for example, drop in customer loyalty, attrition from the project, or low knowledge retention, it can be improved using this parameter.

- *Strength.* Defined as the extent to which the object is able to resist changing in response to force. This will be the improving or worsening parameter if the problem is related to resisting an external or internal force. *Example: Ability to resist frequent changes to the project scope; inability to make the team flexible in accepting change for process improvement.*

- *Duration of action (durability).* The time the object can perform the action, or mean time between failures. This will be the improving or worsening parameter if the problem is related to durability. *Example: On average an employee stays in an organization for eight months; the project plan needs revision every 10 months; standard operating procedures change within four months.*

- *Temperature.* The thermal condition of the object or system, and other thermal parameters, such as heat capacity, that affect the rate of change of temperature. Heat is also seen as a form of energy arising from the random motion of the molecules of bodies. Hence, if the problem is related to the improving or worsening of conflicts or excitement between stakeholders, temperature is the parameter that we would look at. For example, if there are constant heated communications between the supplier and buyer, or an excited team who voluntarily communicate, brainstorm, and actively come up with ideas for improvement. The triggers for excitement could be conflicts, motivation, teamwork, purpose, disagreements, and so on.

- *Illumination intensity.* The light flux per unit area, also any other illumination characteristics of the system such as brightness, light quality, and so on. As you can see, this parameter is all about the visibility of the object and will be used if the visibility of the object has to be increased or decreased. *Example: The product is not visible in the market as the competitors' products have better visibility; it is hard to see risks and issues in the process.*

- *Use of energy.* The measure of the object's capacity for doing work. It is the physical energy given out by the employee or machine to perform the work. We all learned that energy can be converted from one form to another. The work done by the employee gets converted to a finished product and comes back to the business in dollars, pounds, euro, and so on, in the form of revenue. The business then pays the employee salary and benefits. If your improving or worsening parameter is the amount of energy or cost consumed by the components of the business, this is the parameter that will be used. *Example: Operating cost; energy consumed through physical labor; direct and indirect cost.*

- *Power.* The time rate at which work is performed, or the rate of use of energy. If the problem's improving or worsening parameter is the time rate of consumption or approval of cost or effort or organizational resources, this parameter will be used. For example, getting an approval to buy a $100 item is much easier than for a $10,000 item. The approval for a $10,000 item would require sign-off from someone from the top of the organizational pyramid relative to the person responsible for the $100 item. Hence, the power of approval or consumption is different depending on the approval hierarchy.
- *Loss of energy.* The use of energy that does not contribute or add value to the customer or the job being done. This parameter will be used if the problem is to reduce non-value-added costs or activities, which consume effort in the process without adding any value, for example, penalties paid to the supplier for not adhering to the contract terms and conditions, or repair and warranty costs.
- *Loss of substance.* The partial or complete, permanent or temporary, loss of some of a system's materials, substances, parts, or subsystems. If the problem is related to reducing the loss of physical substances either in the input or output or during the process itself, or improving the process yield, this parameter will be used. Examples for waste of physical substance could be scraps, defects, lower process yield, and so on.
- *Loss of information.* The partial or complete, permanent or temporary, loss of data or access to data in or by a system. Frequently includes sensory data such as customer emotions, inability to capture customer information related to sales, or data to forecast, to name a few.
- *Loss of time.* Time is the duration of an activity. To improve the loss of time requires reduction in the time taken for the activity. Cycle time reduction is a good example. Any time that does not contribute or add value to the end customer is a loss of time. This parameter must not be confused with *speed. Example: Wait time is a good example, but it is relative to the viewpoint from which it is seen in the system. For a customer, the time elapsed from the*

time she orders a pizza until she receives it is wait time, but in the pizzeria, for the chef, the process of making the pizza is lead time.

- *Quantity of substance/matter.* The number or amount of a system's materials, substances, parts, or subsystems that might be changed fully or partially, permanently or temporarily. If the problem is to reduce the inventory, this parameter will be considered.
- *Reliability.* A system's ability to perform its intended functions in predictable ways and conditions. This parameter describes the ability of a person or process to perform a function for a longer duration by maintaining set standards.
- *Measurement accuracy.* The closeness of the measured value to the actual value of a property of a system. If the problem is related to measurement error, this feature can be used as the improving parameter.
- *Manufacturing precision.* The extent to which the actual characteristics of the system or object match the specified or required characteristics. If the problem is related to inability to produce the required output as per the customer's requirements, such as scope variance, this feature will be the improving parameter.
- *Object-affected harmful factors.* Vulnerability of a system to externally generated (harmful) effects. If the problem is related to the external factors that are affecting the object's performance, such as eternal risks, this will be the improving parameter.
- *Object-generated harmful factors.* A harmful effect is one that reduces the efficiency or quality of the functioning of the object or system. These harmful effects are generated by the object or system as part of its operation. These are the risks generated by the system.
- *Ease of manufacture.* The degree of facility, comfort, or effortlessness in manufacturing or fabricating the object/system. If the problem is effort reduction in manufacturing the desired output, this will be the feature that must be improved.
- *Ease of operation.* Simplicity: The process is *not* easy if it requires a large number of people, a large number of steps in the operation, special tools, and so on. "Hard" processes have low yield and "easy" process have high yield; they are easy to do right.

- *Ease of repair.* Quality characteristics such as convenience, comfort, simplicity, and time to repair faults, failures, or defects in a system.
- *Adaptability or versatility.* The extent to which a system/object positively responds to external changes. Also, a system that can be used in multiple ways or under a variety of circumstances.
- *Device complexity.* The number and diversity of elements and element interrelationships within a system. The user may be an element of the system that increases the complexity. The difficulty of mastering the system is a measure of its complexity.
- *Difficulty of detecting and measuring.* Measuring or monitoring systems that are complex, costly, require much time and labor to set up and use, or that have complex relationships between components or components that interfere with each other all demonstrate "difficulty of detecting and measuring." Increasing cost of measuring to a satisfactory error is also a sign of increased difficulty of measuring.
- *Extent of automation.* The extent to which a system or object performs its functions without human interface. The lowest level of automation is the use of a manually operated tool. At intermediate levels, humans program the tool, observe its operation, and interrupt or reprogram as needed. At the highest level, the machine senses the operation needed, programs itself, and monitors its own operations.
- *Productivity.* The number of functions or operations performed by a system per unit time. The time for a unit function or operation. The output per unit time, or the cost per unit output.

The eight parameters (weight, length, area, and volume of a moving and stationary object) are applied on an object, that is, a material that can be seen and touched. Hence, we need to create a dummy object that can take these parameters. I will use a cuboid as the object and name it *project* (see Figure 5.2). This object called project has no meaning unless some characteristics are given to it. We will take one TRIZ parameter at a time out of the eight, understand the meaning of the parameter, and identify the metaphor from project management to create an analogy.

For each parameter, additional synonyms and definitions are provided that will help you in creating more analogies to the problem you are trying to solve.

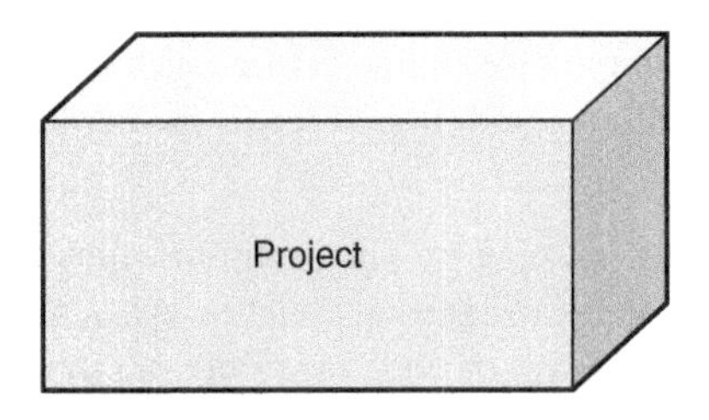

Figure 5.2 An object called "project."

Weight of the object. In physics we define weight of the object as a body's relative mass or the quantity of matter contained by it, giving rise to a downward force; the heaviness of a person or thing. In simple terms I call it *heaviness.* Heaviness is anything that makes the object consume more physical effort to move. What makes your project heavy? It is the components of the project. And what are the components of the project that make the project hard to move forward? It is the scope, schedule, risks, and complexity, to name a few (see Figure 5.3).

Hence, I can visualize my project as a physical object that has one big component—the scope. The scope is further made up of smaller components like activities, risk, effort, and so on. The more components, the heavier the project, and the analogy holds true.

Additional definitions and synonyms. The force exerted on the mass of a body; the quality of being heavy; a unit or system of units used for expressing how much an object or quantity of matter weighs; a piece of metal known to weigh a definite amount and used on scales to determine how heavy an object or quantity of a substance is; heavy object, especially one being lifted or carried; the ability of someone or something to influence decisions or actions; the importance attributed to something; hold (something) down by placing a heavy object on top of it.

Length of the object. Length has two meanings; one is the measurement or extent of something from end to end, that is, to measure some parameter from the start to the end of my project. The best parameter that can depict the beginning and the end of the project is the *time.* The difference between the start time and the end time of the project is the project duration (see Figure 5.4). Hence, another meaning of length is the amount of time occupied by something.

A Gantt chart is the most popular way of measuring and managing project duration. This is done by measuring and managing the length of the bars, with each bar representing the difference between the start and end times of an activity (see Figure 5.5).

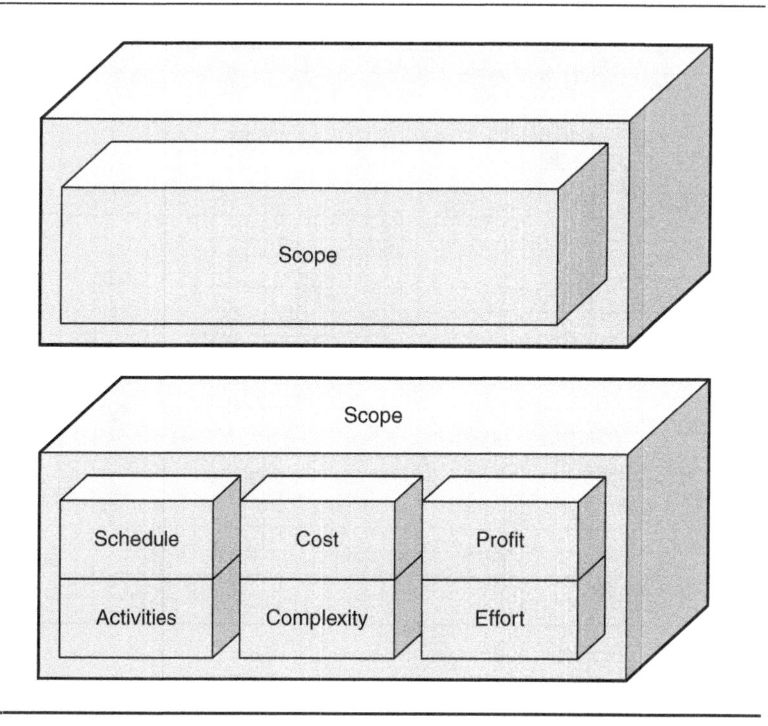

Figure 5.3 The physical object "project" with another object inside called "scope."

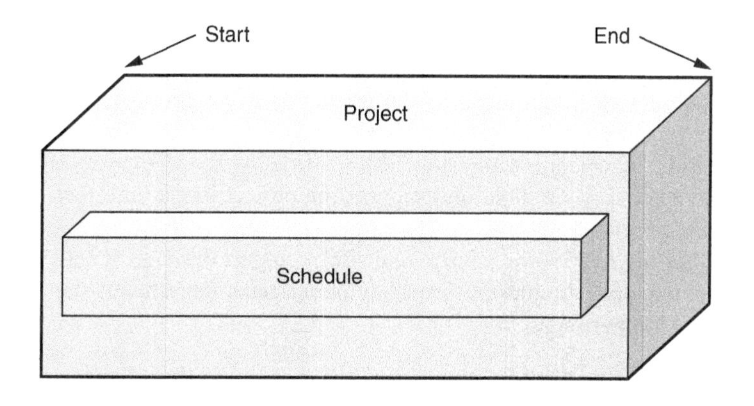

Figure 5.4 Object "project" with clear start and end boundaries.

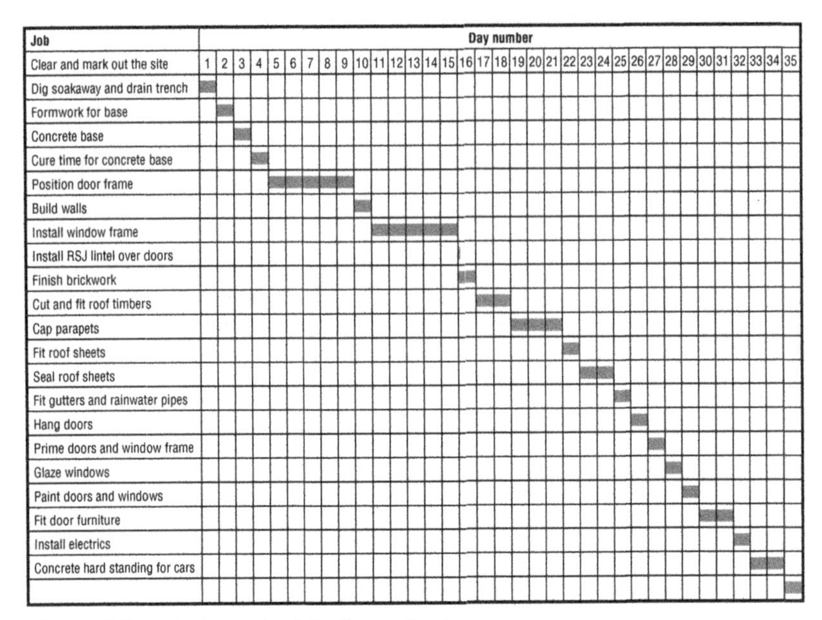

Figure 5.5 Project schedule Gantt chart.

Additional definitions and synonyms. The measurement or extent of something from end to end; the greater of two or the greatest of three dimensions of an object; the amount of time occupied by something; a piece or stretch of something; an extreme to which a course of action is taken.

Area of the object. Area is defined as the extent or measurement of a surface. Everything related to the project and that covers or holds the project together becomes the area. For example, the support functions for project management like the PMO office, budget, Finance, Human Resources, and so on, hold and support the project like a tank that holds water (see Figure 5.6).

Additional definitions and synonyms. A subject or range of activity or interest, expanse, extent, size, scope, domain, sector, department, province, territory, compartment, line.

Volume of the object. Volume is defined as the amount of space that a substance or object occupies. If area is the surface of the project, everything related to the scope, which is the core purpose of the project, becomes the volume of the object. There is a possibility that a tank might have very thick walls and an asymmetric inner surface, which makes the area big but the volume of water it can hold less. Similarly, a project might have too many

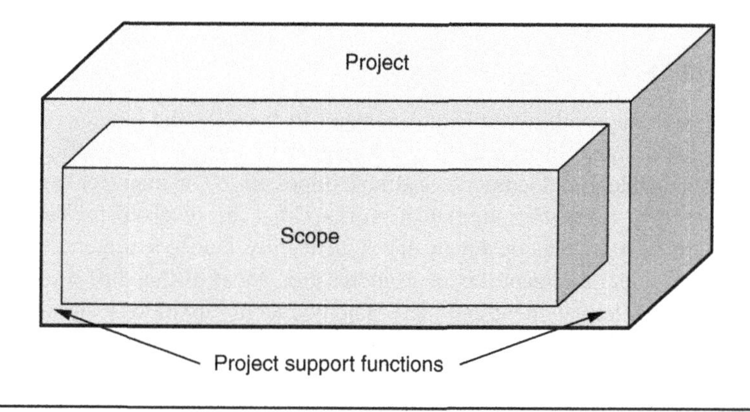

Figure 5.6 Area occupied by the object "project."

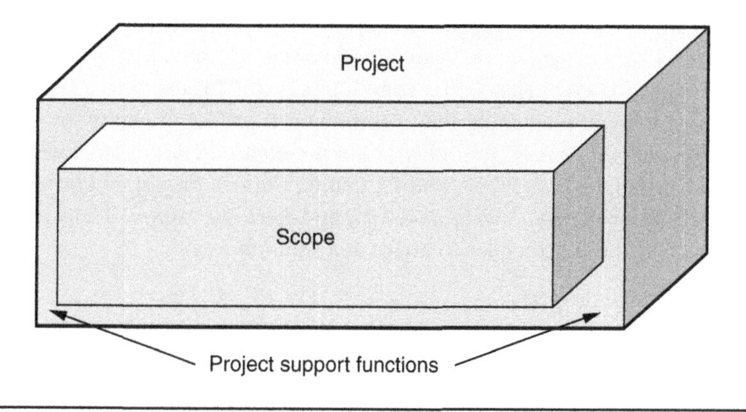

Figure 5.7 Volume of the object "project."

support functions and factors that hold or wrap the project, like internal compliance activities, but that does not mean the scope of the project is too large (see Figure 5.7).

Additional definitions and synonyms. The amount of space that a substance or object occupies, or that is enclosed within a container; capacity, cubic measure, size, magnitude, largeness, bigness, mass, bulk, extent, extensiveness.

You now know all the 40 principles and 39 features or parameters (Terninko et al. n.d.) (Miller et al. 1998).

Lets us look at some examples to see how the contradiction matrix can be used.

EXAMPLE 1

I had a meeting with a municipal manager in Iran. As the bureaucracy is quite impenetrable in Iran, having a foreigner in a government office and sharing confidential documents is almost impossible. The manager kept the problem very short: the number of requests that are received for various issues has been increasing day by day significantly. Due to the international sanctions, unemployment has been increasing. Most of the staff are contractors and relatively new, and there is no budget to hire more-experienced people. The productivity of these staff is quite low, and hence the requests are piling up and customers have started to complain about longer wait times and defects, to name just a few. A month back he received another communication that the inventory of untouched cases must be closed within a target date.

We all have come across this scenario, or will probably come across one in future. Every organization wants to maximize its productivity with minimum operating cost. Hence, the contradiction was Productivity (39) to be improved without worsening the operating cost, or Use of energy by moving object (19). For this contradiction, in the contradiction matrix we will see four principles, 35, 10, 38, and 19, that is, *Change property (Parameter change)*, *Prior action*, *Strong oxidants*, and *Periodic action*. The way we used each of these principles to arrive at a solution was:

1. Change property
    a. Implement a low-cost, simple workflow in the next six to 12 months.
    b. Design a clear workflow and standard operating procedures rather than depending on the intuition of the employees.
    c. Translate the guided workflow to a mobile application that can be used by end customers for 58% of the requests.
    d. Train and assess employees on their roles and responsibilities.
    e. Measure and monitor key process indicators (KPIs) at different stages.
    f. Level load the team, considering the bottleneck processes.
2. Prior action
    a. The request forms were redesigned according to the process flow to avoid unnecessary motion.

   b. All the information required from the customer is taken in the first go.

   c. Classify and assign all the requests depending on type.

3. Strong oxidants

   a. The team was continuously monitored and motivated.

   b. Team leaders constantly cheered the team.

   c. All the customer data were made accessible in a central repository.

4. Periodic action

   a. Periodic reviews of the world done every day so far.

   b. Periodically review the queue and reschedule the resources from one process step to another.

You might now have a question in mind—are many of these not lean tools? Yes, there could be many lean or Six Sigma practices that are used with a principle as they are all problem-solving approaches using different techniques. The client went ahead and started implementing these solutions. In a month, productivity went up by 65%. I recently got an e-mail from the client that they have implemented the workflow and their productivity is now 3.5 times more than it used to be. If any of you happen to go to the municipality of Iran to get your work done, please do me a favor by letting me know about your experience.

EXAMPLE 2

I was asked to conduct a remote training on TRIZ for a South American steel manufacturing company. After introducing them to the contradiction matrix, the vice president of quality volunteered and shared a problem. The company manufactured steel bars in three sizes, large, medium, and small, with a square cross-section. The problem was that the medium-sized bar had a slight shift of 3 degrees in its cross-section (see Figure 5.8). They do not recollect the history of the problem as none of the customers came back, except in the last three months one customer started observing it and returning product to the company as it did not meet their requirements. All the steel, worth thousands of dollars, was scrap. The company did not have a process in place to measure such a small variation. Secondly, they argued

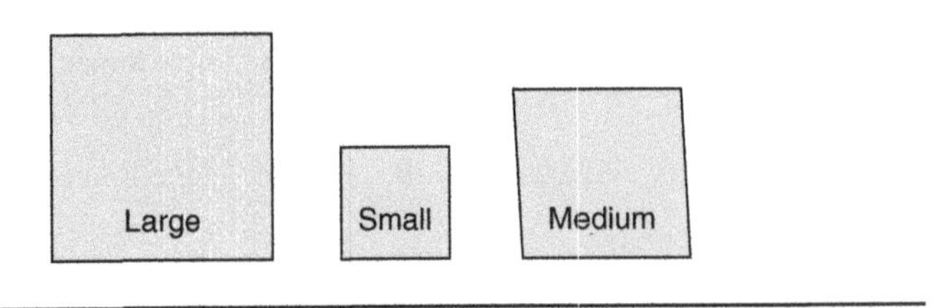

Figure 5.8 Different cross sections of metallic bar.

that the process that was used to manufacture all three types of steel was exactly the same and there was no difference. They wanted to use TRIZ to identify the cause and resolve this problem.

By listening to the customer's problem, I understood without much effort the parameter of the object that had to be improved was Shape (12). I was not sure about the worsening parameter. As per the voice of the customer, the process used for all three types of steel was the same. Hence, the difference between a medium-sized bar and the large- or small-sized bar is just two characteristics:

1. Area of the moving object (5)
2. Weight of the moving object (1)

We first looked at the contradiction Shape/Area of the moving object or 12/5 in the contradiction matrix. The principles we found in the contradiction matrix were 5, 34, 4, and 10, that is, *Merging*, *Discarding and recovering* (also called *Rejection and regeneration*), *Asymmetry*, and *Prior action*. *Merging* is about bringing two or more processes together in space or time, so I asked the client if there is any process step that is done separately for the medium-sized bars, but at the same time or space for the large- and small-sized bars. The answer was no, the process steps are the same for all. *Asymmetry* is a principle where we make symmetrical processes or parts asymmetrical. For this problem, one of the solutions that this principle is suggesting is to create asymmetry by applying a +3-degree shift to the equipment that creates the shape, which was an important indicator. *Prior action* and *Discarding and recovering* principles did not give any direction and hence were dropped. We repeated the same for the next contradiction, *Shape/Weight of moving object*, or 12/1, and the principles we found to resolve them were 8, 10, 29, and 40, that is, *Counterweight*, *Prior action*, *Pneumatics and hydraulics*, and *Composite materials*. Similarly, Counterweight was the only principle that was applicable to the weight of the medium-sized bars that differed from the small and larger ones. As per the Counterweight principle, an additional weight needed to be added somewhere in the operation to make the shape right, which also meant an additional weight was being created in one of the process steps and needed an immediate fix. The other principles were the same for all three.

The team had to answer just two questions:

1. Is there any asymmetry in the equipment that is causing this 3-degree shift?
2. Is there any additional weight that is applied at any point in the process just in medium-sized bars that would be fixed through counterweighting?

The team immediately answered no and said everything was the same for all three processes. They were disappointed, and we all went for lunch. During the lunch break one of the participants approached the production manager. She had gone through the whole process looking to fit just two principles, *Asymmetry* and *Counterweight*, and was able to zero in on the exact problem. After lunch she brought the production manager to the training, and he said that one process step applied excess stress on the medium-sized bars but not on the small or larger ones. A simple correlation and regression resolved and fixed the problem. They could not believe such a complex problem was solved in a few hours using TRIZ methodology remotely. This was a direct bottom-line savings of thousands of dollars per month.

EXAMPLE 3

In Portugal a wine company selling sparkling wine had a problem with the bottles that came from their supplier. Wine and gas were put inside the bottle under high pressure and then sealed. During this process, some of the bottles were unable to withstand the pressure and broke. This happened to 6% to 8% of the bottles. So, it was huge waste of wine and money because the bottles cracked after the wine went inside the bottle, and the wine spilled when the bottle cracked. Changing the suppler was not an option as no other suppliers were able to provide the bottle for the same price. The contradiction in this problem is the improving parameter is Stress or Pressure (11) and the worsening parameter is Strength (14), and the principles to resolve them are, 9, 18, 3, and 40, that is, *Preliminary anti-action*, *Mechanical vibration*, *Local quality*, and *Composite materials*. The owner made it very clear that there is no way he is going to change the machine or the bottle, so Composite material and Mechanical vibration were ruled out. I was left with Preliminary anti-action and Local quality. We used an elastic rubber band around the middle of the bottle where the pressure was highest before the bottles went into the machine for filling as an anti-action against the pressure coming from inside. The problem was solved with the small effort of putting the bands around the bottles. Now the breakage is down to 1%.

EXAMPLE 4

For an insurance business, my role was to reduce the cycle time of a quote generation process. This process was very crucial for the company. The customer would approach the insurance company for a quote and at the same time would be shopping to get a quote from other insurance companies as well. The speed at which the quote is generated is one of the key factors in converting the quote into a sale. There were two aspects here: generating the quote quickly and at the same time accurately. The agent has to gather all the information from the customer on which the risk is assessed and the quote is generated. If the information is gathered incorrectly, then risk is assessed incorrectly and hence the quote is incorrect, which will put the insurance company at a loss. Hence, the improving parameter here is Speed (9) and the worsening parameter is Measurement accuracy (28), and the principles are, 28, 32, 1, and 24, that is, *Replace mechanical system*, *Color or optical change*, *Segmentation*, and *Mediator*.

1. *Replace mechanical system.* 40% of the customers were return customers, and a lot of information was available online. Hence, all the information available online was captured before the agent went to meet the customer to collect all the information.

2. *Color or optical change.* The factors that increase the risk and quote to the customer were highlighted in red so that they could check and confirm if the information was right. The same was done with the back-end team, where the team had just to check the information highlighted in red on the application rather than going through the whole application. Even key decisions were taken based on colors.

3. *Segmentation.* The customers were segmented by industry type, location, job role, and so on, and based on these parameters the risk was assessed and the form was generated for each customer. The fields in the form were customized based on this information.
4. *Mediator.* Having a representative available for the top-priority customers, working from the customer's location with the most recent information regarding the customer.

Exercise. Identify the improving and the worsening parameters for the following scenarios and how you can apply the principles in your business.

1. Decrease the operating cost without putting any pressure on the employees.
2. Reducing the cycle time is leading to a decrease in reliability.
3. Reducing the complexity of the business is leading to an increase in customer waiting time.
4. Attempting to reduce the inventory at the bottleneck process steps increases the effort utilized by the resources.
5. Multiple handoffs in the business had made operations extremely difficult.
6. Micromanagement by the supervisor is putting a lot of pressure on the employees.

Answers

1. 19, 11
2. 9, 27
3. 36, 25
4. 26, 19
5. 36, 33
6. 10, 11

BEEN THERE, DONE THAT

It's February 2016; we have just entered Vietnam from Laos and will cycle through the country into China; the roads here are much better than in Laos (even going uphill is such a breeze); the scenery is beautiful, with bamboo forests on both sides and a shimmering blue river appearing occasionally to the left side. Everything's perfect, but Sunil seems distracted.

It's only after some hours that I realize that he's looking for an ATM. We didn't exchange money at the Laos border to avoid unnecessary conversion charges. We assumed we would find an ATM on the other side of the border, but we didn't.

You see, Valentine's Day was upon us, and a month earlier Sunil had promised me that he would do something special for me. But we didn't have a single penny and he was fretting.

When we finally found an ATM in a small town, we were told it was closed for the holidays and the nearest ATM was another 105 km away. Seeing our disappointment, a man standing next to the ATM invited us to his house. His wife prepared a Vietnamese New Year feast; they even served French wine. We were stuffed and became very cheerful. We got back on the road after the meal, and Sunil soon started to cycle like a drunk man. So, we took a one-hour nap under the bamboo trees by the road and woke up to the sounds of birds. It was very refreshing.

We soon came upon a small village, and a petite old lady asked us to come over for tea. When we asked her if we could pitch our tent, she insisted that we sleep inside the house. Unlike other houses in the village, her house was bigger and not made of wood and bamboo. She served sweets and water; her husband brought out the local brew. Village women with babies stopped by and had tea. The two prepared a big feast for dinner. The lady cooked small fish; the husband made a delicious fluffy omelet with lots of herbs. Fried green vegetables and vegetable soup were also on the table.

Suddenly, the husband put on loud music. "Dance! Dance!" the lady asked us. The husband cranked up the volume and brought out disco lights from his room. The neighbors also joined us. The lady disappeared and came back with the traditional dress so we changed into yukata *and* lungi. *We kept dancing. People laughed and took photos. At some point, Sunil put on the traditional ladies' costume and danced with the drunk village men.*

It was Valentine's Day and we were having a cheerful night. Maybe not romantic, but cheerful.

Suddenly, the lady insisted that Sunil and I should sleep in different rooms. We told her we were married, but she would have none of it. She came and slept next to me and two local ladies chased Sunil off. Sunil gave up and said, "Good night. Happy Valentine's day!" I shared the bed with the lady that night.

6
The Idea Generator

Be there a problem to solve or a process or product to improve, there are numerous techniques for generating ideas, and the most common one is *brainstorming*. As I mentioned in the first chapter, all the ideas that come out are purely based on the past experiences of an individual or group. Our past experiences develop the thoughts, these thoughts produce ideas, and these ideas become innovation (see Figure 6.1). Hence, if you want to produce a good yield of innovations it is very important to have a very high concentration of past innovative and creative experiences, which can be partly achieved by being surrounded by creative people, working in a problem-solving environment, being curious, reading books, and so on. We cannot ask life and the people around us to be innovators and problem solvers. Given a chance I would love to have Einstein, Feynman, and Da Vinci as my project team members, but in reality I have very limited options due to different constraints in choosing my project team members. The question now is, how can I make the existing project members think like Da Vinci or Einstein?

By using TRIZ principles we can increase the yield by a hundred times or more. If, instead of channelizing our thoughts based on our past experiences, we can replace this with the 40 TRIZ principles, we will be able to think similarly to 200,000 Soviet innovators. By doing so, the yield will increase exponentially.

While I was in Athens I was invited to conduct a boot camp on TRIZ, and the audience consisted of MBA students with specialization in total quality management. After introducing them to the nine windows tool and 40 TRIZ principles, I presented a fictitious problem to be solved in groups of three. One such problem was as follows.

Brompton is a folding bicycle company in the United Kingdom and a renowned brand. They were planning to launch electric folding bikes to the market and needed an effective social media marketing strategy for Europe.

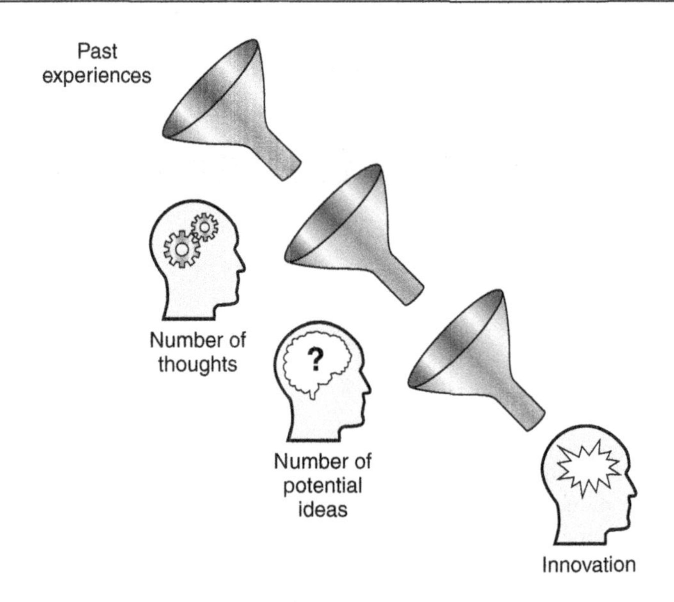

Figure 6.1 Thought-to-innovation cycle.

Table 6.1 Nine windows for building social media marketing strategy.

	Past	Present	Future
Super or macro system	Competition, other brands, the need (demand)	Customers, social media	Customers, social media
System	Product (electric folding bicycles)	Social media marketing strategy	100,000 people engaged on social media (digital customers)
Sub or micro system	Cost of the productions, components	Markets, target groups, demand factors, contents, digital strategy	Like, posts, shares, comments

None of the team members had any prior experience in social media marketing. They started by first creating a simple nine windows (see Table 6.1).

Then they started applying the top 10 TRIZ principles for each parameter in each window. They came up with hundreds of ideas within 60 minutes. Table 6.2 shows some of the ideas that were generated.

As you can see, this approach is very effective in generating high-quality ideas in a short duration of time. The total number of ideas generated depends on the average number of parameters in each window in the nine windows (see Figure 6.2).

If there is an average of one parameter per window, we have 360 creative ways to think. Normally, on average there are six parameters for a simple product, which means we will have 2160 creative ways to think.

Table 6.2 Ideas and principles used.

Ideas created	Principle
Divide the market by existing bike users in order to determine the demand for electric folding bicycles (Normal bike, electrical bike, folding bike and all of their combinations)	Segmentation
Division of target groups by age and income	Segmentation
Division of target groups by geographical area (Amsterdam, rest of Europe)	Segmentation
Division of target groups by areas with high levels of bicycle thefts	Segmentation
"Take out" from our competition all the other brands that gain small pieces from the pie of "demand"	Taking out
"Take out" the digital strategy and the content from our social media campaign that do not have strong engagement with the audience	Taking out
Promote features like the option to switch on the motor when traveling uphill within the content	Local quality
Create a schedule of bike marathons and promote our product there, or create lotteries in social media	Local quality
Evaluation of target groups by age and split them asymmetrically (younger—fewer campaigns, older—more campaigns)	Asymmetry
Asymmetrical approach and reevaluation of the content of the digital marketing strategy according to results every month	Asymmetry

Continued

Table 6.2 *Continued.*

Ideas created	**Principle**
Analysis of comments /shares/ likes/ follows social media posts in order to evaluate the engagement of consumers according to the relative strategy implemented by the company	Merging
Implementation of decreasing marketing cost strategy in collaboration with digital marketing strategy	Merging
Consolidating the audience engagement from different channels into one	Merging
Using the user engagement data to forecast sales	Universality
Use the audience comments as a feedback for process improvement and product design	Universality
Identify the target group, split the target group by geography, break down the geography by age, sex, and income, and then allocate the campaigning budget depending on the total population size of each group	Nested doll
Launch a new social media customized strategy when likes, comments, or shares decrease periodically	Anti-weight
Aggressive video advertisement on social media to sarcastically compare bicycles, motorcycles, and electric folding bikes	Prior counteraction
Release posts, hash tags, pictures, and videos as teasers to create eagerness before the launching of the product	Prior action
Prepare calendar and schedule posts in advance.	Prior action
Exchange of advertisements of comments on social media with other companies' sites on a permanent basis	Anti-weight/ equipotentiality
Make the content interactive, for example, ask audience to comment on the answer to a question	Dynamics
Contents of the campaign must use the colors of the brand, and highlight the uniqueness of the new product	Color change
Change the color composition of the content depending on the target group	Color change

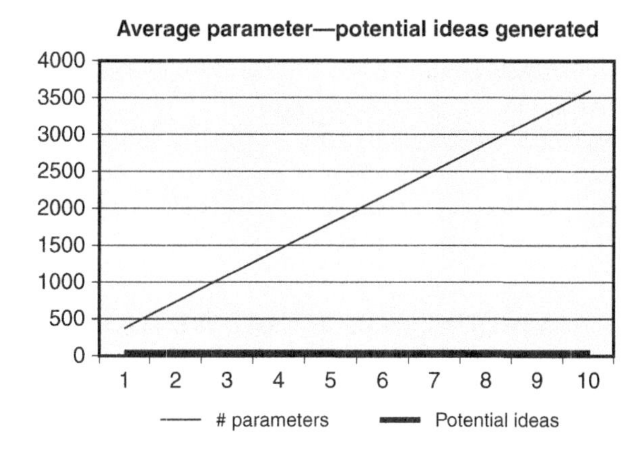

Figure 6.2 Number of parameters in the nine windows versus total ideas generated.

A NIGHT AT THE POLICE STATION

When we left Hanoi we thought we had been spoiled by our host. But as the scenery started to change from the busy city to rice fields, so did our natural instinct. We saw an old man behind his house gate and asked him if we could pitch our tent for the night. He invited us in and served snacks and drinks.

In the evening the family served us dinner—pork, vegetable soup, rice, and beer. They had a karaoke set, and the old man's wife started to sing. Sunil, always generous with compliments, said, "Wow! You sound like a pop star." And that was it. She didn't stop singing.

Suddenly, the atmosphere changed. Around 11 p.m. the family asked us to go to the police station. They told us it was illegal to let foreigners stay in a house, and the neighbors would report on them.

It was dark, and we were slightly tipsy, but we followed the old man. After 20 minutes we arrived at the police station, where a policeman asked us for our passports.

"Stay in hotel," he said. "But we have no money," we said. He made several phone calls and then insisted that we stay in a hotel. "Can we stay in the police station," I asked. He made another call and agreed. "Tent OK. Give passport."

A MONKEY DOLL THAT WE TOOK AROUND THE WORLD

We were close to Lào Cai, the city along the Chinese border. The road was muddy, but we were enjoying the ride. About 10 minutes later we passed by a school, and a boy on a Vietnamese motorbike accosted us.

"Where are you from?"

"I am from Japan and he is from India."

"What is your name?"

He kept asking us questions as he rode alongside. After about five kilometers the boy pointed to a house and said that was his home. He invited us in, where his pretty mother welcomed us with biscuits, chocolate pies, and tea. The boy and his mum used Google translator to speak with us. They asked us to have lunch with them, and when the boy's younger sister returned from school she was very excited to see two foreigners in her house. The family had a kitchen garden and hen house from which they sourced raw materials for their food. The mother made an omelette with spring onions and mooli *just like we do in Japan. She also cooked a pork dish. The girl offered us two Vietnamese chocolate boxes. She then made a monkey from her model-making kit for us. We were so touched by the gesture that the monkey doll has been with us ever since.*

7

System Evolution

As a consultant, one of my key deliverables is to understand the customer's pain areas and design a future-state system that can overcome all these pain areas and be more efficient. I ask the stakeholders of each department to list their pain areas, and most of the time they respond that they do not have one! I try to get the answer by framing the question in different ways, but this is usually not much more effective. Once, I asked them, suppose I am a genie just out of the lamp and I can help you with anything related to your work, literally anything—what would you ask for? A supply chain analyst answered that she would like to complete her everyday mundane tasks with the click of a button, a procurement manager said he would like to purchase materials at the cheapest price without doing any research, a floor operator said he would like the assembly line supervisor's mouth to be shut while at work, and so on. These were the answers I was looking for. At this point none of us knew that we were talking about *ideality*.

Ideal final result is a TRIZ concept. The law of ideality states that any technical system moves toward ideality, that is, it becomes more reliable, simple, effective—more ideal. As we get closer to ideality, it costs less, it is simpler and more efficient. The ideal product is one that performs its function without even existing. The ideal process delivers the necessary action without expending energy and time. An ideal system will:

- Have only benefits
- Not cause any harm
- Not require costs for operation

The equation for ideality is

$$\text{Ideality} = \text{(Perceived) benefits} / (\text{Cost} + \text{Harm}).$$

For example, an ideal procurement process will be able to procure the cheapest materials with 100% accuracy without spending a penny on the procurement team or process itself. Take any department in your company and ask what its core function is. Or take any object that you see around you, for example, a cell phone. An ideal communication device must resolve contradictions like zero noise, zero delay, easy maintenance, and so on. Let us travel a few centuries back—the mode of communication was through letters, and the harm in the process was delay in receiving the information. To bridge the delay, telegraph took over, but still there was delay and the messages were short. Then wired telephones were developed, which was a breakthrough, but the harm was you had to stay near to where the phone was. Then cell phones solved this problem, but they were expensive. Then the price per call started to drop drastically. To stay competitive in the market, cell phone manufacturers started adding more features and functionalities into the phone, like Internet, games, movies, and other applications. Now a cell phone is not just a device to make and receive calls but a bunch of devices combined into one device. One by one the contradictions were resolved from the time of smoke signals and drums to the age of smartphones. So, what happened over the decades was the system started to reach ideality by minimizing the cost and harmful factors and maximizing the benefits. Hence, irrespective of whether you, your company, or the industry decides to move toward ideality or not, the market and customer needs will move toward it.

So, to stay competitive in the market, ideality is the key. One of the quality methodologies used to create a strategic plan in a company is *hoshin planning*, and one of its key steps is to develop breakthrough objectives. Many major brands follow it, but why do many fail and few succeed? These breakthrough objectives are established purely through tools like the Ansoff matrix, which helps to show the gaps in the products or services offered to existing consumers and the offerings of the competitors. The entire process of innovation is seen through a very small lens, and secondly it is focused on the existing product rather than the functionality. According to the concept of ideality, the ideal state of the system is where all of its functions are achieved without causing problems. The ideal system is better, faster, costs less, commits fewer errors, and requires less maintenance. In other words, an ideal system consists of all positives and no negatives. The breakthrough objectives established during hoshin planning should not be based on the gap between the existing business metrics and the competitor benchmark, but rather the gap between the existing functionalities and the ideal functionalities. Products are the channels through which the functionality is met, and thus the focus should be on the ideal functionality rather than existing product functionalities. Eventually, every product will move toward ideality. The ideal solution is realistically not achievable, but is used as a reference point in order to conceptualize the obtained solutions. The ideal solution is a solution that does not create any negative effects.

By understanding the movement or evolution of the product toward ideality we will be able to predict what will happen next to the product or the market. The good news is that there are laws that direct the increasing degree of ideality in system evolution.

The first law states that a system can evolve by increasing the degree of system dynamics. This can be done by moving the system from the macro level to the subsystem level, for example, by making the size of the product, business, or project smaller and smaller to be more dynamic. Let us look at the evolution of business models. A large, rigid company broke into flexible business units, which further broke down into well-connected independent companies, which further broke down into interim management teams, which further broke down into a startup created to deliver a function and disappear, which further broke down into a single mobile application (see Figure 7.1). If a product or service is well received by customers because it is smaller than its previous version, the trend will continue.

Another way of improving the system dynamics is by increasing the degree of fragmentation. The business system can be monolithic or non-monolithic (consisting of several parts). A system can transition to a micro level through continuous fragmentation. For example, solid to liquid to gas to fields. Look at the evolution of the computer (see Figure 7.2).

The second way of improving the system dynamics is by transforming the system into more energy saturated forms. This can be achieved in many ways. Increasing specific energy levels of the working unit makes it possible to raise the effectiveness and quality of manufacturing processes and also to create new manufacturing processes. Keep the budget, resources,

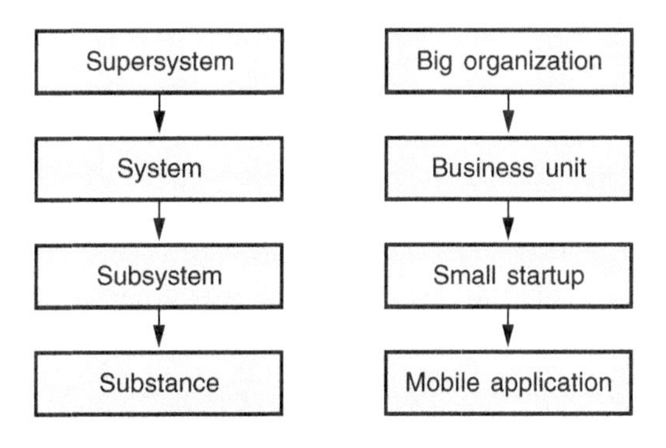

Figure 7.1 Transition of system to micro levels.

Figure 7.2 Evolution of the personal computer.

and capacity at the maximum for units, processes, or process steps that are critical for the business or product, especially those that have a direct impact on customer satisfaction. Increasing the control over the units will improve system performance. For example, by replacing a field type with a field that has a higher degree of control will increase the efficiency and performance of the process. In business we try to convert the mechanical energy of human effort into electromagnetic fields through automation. If automating a process directly from mechanical to electromagnetic is hard, we can convert the mechanical process into optical information, and the system can take decisions based on color and automate the process. Not just energy, but even saturating a particular business unit with information will improve system performance and move them toward ideality. By providing a system with all the information that it needs with the necessary feedback loops, a system can be transitioned to a self-educational and self-organizational system, and, finally, to a self-evolving and self-reproducing system. The "Internet of things" and machine learning are doing the same, they are fed with all the information and complete feedback loops to educate themselves.

The system can also evolve and move toward ideality through proper coordination between the system, subsystem, and supersystem. What did Amazon retail do? They just increased the coordination between the numerous suppliers (subsystem) and the consumers (supersystem) around the globe. It is a retail store that is close to ideality, where we can find maximum consumables with a click of a button, with competitive pricing, and without any real estate or high operational expense.

Lastly, a system can evolve by merging with a supersystem. For example, merging of printer and scanner. Who would have imagined a major competitor for the camera industry would be mobile phone companies?

You might be wondering by now, while these laws might hold good for technical systems, are they applicable to business systems that involve human interactions?

Valeri Souchkov, a TRIZ master, explains in one of his papers (2015):

> *There have been many discussions if TRIZ can be directly applied to innovating business systems and business models. One of the arguments against it due to the fact that the business systems operate with people and therefore they have different principles of evolution rather than technical systems. Unlike technical systems which are based on the laws of sciences like physics or chemistry, business systems depend a lot on psychology, especially on human decisions which can be irrational. As a result, when we use a model of a technical system we can predict its future behavior more or less correctly while when using a model of a business system we may not produce a correct prediction of its behavior.*
>
> *In part, it is true. However today most of the business systems operate on the basis of business processes which clearly define various aspects of a business system functioning and behavior. A modern business system possesses a well-defined structure and well-described relationships between its internal parts and their external system: a supersystem.*
>
> *Studies already demonstrated that the fundamental TRIZ principles could be observed in a number of different non-technical areas. Research by B. Zlotin and A. Zusman on evolution of organizations also revealed trends and patterns very similar to those which were found in technical TRIZ for evolution of technical systems.*

Key Takeaway

During its evolution, the technical system tends to improve the ratio between system performance and the expenses required to achieve this performance.

Main directions:

1. Improvement of the system performance without additional expenditures

2. Decreasing the expenditures without performance decreasing

3. Transition to the supersystem

This law is always true.

It is a perpetual design direction. It must be considered as a concept, an ultimate goal.

Some linked concepts:

- *Ideal machine.* There is no machine, but the required action is performed.
- *Ideal process.* There are no energy expenses and no time expenses, but the required action is performed.
- *Ideal substance.* There is no substance, but the function is performed.

(Souchkov et al. 2016)

A business can be idealized (taken close to ideality) by the following methods:

- Remove non-value-added processes, resources, customer segments, services, features, or anything that doesn't add value to the customer. Or simply, "make it lean."
- Increase the number of functions that add benefit to the customer, or keep adding benefits to the customer.
- Increase the value of the parameters that add value to the customer, such as delivery time, cost, and other KPIs.
- Use advanced processes, technology, and materials that reduce complexity and human involvement and increase customer experience in delivering value to the customer.
- Eliminate the parameters and functions that make the customer uncomfortable or unhappy.
- Use the TRIZ principle of *Cheap disposables* wherever applicable.
- Optimize the entire business.
- Use expensive materials if it adds value to the customer.
- Use more resources if it adds value to the customer.

Ideality is one of the most important concepts in TRIZ, and crucial for innovation and business transformation. We will be discussing more on this as we move forward, but just remember that the *ideal final result* might sound like an extremely aggressive goal, impossible to achieve, impractical, unfeasible, and unattainable. Look around you, and realize that all the innovations that you see were once the same but now are reality. Though ideality does not provide the solution, it will tell you how far you are from the ideal system and guide you in the direction of improvement. Still not convinced? I always end my lecture on ideality by quoting this example that I came across. Sailors used stars in the sky as the directional orientation for a long time, but have any of the sailors reached a star? However, think about how many ships have found the harbor without going astray, and how many human lives have been rescued, thanks to this directional orientation. Similarly, you will not be able to achieve ideality, but an attempt to achieve an ideal business will take you in the right direction.

Assessment

Define an ideal:

1. Project manager
2. Operations manager
3. Customer
4. Stakeholder
5. Process improvement manager
6. Business
7. Supply chain process
8. Sourcing process
9. Employee

Once you have defined the ideal, identify the contradictions in your organization that are stopping you from taking each of these toward ideality. Apply the laws and methods for taking a process toward ideality. Come up with SMART action items. You will be a star in your organization.

> ***Activity:*** *Define the ideality of any process, product, service, or result that you want to improve. List all the benefits, costs, and harms in the existing system and think about how you can take the process close to ideality. Also think about what could be the future of the system and what the ideal system would look like.*

(Cascini n.d.)

HELLO CHINA

We were running out of time, so we took a train to Kunming, China.

"Are you a yoga practitioner?" Lisa asked me at the platform while we were waiting for the train.

"Umm, I do yoga." Lisa saw my tent mattress and assumed I was a yoga teacher.

She got chatting with us and invited us to stay with her in Kunming. A young soldier seated next to us got so curious that he asked Lisa if he could come stay with her too.

"Yes," she said. When we reached Kunming, the young soldier carried our two bikes as if he were carrying two pillows.

Over the next few days she showed us some beautiful places. One of the memorable experiences was attending a Chinese tea ceremony. Each time the master poured the tea in small cups, he talked about some lesson for life. He taught us the importance of having some peaceful moments in our lives.

Lisa was involved in a lot of activities, including volunteering. She took us to the family of a young man whose brain had not grown as fast as his body. When Lisa told him about our cycling trip, he showed us how to write bicycle *in Chinese. Then we had origami and Indian dance sessions. The boy and his father put on* lungi *and we danced until we all got tired. "Let's have chai," Sunil said. They had never tasted chai before but they loved it.*

GOOD-BYE CHINA

It was still a long way to the border; it was getting dark and we were in the middle of nowhere. We could see the snow-capped mountains and some abandoned tombs. We finally saw a van and it stopped for us. When we told the driver we wanted to go to Bishkek, he said, "I don't think you can. You need to take a local taxi from the border as there is still thick snow in the mountain."

He dropped us near the border, and we cycled toward the immigration office, looking at the imposing mountains ahead of us. I was totally unprepared for snow in April, but Sunil seemed optimistic.

"Ready for the snow?" he asked.

"Not for the snow, but definitely curious to see Kyrgyzstan."

8

TRIZ for Entrepreneurs, Business Plans, and Proposals

TRIZ is a wonderful tool for someone looking for an idea to start a business, and it can help in creating a business plan, identifying potential customers, and managing financial and operational risks, and so on. Wikipedia beautifully defines a business plan as "a formal statement of business goals, reasons they are attainable, and plans for reaching them. It may also contain background information about the organization or team attempting to reach those goals." Though business plans were used purely to attract investors and get bank loans in the past, today their scope and usefulness goes far beyond that. First off, writing a business plan is a journey through one's idea. If you had an idea that you planned to materialize as a successful business venture, the first step should be to write a business plan. This will throw a lot of light your goals and help you understand the nitty-gritty of converting your idea into a successful business venture. Secondly, this plan will help investors understand your idea and all aspects of your business in detail, and provide a strong reason to invest in your business. Most of all, it will give you much clarity and help you decide if it is worth taking a shot or to just drop the idea. The probability of raising money is higher if you can answer as many questions from potential backers as possible. The TRIZ contradiction matrix can help in creating a strong business plan, from identifying an opportunity to answering some of the difficult questions that need a creative thinking process.

A business plan should contain at least the following basic components to attract investors:

- Identify the problem
- Business description
- Business accomplishments
- Product description

- Market analysis
- Pricing
- SWOT analysis

Now let us look at how each of these components can be addressed using TRIZ.

Identify the Problem. The most common problem most startups face is not the operational challenges or getting investors or selling the product or managing risks. If you want to be a businessperson you have to sell a product, service, or result, and entrepreneurs are finding it extremely hard to identify one. The product or service that is to be sold must solve some serious problem that the customer is ready to pay to have solved, or simply, the product must resolve a contradiction. Have a look at any of the objects around you, and ask yourself which product it replaced and what the contradiction is that it resolved, and you will be amazed to see the magic. But just resolving the contradiction alone is not enough. For example, I could invent an electronic gadget that would boot my computer 10 seconds faster, and if I price it at $300, how many people do you think would buy that? Probably not many, and the reason is because this product does not impact the ideal final result much. But if I can invent a gadget that would let me boot the system through my cell phone and price it reasonably, there is a high chance for the product to be successful because this resolves one of the contradictions that will help the system to move closer to ideality. TRIZ can help you in finding the contradictions in the existing system, check whether they will take you closer to ideality, and then help you resolve them.

Here is a step-by-step approach that will help you in identifying or inventing your product or service:

1. Choose an existing product or service that is close to your heart, something that you are passionate about, something that you know a lot about but that you would like to change.
2. Define the *ideal final result* of that product.
3. Identify the contradictions that are stopping it from reaching ideality.
4. Create a nine windows chart for the product.
5. List all the contradictions that you think you can control with the help of the nine windows, contradiction matrix, and TRIZ principles.
6. Try to resolve as many contradictions as possible.

7. You might have more than one solution for many contradictions; optimize them based on feasibility, cost, risk, ease of operations, and so on.
8. Identify a way to package your solutions into a product or service.
9. Perform a cost/benefit analysis and calculate how much you will price the product or service.
10. Test out whether the customer is willing to pay the price you calculated for your product or service.
11. If not, try repackaging the solutions and repeat the process from step 6 until you reach the ideal final result.

I was hosted by a truck driver, Azim, in Iran in a small village during our year-long cycling tour, and he was extremely passionate about massage. He had been trained to be a masseur, and shared his passion of inventing something for the old people in the village that would help them get a massage at home without spending any money. He had been trying for a couple of years now and had a few designs that used old plastic bottles filled with warm water that can be rolled on the back and shoulders to ease pain and promote relaxation. I was amazed and impressed at the innovation, but the problem was that it was not packaged well, and the device was unattractive. I spent two days with his family trying to improve the design and finally designed a holder. The holder can take up to five 500 ml used plastic bottles filled with warm water, and the small wheels in the holder help the bottles to roll on the back and shoulders. This small device would not cost more than $2–$3, and it resolved many contradictions and took the system close to ideality, but Azim was not interested in commercializing it or patenting it.

Business Description. As you already have your product in this section, you will explain what your company is all about and its mission statement.

What is the mission of Train and Trot (a company I used to own)? In TRIZ terminology I would say it is to provide an *ideal training solution* to the customers by resolving the contradictions in the business. Hence, in the business plan it will translate to "To provide high-quality training at the lowest possible cost and help the customers reap maximum benefit. The company will begin with a small group of subject matter experts and trainers to provide training related to TRIZ, and over time we will expand the offering. We will be an LLC when we start."

Business Accomplishments. What are your past accomplishments? In TRIZ terms the question is what contradictions have you resolved in the past? And the answer is "as a freelancer I have helped organizations execute

LSS projects faster (Speed) with lesser effort and cost (Use of energy) and helped organizations reap benefits much faster." You can also include the specific client information, if they agree, and the value that you delivered.

Product Description. In this section you will clearly define the contradictions your product or service will resolve, and the TRIZ principles used. You can take all the details from the Problem section and use them here. In TRIZ terms the course my company provides resolves the contradiction *Speed/Manufacturing precision*, and the principle used is *Prior action*. This means that my clients will execute lean and Six Sigma projects much faster by using TRIZ, and this in turn will help my clients to perform more projects in a shorter duration of time. By doing more projects, they will be able to save more cost, effort, and all the other affected metrics. By saving more cost in less time, they will be reducing the operating cost.

When I started, my idea was just to resolve one contradiction, but as you can see, TRIZ has numerous benefits and helps in resolving numerous contradictions that I never thought about before. Here is a technique that can be used to capture all the benefits of the products and services that are offered.

The principle *Prior action* helps in resolving close to 548 contradictions in the contradiction matrix. But all 548 need not affect my client's business, or they may not be adaptable to my idea. Hence, you will short-list all the parameters that affect the client's business. In my product the parameters that affect my client's business are:

- Adaptability or versatility
- Device complexity
- Difficulty of detecting and measuring
- Duration of action of moving object
- Ease of manufacture
- Extent of automation
- Loss of energy
- Loss of information

Plus, there are 30 contradictions that get resolved using the principle Prior action. There is a strong possibility that though the principle is Prior action, the way it is used in the contradiction need not be related to my idea, and hence the feasibility has to be checked. I validated all the 30 contradictions, and my product helps in resolving all 30 of them. Though the idea is just one, it has 30 fundamental applications to my customers, and all this has to be elaborated and described in detail in the business plan.

Market Analysis. This is where the product description again comes into play. Take all the contradictions that your product or service resolves and compare them to the top competitors who offer a similar product or service; identify the gap and clearly describe how your products are superior to the competitor's products. Using the contradiction matrix, identify the contradictions that the product resolves and then identify the opportunities in the market that have these contradictions. That becomes your potential market. In my case, I would clearly state the training duration, user experience, and the methodology, which has never been used in the past by any of my competitors and is a huge differentiator. My potential market is any organization that is looking for quick-fix methods to solve complex problems. All the companies that have this requirement are my target market.

Pricing. Pricing the product is a very crucial parameter for the product's and the startup's success. *Cost* is what the company has incurred to create the product, and the *price* is what the customer is willing to pay for the service. When I started my company my pricing was purely based on the training hours, and I had an hourly rate. Over a period of time the number of people attending the training and the business impact of my trainings kept growing exponentially, but my price remained the same. There was so much value I was creating, but my pricing remained the same. I was scared to move to a different model where the customer would be charged not on the number of hours I spend but the number of employees who attend the training. The fear was of losing the customer. But still I decided to do it one day. Surprisingly, the customers did not mind at all as the value the training provided was worth much more than the pricing, or simply, there was value for money. So, the key to pricing is to make sure the customers feel there is value for every single penny they are spending on the product or service. The method I used to arrive at the pricing was, I asked a customer what contradictions existed in her business and approximately what the loss was that she was incurring due to these contradictions. I then researched how much impact my trainings could create to reduce the loss, if not to make it profitable. I took a conservative number and then put a percentage as my pricing. If I am more confident in resolving the contradictions, I use an outcome-based pricing, that is, calculating the total business impact I have created by helping the team solve problems and then taking a share from the impact.

As you can see, the pricing depends on numerous factors, such as the maturity of the product market, customer requirements, and so on. One important activity to perform so that you do not lose a customer due to pricing is pick the improving parameter of your product for which your client is willing to pay, and choose the worsening parameter as the *Use of energy* principle (the money he is spending on your product). Keep a watch on the principles and these two parameters and ask the following questions regularly:

- Do the contradictions still exist with my customer?
- Do my products still resolve the contradictions?
- Is there any other similar product on the market that is able to resolve the contradictions?

Depending on the answers that you get, change the pricing model. In my product, the improving parameter was speed, and the principles the customer could use to drop my services were (worsening parameter—Use of energy) Counterweight, Dynamicity, Change property, and Using strong oxidizers, and many of my customers did so. They hired more Six Sigma Black Belts, increased the frequency of lean and kaizen workshops, and held many process reengineering workshops, and so on. These were the pricing-related threats to my business.

SWOT Analysis. In this section we need to clearly define why you or your organization is capable of resolving the contradictions. You will break the contradictions into action items, and each action item must be categorized as a *strength*, *weakness*, *opportunity*, or *threat*. Strengths are great, and if you believe your strength is resolving a certain category of contradictions, you must exploit this opportunity in businesses that require skills resolving similar contradictions. If you are weak in particular skills, identify and resolve the contradictions and convert the weakness into strength. If you foresee threats, identify the contradictions that are causing the threat and resolve them so that they become opportunities, and also have proper risk mitigation strategies to manage the threats better.

TRIZ FOR REQUIREMENTS GATHERING

Understanding the objectives, gathering the requirements, and translating the requirements into a scope statement is a crucial process for any project's success. The traditional approach to gathering requirements is to involve a group of key stakeholders and use tools like brainstorming, interviews, focus groups, mind mapping, user stories, *as is* and *to be* process modeling, case diagrams, and so on. Once the requirements are gathered, each requirement is analyzed and selected or rejected through voting or unanimity, majority, plurality, or dictatorship. This method has many disadvantages, the core being that there is no guarantee that the collected requirements are solving the business problem as the techniques used to gather them are based on an individual's or team's past experiences. I have personally come across situations where many of the requirements were "not said" by the customer explicitly as he thought they were self-explanatory, but on the other end for someone who is trying to define scope, every word in the scope matters, and anything that is not mentioned in the scope statement is null and void. Just imagine and extrapolate this. If there are 100 stakeholders who provide requirements, and each stakeholder fails to explain one small requirement as he thinks it is self-explanatory, we have lost 100 requirements in the scope statement. I have personally seen many projects being "successful" but failing to solve the business problem at the end of the day.

John is a project manager in an organization, and his company is finding it difficult to manage their supplier payments due to an increase in volume. A senior stakeholder explains this problem to John in one or two sentences and asks him to find economical software that can take care of this requirement. Immediately, John created a project charter and started collecting the necessary high-level requirements like budget, risks, milestones, and so on, from senior stakeholders. The approval of the project charter took a week's time due to stakeholder availability and other factors. The next step was to identify the right stakeholders and gather the requirements using some of the tools that I mentioned above. As every stakeholder wants to reduce effort in his or her own department, the requirement did not just focus on managing the payment system but also on generating invoices, keeping a database of suppliers, updating supplier contact information, and so on. John was not surprised to see some conflicting requirements, where one stakeholder needs a certain functionality while the other stakeholder doesn't need that functionality. John did further analysis on the collected requirements, refined it, got approvals, and built a software application. The project was successful, but did it really solve the business problem is the big question.

TRIZ can solve this problem. TRIZ can guarantee a solution, yes 100% guarantee! Tim is another project manager who knows TRIZ. Let us see how Tim manages the same project using TRIZ. Once the stakeholder explains the problem and the solution of buying or building software, Tim will take a step back. What is a business problem? It is nothing but a contradiction. Once the senior stakeholder explains the problem, Tim will go to his desk, open the TRIZ contradiction matrix, and identify the contradictions:

- *Improving parameter.* Pay too many suppliers—Amount/Quantity of substance
- *Worsening parameter.* Difficulty in managing the payments—Ease of operations

Now, the principles that can resolve this contradiction are:

1. *Parameter change.* What are the components in the current process whose parameter change will improve my existing payment process?
    a. Process used to manage the payment system
    b. Volume
    c. Software
    d. Person managing the process
2. *Pneumatics and hydraulics.* What are the components in the current process where I use solid parts that could be replaced by liquid or gaseous parts?
    a. Use electronic invoices instead of physical paper.
    b. Save the invoices in a common web folder rather than e-mailing them.
3. *Self-service.* What are the components in the current process where an object is unable to service itself by performing auxiliary helpful functions?
    a. Can we ask the individual suppliers to manage the payment process and have the company just audit the information?
    b. Can the project managers of each project manage the payments to the suppliers rather than the procurement team?
4. *Prior action.* What are the components in the current process where the required change of an object is not performed in advance or objects are not prearranged in a way such that they can come into action from the most convenient place and without losing time for their delivery?
    a. Payment history
    b. Supplier classification

c. Standard documents and templates

d. Standard operating procedure and workflow

Now Tim will perform a high-level feasibility study on implementing each of these solutions, the cost that will be incurred, the stakeholders who will be affected, risks, milestones, and schedule, and so forth. He will include all this information in the project charter and send it for approval. As you can see in Figure 8.1, Tim has more or less gathered the requirements that will resolve the contradiction himself using TRIZ. All the stakeholders need to do is to choose one or more approaches from the ones proposed by Tim. There is also a possibility that a few additional requirements might be included, secondary requirements that support the primary requirement. Now Tim will write the project scope with all the analysis and the information gathered. Imagine the time, effort, and ambiguity that are saved here! If you had an option to choose a method, whose approach would you choose? Tim or John?

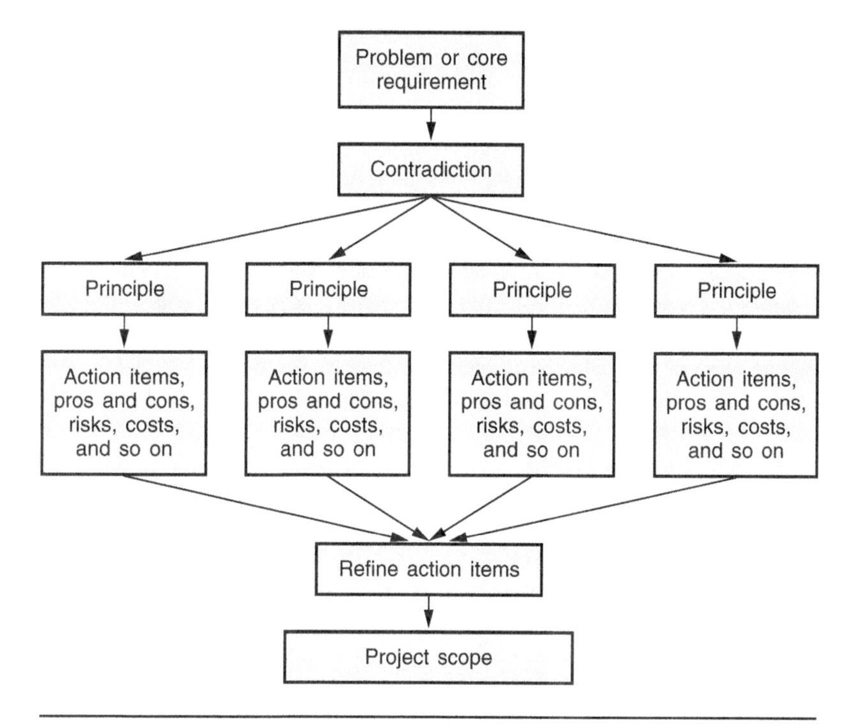

Figure 8.1 Requirements gathering using TRIZ.

Here is a step-by-step guide to gathering requirements using TRIZ:

1. Understand the problem or business objective.
2. Define the *contradiction* that the problem is trying to resolve. It is absolutely fine if there are more than one.
3. Based on the principles used in the contradiction matrix, identify the possible solution at a very high level.
4. Conduct a feasibility study on implementing the solutions, and also try to gather more information that will help in taking quick decisions, such as milestones, risks, estimations, and so on, and create a project charter.
5. Explain the options to the stakeholders and decide on the final list of requirements.
6. Get the necessary approvals.
7. Consolidate the requirements and create a project scope statement.

You have just improved an existing software application developed by your company with 10 addition functionalities, and you're sure all your existing customers, 500 of them, will be more than happy to upgrade and pay for it as these functionalities are extremely important for their business. You can package the new upgrade in a single version and sell it to the clients for $100 and get $50,000. There is another option: you can release one functionality every month for $15, and for 10 releases over a year you would get $75,000, that is, $25,000 more just by delaying the release of innovation over a longer period. There could also be another possibility: you could categorize the functionalities into different categories like Silver, Gold, and Premium, where Silver users can use three functionalities for $50, Gold can use six functionalities for $90, and Premium users can use all 10 functionalities for $150. If you are confident that over a period of time customers from the lower Gold and Silver levels will move to the Premium level, this model would be profitable. There can also be a model where the customer can pay a minimum base fee for a certain number of basic functionalities and an additional fee for additional functionalities. Do these strategies sound familiar to you? Yes, brands like Microsoft, Apple, Samsung, and so on, have an inventory of innovations, and they strategically release these innovations to the customer in a way that brings maximum profit to their shareholders. Apple knows the needs of an iPhone user, and also knows that the customer will likely move to higher models over time; hence, the release of attractive functionalities in every model is crucial. This is called *strategy*, that is, a method or plan chosen to bring about a desired future, such as achievement of a goal or a solution to a problem.

Middle managers are mostly involved in the day-to-day operations of an organization, while the CXOs, that is, CEOs, CFOs, COOs, and so on, think and take strategic decisions, for which the TRIZ contradiction matrix can be a very good stand-alone tool. Here is a step-by-step approach:

1. Define the *ideal* product, service, or result for which the strategy is being built.
2. Identify all the contradictions that are stopping the product from reaching the ideality (see Figure 8.2).
3. Identify the action plan, risk, cost, benefit, dependency, effort, and resource requirements in resolving the contradictions.
4. Prioritize the contradictions using tools and techniques that are best suited, for example, SWOT analysis or prioritization matrix. One of my favorites is Steven Covey's time management grid, purely because of its simplicity and effectiveness (see Table 8.1).

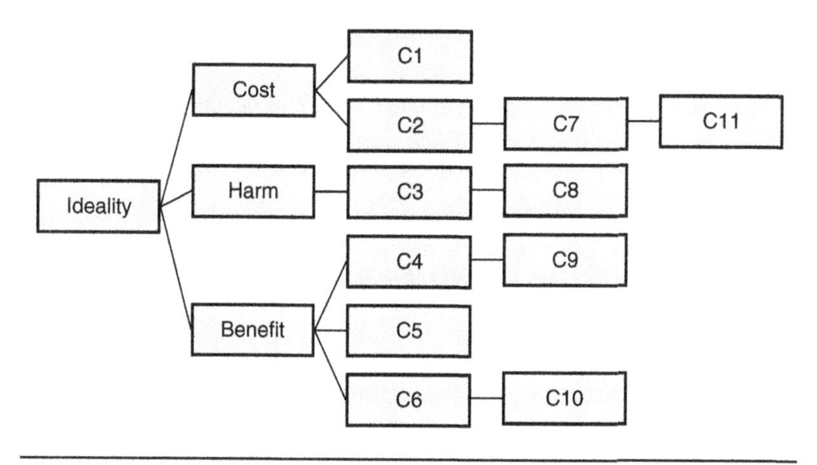

Figure 8.2 Contradiction tree.

Table 8.1 Contradiction prioritization.

	Urgent	**Not urgent**
Important	C1, C2,	C6, C7, C8,
Not important	C3, C4, C5	C9, C10, C11

In this simple grid you will enter the contradictions based on their urgency and importance to the end business objective. Contradictions C9–C11 are neither important nor urgent and should not be worked on intensively, and this information should be communicated to the lower levels of the organization as they might not have the visibility and understanding of the strategy and top-level priorities. Contradictions C3–C5 are not important but urgent, for example, they might not bring in a huge amount of revenue but must be resolved immediately; if not, competitors might resolve them first, or it could be needed by the customer soon. Hence, the leaders have a choice to do it or drop it depending on the payoff. The contradictions C1 and C2 are important and urgent and hence must be the top priority. Contradictions C6–C8 comprise the most important block in the grid, that is, contradictions that are important but not urgent, but if they are not prioritized will move toward the adjacent block—urgent and important. It is always wise to keep the important/urgent block as empty as possible as this block creates a lot of stress and panic and promotes a toxic environment. The only way to keep this block empty is by prioritizing the contradictions in the important/not urgent block.

There are numerous ways to build strategies depending on the organization's goals and objectives. I will just touch on a few tips to give you a perspective; you are free to innovate your own techniques and strategies.

- Always try to resolve the mother contradictions rather than the children. If contradiction C2 is resolved, C7 and C11 disappear automatically.
- Make a watch list of external dependencies like technology, market price, economy, and so on, that are affecting the contradictions, and take timely action.
- Organizations may also *not* resolve the contradictions to their benefit. When Mark Zuckerberg had the first thousand, ten thousand, or hundred thousand users on Facebook, Facebook as an ideal system had lots of harm and no benefits as a lot of time, effort, and money were spent without any return. He could have changed the business model for short-term benefit by charging a membership fee to the users. If they had done that, it would have been a disaster, and millions of users would have dropped out. But Facebook moved on, with the contradiction of not charging

actually helping keep competitors at bay, and today there are over 1.7 billion active monthly users, revenue of $1 billion, and a market valuation of over $300 billion. Hence, not resolving some of the contradictions can sometimes be a good strategy for long-term benefit.

- Drop the contradiction if it consumes cost and does not bring any benefit or reduce any harm significantly.
- Treat each contradiction like a project, with a clear beginning and end, rather than accepting it as part of the process, and treat related contradictions like a program.
- For every contradiction, evaluate the cost and benefit and the time value of money spent to resolve it.

5. Create a strategic plan with action items to resolve the contradictions in a sequence that meets the business objectives.
6. Monitor and control the strategic plan.
7. Keep a watch on the external and internal parameters that might impact the plan.

TRIZ FOR EFFECTIVE COMMUNICATION AND BRANDING

Exchanging or imparting information, also called *communication*, is an integral part of any project. Many more projects have failed due to the lack of communication than due to lack of planning or execution. Communication can also help to get a sinking project back on track. The best example is the story of Apollo 13. En route to the Moon, 330,000 km away from Earth, the crew gave a live broadcast for six and a half minutes. When the team in the spacecraft was asked to turn on the hydrogen and oxygen tank stirring fans in the service module, they heard a loud bang. The service module was seriously damaged, which made the return trip virtually impossible, but all the astronauts returned safely purely because of effective communication. Everyone—the crew, the project manager, experts, scientists, and even President Nixon—was in the communication channel. Quick decisions were taken, and the even more fascinating part was brainstorming and solving the problem with the huge constraint of using the materials available on the spacecraft and communicating the solution to the astronauts 330,000 km away. The astronauts had to gather all the required components and set them in the right order, follow the process, and perform the activities in the right sequence in spite of all the noise in the communication system. Finally, all the astronauts were brought back alive though the project was a failure. Apollo 13 is considered one of the biggest successfully failed projects in history, and it was purely because of the efficient communication between the stakeholders.

TRIZ can help you communicate innovatively and help in solving problems related to communication. Why do we communicate? To exchange information, in other words *enlighten* someone. The primary goal of communication is to bring something from dark to light, and that something is information. How can we enlighten an object? By throwing light on it or increasing its illumination intensity. Improving the parameter *Illumination intensity* will increase the visibility of the information, and by decreasing this parameter confidential information can be hidden. To improve the effectiveness of the communication in your organization you can:

- Identify and select the process or project where you would like to increase the communication.
- From the TRIZ contradiction matrix, choose *Illumination intensity* as your improving parameter.
- Go through each of the 39 worsening parameters in the contradiction matrix and choose the ones that are relevant to your project.
- From the short-listed worsening parameters, choose one contradiction at a time and apply the principles to resolve them.

This approach can be used to improve the effectiveness of communication, create communication plans for a project, and also for improving the brand value of an individual product or service, as brand value is nothing but improving the visibility of an object. There are enormous contradictions when it comes to how a brand should be seen by the customer and how it should not. When you observe brands you differentiate their products through the look of the products, including shape, color, style, fonts, and so on. That is the way of communicating to the customer, and the consumer receives the information through these fonts, colors, shapes, and so on. The Olympics is one of the oldest and the biggest brands, older than Christianity, and it has a lot of contradictions. One of them is that it communicates as a humanitarian brand to unite countries through sports, and is seen as something similar to the United Nations, while at the same time it partners with many commercial brands like Coca-Cola, McDonalds, and so on, and has been successful so far in resolving the contradiction. Let us look at this example through the TRIZ lens: the improving parameter is the *Illumination intensity* of the commercial factor, that is, brands like Coca-Cola and Nike must promote their products through the Olympics as they are the sponsors and need a return on investment; but the worsening parameter is if the Olympics promotes these brands instead of the sport and the unity of the countries, it will be a disaster, and the core existence of the Olympics as a brand will be gone, which in TRIZ terms is *Object-affected harmful factors*. The principles that can resolve this contradiction are:

1. *Dynamicity.* Sports stars promote commercial brands and the Olympics, and commercial brands promote the sport, sportsmen, humanitarian values, and the Olympics in their advertisements. That way the communication of both brands has a good mix and is seen as one by the customer.
2. *Periodic action.* Do you see a series of advertisements with the sport sandwiched in between for a few minutes, or the other way around? Yes, we have advertisements during the breaks, but they carry a strong brand value and communicate effectively at the same time.

You can use the same contradiction to promote a brand on social media in a humble but effective way through these two principles—communicating the information to potential customers while at the same time not sounding like a salesperson or someone bragging about the product. There was an employee who used to report to me. He was reliable, smart, and extremely dependable, and someone I could delegate complex tasks to. But he expected a return in the form of recognition. So, every time he did a good job he insisted that I send an appreciation e-mail to the senior leaders, his peers, and the whole department. Every time I did this he was a star on the floor and was seen as a celebrity, which was a huge motivation for him. This also motivated other team members, who started coming to me to take up more responsibilities, which they accomplished, and I happily sent an appreciation e-mail to the entire department. This way, everyone from the leaders to the new joiners knew everyone on my team, and after some time it became a best practice in the organization. This way we increased the brand value of the team members, the team, and the department within the organization. Whenever there was an internal job requirement, the managers approached me to see if any of the resources on my team were releasable to work for their team.

So, I hope you improve your brand value and communication effectively.

TRIZ FOR INTERVIEWS

Let us be clear here, interviewing is very subjective. Any amount of time taken to understand a candidate is insufficient, and there is always a potential for personal unfairness to emerge. But in spite of it all, the goal of an interview is the same, to assess the suitability of each applicant for the job and decide on the most appropriate one. Most of the jobs in management require people with good problem-solving skills, and TRIZ is a wonderful tool that will help you in cracking the interviews. But let me be very clear and reiterate—interviewing is very subjective, and so are the selection criteria. Hence, TRIZ will help you answer the questions creatively, but will not guarantee you a job for various reasons, for example, you are good at problem solving but you do not have enough technical expertise, or you do not meet the basic requirement criteria, and so on. So what TRIZ can do for you, provided you have met all the criteria, and when you are compared with other candidates who are not aware of TRIZ, is give you a better chance at success.

I have short-listed some of the common interview questions and have provided the answers for a few, and directions for the rest on how I would make use of TRIZ to answer the interviewer. I would recommend that you complete the exercise. Referring to this exercise might help you if you are attending an interview in future.

- *Interviewer.* How did you work with underperforming staff members, for example, an employee who is always late in delivering the task that is allocated to him?

  Speed—Force is the improving and worsening parameter, and the principles I would/could have used are:

  - *Inversion.* Instead of me trying to improve his speed, I asked the employee to come up with action items to improve his speed.
  - *Replace mechanical system.* I provided necessary training and helped him use some automation tools to increase his speed.
  - *Dynamicity.* To manage some of the complex process steps that he was not good at, I mentored him.
  - *Periodic action.* I reviewed his performance periodically and prescribed corrective and preventive actions.

- *How do you evaluate success?* The dictionary meaning of success is "the accomplishment of an aim or purpose or an undertaking." Define personally what accomplishment of professional undertaking defines your success. For example, if I am able to manage and deliver project results consistently, that is my definition of success. In terms of contradiction it will be defined as:

Volume of moving object—Reliability is both the improving parameter and worsening parameter, and the principles to be used are:

- Spheroidality
- Segmentation
- Composite materials
- Cushion in advance

Describe how you can use each of these principles to solve the problem.

- *How do you handle stress and pressure?* For example, if you have handled cost-related pressure, then the contradiction would be:

  Use of energy by moving object—Stress or pressure:

  - Feedback
  - Spheroidality
  - Self-service

- *Share some examples of the ways in which you've impacted your process.* I have worked on many projects to reduce the operating cost without affecting the reliability, hence, I would choose the contradiction:

  Use of energy by the moving object—Reliability:

  - Periodic action
  - Rush through
  - Cushion in advance
  - Cheap disposables

- *What do people often criticize about you?* I have often been criticized for being:

  Less adaptable to situation—which has led to some Risks (Object affected by harmful factors). But I have overcome it by taking the following actions:

- Change property
- Cushion in advance
- Color change
- Porous materials

- *What is your greatest weakness?* For example, I have the weakness of focusing too much on productivity while ignoring risks. But I am able to overcome this weakness by using:
  - Harm to benefit
  - Change property
  - Inversion
  - Mediator
- *What is your greatest strength?* I have the experience of reducing the most complex of processes without affecting the operating cost. These are the principles I used:
  - Cheap disposables
  - Taking out or Separation or Extraction
  - Pneumatics and hydraulics
  - Replace mechanical system
- *What can you contribute to this company?* I can help your organization to move toward ideality with the help of continuous improvement and innovation. This is how I will do it:
  - I will understand the product/service/result.
  - I will define the ideal final result for your offering.
  - I will identify the contradictions.
  - I will resolve the contradictions through innovative problem solving.
  - I will create a watch list for items with open contradictions.
- *What are you looking for in your next job? What is important to you?*
  - I am looking for an opportunity to make the customer happy by improving the offerings.

- I am looking for an opportunity to innovate and solve complex problems that have an impact at project, business, and market levels.
- Add other advantages of TRIZ.

- *Tell me about a time that you took the lead on a difficult project.*
  - Describe all the projects you have handled, the contradictions that they had, the solutions you implemented, and the solutions that you could have implemented.

- *Describe a time when you had to ease a personal disagreement between two staff members.*

  Every contradiction has the possibility that it might lead to a conflict. For example, your department performs too much manual labor and wants to automate the processes, but the finance team does not want to spend on automation. You can resolve the conflict through the following principles:
  - Taking out or Separation or Extraction
  - Color change
  - Inversion

- *Describe a time when you were running short on a deadline and your next steps.* This is a contradiction where the improving parameter is *Speed* and the worsening parameter is, for example, *Manufacturing precision.* The principles that could be used to resolve them are:
  - Prior action
  - Replace mechanical system
  - Color change
  - Self-service

- *Describe a time when a client/customer was treating your staff unfairly.* This is a clear contradiction between *Pressure* and *Object affected by harmful factors*, and the principles used to resolve them are:
  - Harm to benefit

- Taking out or Separation or Extraction
- Thermal expansion

- *Describe how you have handled priorities for multiple projects.* For example, I want to deliver all the projects faster, but the number of projects makes it harder. Hence, the contradiction will be *Speed/ Quantity of substance* and the principles are:
  - Prior action
  - Periodic action
  - Pneumatics and hydraulics
  - Strong oxidants

Congrats, you have done a great job in answering the interview questions. If you come across more interview questions, try to convert them into contradictions and answer them using the TRIZ principles. All the best!

USING TRIZ TO COMPLETE LEAN AND SIX SIGMA PROJECTS FASTER

During a training session on TRIZ as part of a Six Sigma Black Belt program, a participant jokingly asked me if the participants had solutions for the contradictions readily available, in which case the class had wasted 10 days on the training program. Though the comment was a joke, it made sense and put a thought into my head.

From then on I began fantasizing about solving complex problems that required lean and Six Sigma (LSS) expertise, lots of manpower and time, and had to be solved quickly. It felt marvelous to me. I began taking baby steps toward it, with the end goal being to achieve the outcome of a value stream mapping (VSM) workshop/Six Sigma project in less than one hour.

I refined my dream even further by asking very few questions to the customer concerning the problem, and in the end telling the customer, "This is exactly where the problem lies, and this is the solution." I kept looking at the TRIZ contradiction matrix, which contains the technical contradictions and the TRIZ principle to be used, trying to create a framework (see Figure 8.3). Finally understanding how to do so, I had to marry Lean Six Sigma and TRIZ.

An ideal TRIZ problem-solving approach, and challenges, follows.

1. Define your specific problem

Degraded feature / Feature to improve	Weight	Length	Area	Force	Speed	Strength	...	Durability	Temperature
Weight						40,3		5,31,34	
Length									
Area									
Force									35,10,21
Speed									
Strength	40,3								
⋮			Inventive principles						
Durability	5,31,34								
Temperature				35,10,21					

Figure 8.3 TRIZ contradiction matrix.

   a. A typical LSS problem/goal statement has the factor that needs to be improved, but not necessarily the factor that is limiting the factor to be improved.

2. Convert your problem to a TRIZ general problem

   a. To convert the problem to a TRIZ problem, the contradictions need to be identified.

   b. Relating a technical contradiction for a service industry problem is difficult due to the terminology used all being related to manufacturing.

   c. A problem can have multiple contradictions.

3. TRIZ-specific solution using contradiction matrix

   a. TRIZ solutions are straightforward for technical problems, and relating them to a transaction-based model or service industry is hard as it is tough to relate the principle to the components of the system.

4. Specific solution to the problem

   a. TRIZ solutions do not point out the exact process step where the problem lies, which needs LSS.

I took previous LSS projects and attempted to fit the TRIZ approach to solving the same problems. The solutions were accurate, but as a consultant, I was still unable to say exactly where the problem existed.

For example, when I had to apply the TRIZ principle *Mechanical vibration*—causing an object to oscillate or vibrate—identifying the object in a nonmanufacturing process was the first challenge. Identifying the exact location of the object in the system without knowledge of the process was much more difficult.

To resolve this, I took an alternative approach—I came up with a paradox: *if for a given contradiction TRIZ has a solution that improves the process, the improved process was the problem area for the customer.*

Now, for any given problem and contradiction, a set of principles can be identified through the contradiction matrix. The next step is to isolate the processes where the principle can be applied, which could be more than one place.

I took the list of components that are part of the system (applications, people, information, and so on), and framed the opposite question of the principle against the components (that is, if the principle was "mechanical vibration," I would ask, "Which component is not oscillating or oscillating slowly?").

This would point to a few components in the system; at that point it was easy to locate the activities needing improvement. The reason the opposite is considered is because it gives the *as is* process, and the principle provides the future state *to be* process (see Figure 8.4).

I also prepared a list of 300 synonyms and adjectives for the principles to create a broader scope of understanding. For example, instead of vibration I could ask about motion, speed, moving, frequency, resonance, fast periodic motion, and so on.

I then formulated an approach using different stages to solve the problem as shown in Figure 8.5. The last block on the right provides the four optional LSS tools that can be used to leverage the approach efficiently.

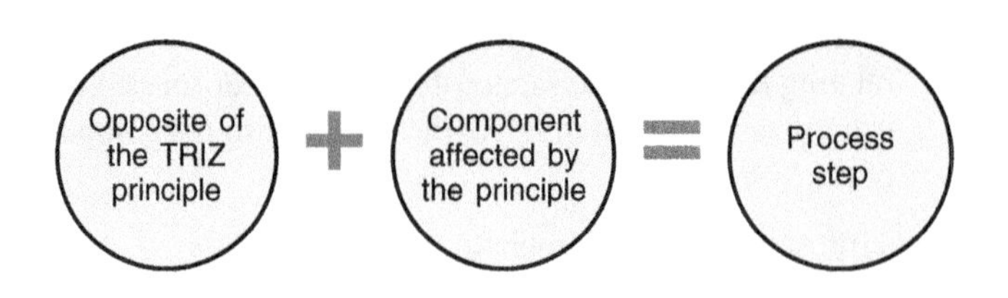

Figure 8.4 Relationship between TRIZ principle, affected component, and process step.

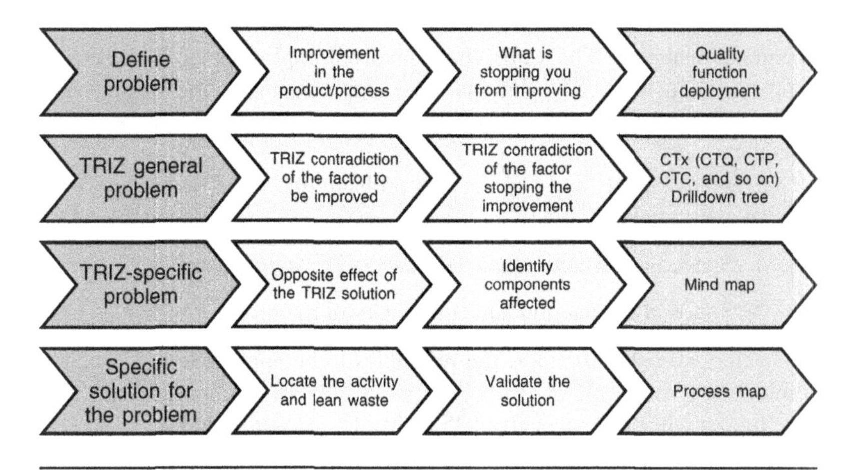

Figure 8.5 Eight steps and four lean tools for solving problems.

After testing this approach on many projects, I wanted to conduct the litmus test with industry experts. I wrote an e-mail to many past students and friends asking them to help with the complex business problems used to improve the model. The response was poor, though, as it involved confidentiality and no incentive.

I sent a follow-up with two carrots the next time. I told the prospective participants that if they could come up with difficult problems that were already solved, I would show them how they could be solved within one hour, and then provide training on the same. This time the response was much better, and I handpicked 14 from a variety of industries, including social media marketing, service, information technology, and sales, to ensure that subject matter expertise would not influence the model.

The first three hours of the two-day session were spent training the participants on the TRIZ contradiction matrix and the instructor's approach. The remainder was spent solving the problems the case studies provided (see below). The ground rule to solving the problem was that the participant who provided the problem would be the client, while the remaining participants would act like consultants asking questions. The client was supposed to provide one-word/generic answers.

Problem 1

A VSM workout was conducted by a Black Belt to reduce order-to-cash cycle time for their energy client. The total schedule took five weeks to complete: two weeks of prework, three days for the workout, and two weeks for implementation. The value chain involved approximately 75 full-time employees. In total, 12 solutions were implemented, with a cycle time reduction of 11% post-implementation, and no significant improvement in accuracy.

The participants and I chose this problem and identified the two following contradictions:

1. Speed of transaction and accuracy of the transaction
2. Speed of transaction and complexity of the process

From the two contradictions, the principles to be applied were as seen in Table 8.2.

In total, the group conceived 25 highly significant solutions in a span of 45 minutes. The solutions will increase cash flow by $800,000 per month.

Problem 2

A software company faced a major challenge where its processes and standards were not being followed in their project work. This affected the end customer deliverables through defects and rework.

Company leaders started by asking project managers to take a closer look, which did not yield much in results, even after a month, due to the complexity of the projects, non-value-added documentation, and stringent deadlines. The leaders then started micromanaging through biweekly meetings, but still things were the same, and the projects started to miss the schedule.

Then the company hired a consultant with a strong knowledge of enterprise resource planning (ERP) and project management to audit the deliverables. After five months, things started to improve before the auditor quit.

The contradictions for this problem are (1) the need to improve the accuracy of manufacturing (development), and (2) the subsequent need for more time, energy, and productivity to deliver the activities related to compliance.

The TRIZ principles that need to be applied from the matrix are:

1. Other way round
    a. Instead of project managers managing the process, let the consultants manage the process themselves; make it part of the internal deliverable so it cannot move ahead without a tollgate review by the stakeholders.

Table 8.2 Principles used and the derived solutions..

1. Prelimary action	**2. Replace mechanical system**	**3. Asymmetry**
• Do you have a customized ordering form for each product? No • Do all the forms have standard format? Yes • Do you have free text fields in the ordering form? Yes • Do you fall short of staff due to high volume? Once in a while • Do you anticipate orders and staff accordingly (forecasting)? No • Do you send forms back to the customer requesting further information? Often	• The mechanical systems are the people who are processing the orders, hence are there any skill misfits? Few • When was the last training conducted? More than a year ago • Do you have a lot of manual data entry? Yes • Does the work involve any human judgment or is everything rule-based? More than 80 percent rule-based	• Do you have guided workflows that help the customer to choose the right options based on the previous selection? No • Does the team have guided workflows that help them to choose the right options based on the previous selection? No • Do the order processing agents get requests that they cannot work on and then send back upstream or downstream (multiple handoffs)? Yes, often • Do the agents receive requests where they do not have the expertise and forward it to the concerned department? Yes • Does the agent wait to get an approval/clarification before processing the request? Yes • Do you have a lot of transactions in queue waiting to be processed? Yes

Continued

Table 8.2 Continued.		
4. Recycling (restoring and discarding)	**5. Optical changes**	**6. Self-service**
• Do you maintain customer's previous order history? Yes • Can the customer reuse the previous order and payment options to expedite? No • Do you manage a lessons learned document from previous mistakes? No • When was the standard procedure document last updated based on what was learned? Never	• Do you have visual management to monitor the order status at different checkpoints? No • While entering information into the system manually, are there any overlooked errors? Many	• What key information is entered by the customer on the form? Product name, delivery date • What additional information does the team gather before confirming the order? Inventory availability, promise date • Can the system show the stock availability and promise date before placing the order? Yes

2. Color change
   a. Have a well-documented process flowchart and visual dashboards of the processes to be followed on the floor.
   b. Provide and monitor the checklist.
   c. Color-code the reports not only by deliverables and activities, but the status of the processes followed.
3. Taking out or separation or extraction
   a. Remove unnecessary process status review meetings.
   b. Remove processes that do not add value to the end customer.
   c. Remove the testing practices that have been causing the defects through permanent fixes.

4. Copying
   a. Create and reuse standard templates for project plan, documentation, and so on.
   b. Document lessons learned from the past and reuse the improved procedures.
5. Replace mechanical system
   a. Retrain noncompliant resources.
6. Mechanical vibration
   a. Institute a communication plan that clearly defines when, what, and how to communicate.
   b. Eliminate noise/delay in communication.
   c. Increase frequency of communication and audits.
7. Preliminary action
   a. Train the team on the processes to be followed well before the project kickoff.
   b. Get all the templates and documents in place before the project kickoff.
8. Inert atmosphere
   a. Create an environment where every deliverable is assumed defective, tested, and only sent to the customer post-conformity.
   b. Reward conformity and punish nonconformity.

These were the actual solutions that were generated with an investment of less than one hour.

Problem 3

For one of the claim coding processes, the average handling time was 30% greater than the target, increasing the backlog drastically and missing the turnaround time. A LSS project was completed over a period of five months to get the handling time back on track.

The contradictions were straightforward: an increase in productivity will lead to a decrease in accuracy. The principles to be applied were:

1. Mechanical vibration
   a. Increase in typing speed
   b. Speed of understanding the request
2. Preliminary action
   a. Training effectiveness
   b. Volumes received and staffing capacity
   c. Absenteeism
3. Color change
   a. Guided workflow for scenario-based procedures
   b. Visual management of the queue
4. Segmentation
   a. Segregate the resources by tenure, knowledge, and skill level
   b. Level load the work based on tenure and skill set

These are the same solutions that were implemented in the *improve* phase. The project team spent eight weeks from *define* to *analyze*, and they identified 28 *X*'s, out of which data were collected from 14 *X*'s, five of which were significant. Using this method, the team did the same within 30 minutes. The accuracy of the contribution can still be validated using hypothesis testing.

Conclusion

Following the workshop one of the participants handling the pre-sales was at the client location to bid on the proposal for a large project. The client had short-listed two companies and detailed the current challenges they had, which would then be transferred to whomever won the contract. They wanted both companies to devise clear solutions as to how they would handle the issues once they got the contract later in the day. The participant called me, we identified the contradictions and came up with many creative solutions in less than an hour, and he was confident that he would surely get the contract. In the evening, I received a call from the participant who said, "Guess what? We got the contract!" and we celebrated the success over the phone. Since then I keep receiving calls and e-mails from him every time he solves a problem using TRIZ, and he asks me to solve the same problem to validate the solution and method. We celebrate when we arrive at the same solution.

Having tested this approach on more than 70 problems with great accuracy, and having trained a batch on the same, I can confidently conclude that this approach can speed up the project schedule by a factor of 10 and save money by executing LSS projects in days, rather than weeks, for the organization. Given the rate at which businesses are transforming, decision making, and problem solving, *Speed* will be one of the key parameters for sustained growth. Figure 8.6 shows how the factors are minimized drastically without the use of any statistical technique, and at the same time how LSS can still be used in the end for very delicate projects.

To revalidate this approach, I applied TRIZ to speed up traditional LSS projects without losing reliability of the solution. The solutions were as follows:

1. *Previously placed pillow (Cushion in advance, or Beforehand cushioning).* Use LSS to validate the results and mitigate the risk of unreliability of the process.
2. *Parameter change.* Transition from LSS methodology by mixing TRIZ principles for faster problem solving.
3. *Cheap disposables.* Train the subject matter experts in the principles of TRIZ and lean to solve most of the process improvement problems.
4. *Replace mechanical system.* Replace the mechanical processes of VSM, data collection, and more with readily available solutions that have already been applied to similar problems in the past.

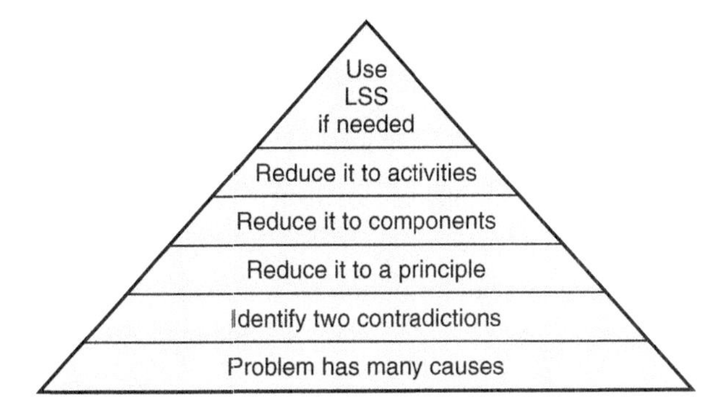

Figure 8.6 The pyramid of process improvement and problem solving using TRIZ and LSS.

DEVELOPING FMEA USING THE TRIZ CONTRADICTION MATRIX

Failure mode and effects analysis (FMEA) is a step-by-step approach for identifying all possible ways in which a design, process, or product or service can fail. Yes, it is a risk assessment tool. The conventional method followed to develop an FMEA is:

1. Study each process or component of a product.
2. Identify the potential failure modes, that is, all possible ways in which the process or product can fail to perform what it is intended to do.
3. Identify the potential effects, that is, the impact of the failure of the process or component on other components, processes, people, and so on.
4. Rate the severity of the effect on a scale of 1–10. For example, 1 does not have any significant effect and 10 might lead to the death of an employee or a customer.
5. Rank the possibility of occurrence on a scale of 1–10, where, for example, 1 means it can happen once in 10 years and 10 could mean it might happen every day.
6. Rank the ability to detect the failure on a scale of 1–10, for example, 1 means it is easily detectable and 10 means there is very little possibility of detecting the failure or there is no mechanism to detect it.
7. Calculate the *risk priority number* (RPN) using the formula RPN = Severity × Occurrence × Detectability.
8. Based on the result, higher RPNs are high-priority risks and need an immediate improvement action plan to reduce the RPN score.
9. Once actions are implemented, the RPN is recalculated.

The problem with the existing process is that there is a high probability of missing some of the key failures, impacts, and risks in the process or part due to the high dependency on the past experiences of the team preparing the FMEA, who might have limited knowledge of the process, product, quality, risk management, or perception. The TRIZ contradiction matrix can provide a complete solution to overcome this problem by following these steps:

1. From the TRIZ contradiction matrix identify all the parameters that affect your process or product, for example, *Speed*, *Measurement accuracy*, and so on.
2. In the contradiction matrix choose one of the identified parameters as the improving parameter and choose *Object-generated harmful factors* as the worsening parameter. This will provide all the failure modes that are generated by the process or component.
3. For the combination, you will have one or more principles.
4. Identify the process steps or components where each of these principles can be applied or are already applied.
5. Those process steps or components—in the absence of the principle applied to them—are the ones that can affect the process or product and are the potential failure modes.
6. Similarly, instead of choosing *Object-generated harmful factors* as the worsening parameter in step 2, choose *Object-affected harmful factors* as the worsening parameter and perform the same actions until step 5. This will provide all the failure modes that affect the process or component.
7. Do the same for all the other parameters that were identified.

EXAMPLE

Sarah works in a pizzeria as a call attendant and has been asked by her boss to prepare an FMEA for her process. Her job is to take the call, explain the menu to the customer, take the order, pass the order to the kitchen, get the customer's delivery details, tell the customer the bill amount, and sometimes answer questions if the customer has any. This is the approach she would be taking if she knew TRIZ:

1. The parameters that affect Sarah's process performance are speed of answering the calls, accuracy in taking the customer order, accuracy in passing the information to the kitchen, accuracy in generating the bill amount, and clarity in explaining the details to the customer.
2. She will first choose *Speed* as the improving parameter and *Object-generated harmful parameters* as the worsening parameter. The principles are:

a. *Extraction and separation.* This principle will be applied if:

   i. Sarah has to collect irrelevant information that is not required.

   ii. Sarah has difficulty in getting the order-related information.

b. *Mediator.* This principle will be applied if:

   i. Sarah cannot speak a foreign language and might need the help of a translator.

c. *Parameter change.* This principle will be applied if:

   i. Sarah has to manually enter any information in a register.

   ii. Sarah has to prepare a separate bill by entering the same information, leading to duplication of effort.

   iii. Sarah spends a lot of time in taking larger orders.

d. *Rush through.* This principle will be applied if:

   i. Sarah spends too much time in calculating the total bill amount, putting the customer on hold.

3. Now Sarah will choose *Object-affected harmful factors* for the same improving parameter *Speed.* The principles are:

   a. *Segmentation.* This principle will be applied if:

      i. Sarah has the same way of collecting information for both new and old customers.

   b. *Replace mechanical system.* This principle will be applied if:

      i. The existing order-taking process is too slow.

   c. *Parameter change.* This principle will be applied if:

      i. The process is too stressful.

      ii. The concentration of old customers decreases.

   d. *Feedback.* This principle will be applied if:

      i. Sarah is unable to identify a regular customer.

      ii. Sarah is unable to pull up a customer's order history.

4. Sarah will do a similar exercise for other parameters.
5. Sarah performs step 3 through step 7, arriving at the FEMA shown in Table 8.3.

DEVELOPING QFD USING THE TRIZ CONTRADICTION MATRIX

Quality function deployment (QFD) was created by Japanese planning specialist Yoji Akao in 1966 to help quality professionals see and compare the offerings of a product or service with the requirements of the customer and the offerings of competitors, and bridge any gaps. QFD is performed by connecting customer needs to components of the product creation process, from design and development to engineering, manufacturing, and service.

Using a series of sequential steps, customer wants and desires are translated into product characteristics. The key step in creating a successful QFD is to understand the voice of the customer and translate it into product characteristics.

EXAMPLE

AXZ is an insurance provider and is having a problem with the quote generation process. The quote generation process includes all the process steps involved from the time a customer shows her willingness to buy a policy until the company provides a quote to her. This process is very crucial, as the longer the time the company takes to generate a quote, the higher the risk of losing the customer to a competitor. Secondly, there is also a risk of providing an inaccurate quote, putting the company at risk of losing the sale. Hence, the company decided to redesign the process, and is open to investing in technology as long as the quote gets generated faster and accurately. The first step the company wanted to perform was to understand the customer's requirements pertaining to the information collected for the application and compare it with the information actually collected at that time by the company and their competitors. Figure 8.7 is a block diagram of a quality function deployment matrix. Let us look at each block of the matrix one by one:

- *Customer wants* contains the voice of the customer and clearly defines what the customer needs. This is often done with focus groups. This section will have the details of information the

Table 8.3 FMEA using TRIZ contradiction matrix.

Potential failure	Impact	Severity	Occurrence	Detectability	RPN
Sarah has to collect irrelevant information that is not required	Loose time	5	2	1	10
Sarah has difficulty in getting the order-related information	Order accuracy	7	4	5	140
Sarah has to manually enter any information in a book	Delay in delivery	8	3	6	144
Sarah has to prepare a separate bill by entering the same information	Delay in delivery	8	5	4	160
Sarah spends a lot of time in taking larger orders	Delay in delivery	8	6	3	144
Sarah has the same way of collecting information for both new and old customers	Drop in customer retention	9	8	5	360
Slowdown in existing order management process	Drop in customer retention	9	1	6	54
The process is too stressful	Sarah might quit the job	8	3	4	96
Concentration of old customers will decrease	Drop in customer retention	9	2	3	54
Sarah is unable to identify a regular customer	Increase in cycle time	6	4	5	120
Sarah is unable to pull up the customer's order history	Increase in cycle time	6	5	6	180

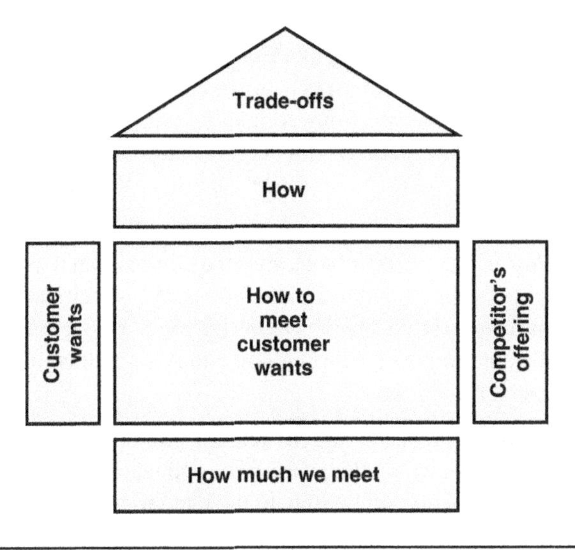

Figure 8.7 Block diagram of a QFD matrix.

customer can provide immediately, the process of submitting the insurance application online, and so on.

- The *How* block lets us measure and evaluate the customer requirements.
- The *How to meet customer wants* block contains a matrix showing the relationships or correlation between the *whats* (the customer requirements) in the rows and the *hows* (the existing characteristics of the product or service) in the columns. It can be a specific measurable number defining the amount of correlation, or just positive, negative, or neutral depending on the complexity necessary to evaluate the customer needs. In the case of AXZ we will have the list of needs from the customer's end, that is, to provide as little information as possible (name, age, sex, city) online and get the quote as soon as possible (a few minutes). AXZ's as-is application process is paper driven, where an executive comes to the customer's location, takes all the required information (name, age, sex, city, past medical history, diabetic or not, weight, and 10 other questions) and leaves, then calls the customer after 24 hours and provides the quote. Hence, the information will carry a negative score on the matrix.

- The *Competitor's offering* block will contain the information regarding the technical aspects of the competitor's product or service. AXZ has one strong competitor, and the information that they gather is (A, B, C, D, E, F, G, H). They do not need (I, J, K) to provide a quote to the customer, and that information is captured in this block.
- The *How much we meet* block shows a comparison between the competitor's specification and the company's specification and how well we meet it. The object of this block is to quantify how well the competitors perform relative to AXZ in meeting the customer's requirement.
- The *Trade-offs* block shows the relationship between the *Hows* and the direction in which the process or product has to improve. It is a very good indicator and will help the team to focus on improving a few characteristics that have a much higher impact on the customer requirements than everything else. In the case of AXZ it would be something like "move from paper to online application submission, and collect information (A, B, C, D, E, F, G, H) that will let AXZ provide the quote within 12 hours, with most of the customer's wants met."

Though QFD is a very good tool for capturing the needs of the customer and mapping them to the technical aspects of the product, it presents some challenges. The most important ones are capturing the voice of the customer and ensuring the accuracy of the information captured (as most of the time the customers do not know what they need), and then getting the customer's need mapped to the technical *hows*. A car manufacturer received an e-mail from a customer stating that every time she buys vanilla ice cream the car starts, but when she stops and buys her favorite flavor the car doesn't start. This e-mail was ignored, but the customer was persistent and kept mailing, and one day the car company was curious to know if it was really true, so the company sent an executive to meet the customer. The customer demonstrated by buying vanilla ice cream and returning to the car, and the car started right up. When she and the agent then stopped for her custom-flavored ice cream and returned to the car, it did not start. The agent was shocked and reported it to the managers and leaders. The car company sent their experts to have a look, and after some root cause analysis they figured out the problem. The vanilla ice cream was pre-packed, and the customer could pick it up and leave in a few minutes, but the custom-flavored ice cream had to be prepared and took more time. As it was winter, the engine cooled down, and when she returned to the car it did not start. This was the real problem, but the customer's VOC was *the car doesn't start when I buy my favorite ice cream*, which is true, as that is how the customer sees the problem, and looking at the technical aspect of the problem is not the customer's business. I am not sure of the authenticity of this story, but it contains some truth about getting the voice of the customer. The problem is always stated from the customer's point of view, and translating it into the technical aspects is a serious task.

Using TRIZ can help in creating a more accurate QFD with little or no customer intervention. Here is the step-by-step process:

1. Define the *ideal* product, service, or result.
2. Identify the parameters that need to be improved to reach ideality, and enter them in the *customer wants* block.
3. The rest all remains the same as for a normal QFD.

The advantage of this approach is that instead of designing the product based on customers, technology, and competition, it is designed based on ideality, technology, and competition:

- *Customer wants block.* Ideality will guide the user to arrive not just at the customer's wants but the future-state function that the customer is not even aware of.
- *How block.* Through its 39 parameters TRIZ can clearly describe how much each parameter has been met.
- *How to meet customer wants block.* By using TRIZ we can easily identify the contradictions that are stopping us from meeting the customer wants.
- *Competitor's offering block.* There is no need to compare the competitor's offering, as our benchmark is ideality.
- *How much we meet block.* Here we will include the contradictions that are resolved and yet to be resolved, and how far we are from ideality.

30 DAYS IN KYRGYZSTAN

The immigration officer couldn't believe his eyes. "Are you Indian?" he asked.

"You are the first Indian to cross this border since I started working here 12 years ago."

"I see Japanese travelers all the time," he continued when he saw Yuka.

"Do you know Bollywood dance . . . ?"

"Yes, I do," I said and started humming the iconic song from the 1982 cult Mithun Da movie, Disco Dancer.

"Now dance. Or I won't stamp your passport," the officer said.

I tried my best to put my hand on my hips and thrust them, just like Mithun Da does. Coupled with a little shoulder movement, I managed to impress the immigration officials, who started cheering me on.

"Welcome to Kyrgyzstan," they said, handing me my passport back.

After that eventful entry into Kyrgyzstan, we started cycling toward its capital, Bishkek. It was April, and yet snow was all around us. After a few hours of cycling, it started to drizzle. We were desperate for shelter, but all we could see were snow-covered mountains.

Suddenly, we heard a vehicle rolling toward us; it was a van heading to Osh, and the driver took pity on us. For the next several hours we didn't find a single soul on the road, and thanked our stars that we had hitched a ride. We reached Osh in the middle of the night and were not sure what to do next in this strange place. As we stood there contemplating, the driver asked us, "Bishkek?"

He called a driver friend of his who was about to leave for Bishkek and asked him to give us a free ride.

Osh to Bishkek. Oh my gosh!

All the men in the van were drinking vodka to beat the cold. "Drink, drink," they said to us, but we were dead tired and soon nodded off.

We awoke with a start. The van had skidded due to the ice and was spinning. The drunk men were shouting at the driver. The men then got out and started pushing the vehicle. Some laughed, others cursed the driver as they kept slipping on the ice. The other women and I were watching their comical movements, and eventually the men managed to put the van back on the road. When we got back in, all the occupants were better acquainted with each other. In the morning all of us played in the snow when the van stopped for a break on the way to Bishkek.

9

Standard Solutions

We have come across the word *system* so many times, and it is extremely important to understand that key word before we try to innovate or improve a system. By defining the system, we will understand the scope of the problem. The dictionary definition of a *system* is "a set of things working together as parts of a mechanism or an interconnecting network; a complex whole." The *set of things* need not be a physical state, it can include processes, procedures, information, documents, and so on. There are a few conditions to be met before we can describe something as a *system*. A system must always contain three components:

1. *Subject.* A person or thing that is being discussed, described, or dealt with.
2. *Action.* The fact or process of doing something, typically to achieve an aim.
3. *Object.* A person or thing to which a specified action or feeling is directed.

Let's look at an example. In Figure 9.1(a) we can define the first system as *table holds the bottle* where *table* is the subject, action is *holds*, and the object is the *bottle.* Now let's zoom in on the beer bottle (b); the beer bottle filled with beer becomes the new system. Now the definition of the system is *bottle* (subject) *holds* (action) *the beer* (object). Let us look at the third picture (c); is the definition *bottle holds the cap*? No—when defining a system, the definition *must* meet three important conditions:

1. The action must *always* change the parameter of the system. In the last example, if we define the system as *bottle holds the cap*, and if the cap is removed, there is no change in any parameter. Suppose we define it as *cap seals the bottle*; then if the cap is removed,

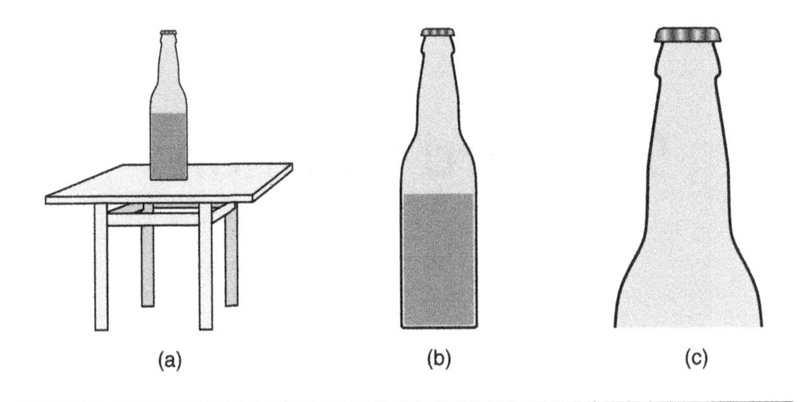

Figure 9.1 A system seen from different perspectives.

there will be a significant parameter change as the beer will spill out or the carbonation will evaporate. Hence, this rule ensures there is a function performed by the components of the system.

2. The definition must include all three components: subject, object, and action. Even if only one of the components is absent, the system is incomplete.

3. Avoid ambiguous actions. *Cap protects the beer* contains all three: subject, action, and object; is this a good definition of the system? No, the action "protect" is too ambiguous. The right definition would be *cap stops beer* or *cap seals the bottle.*

***Activity:** Define at least 10 systems from a project or process that you are associated with and is part of your day-to-day deliverables. For example, Alan (manual tester) finds defects, Bob (project manager) manages risk, Ken (developer) writes code, Laura (HR manager) hires people, and so on. Choose smaller systems rather than larger systems, as larger systems might have subsystems associated with them.*

From the above activity you should have 10 examples with subject, action, and object. What do we do once we have defined the system? The next step is to categorize the action into *useful, harmful, excessive,* or *insufficient* based on your personal experience and expertise with each of the examples. For example, manual tester testing (excessive) defects might be an *excessive* action for me, as I feel this could be automated. Bob managing risks is a *useful* action, as he has foreseen and avoided many risks in the past, Ken writing the code is an *insufficient* action, as there are a lot of bugs and too much rework. This is called the *component model*, and you can further connect all 10 examples into one process map and create a graphical model to visualize the flow of actions and take necessary corrective or preventive actions accordingly.

Activity:

1. *Draw the picture of all the components of the system.*
2. *Clearly label all the components.*
3. *Show the interactions between them.*
4. *Classify the interactions as useful, harmful, excessive, or insufficient.*

From the resulting diagram (Figure 9.2) you can now redesign the process and the flows by increasing the action wherever the action is insufficient, decreasing the action wherever it is excessive, and taking corrective and preventive actions wherever you see harmful interactions. In lean methodology many stakeholders find it hard to identify the non-value-added process steps, but I will give you three simple rules for trimming the process and removing the non-value-added activities:

1. An entire component can be trimmed if the object of the function is no longer required. Once the development is complete, Ken, the developer, can be removed from the process or project.
2. A component can be trimmed if the object of the function performs the function. If code can test itself, then the manual tester can be removed from the system.

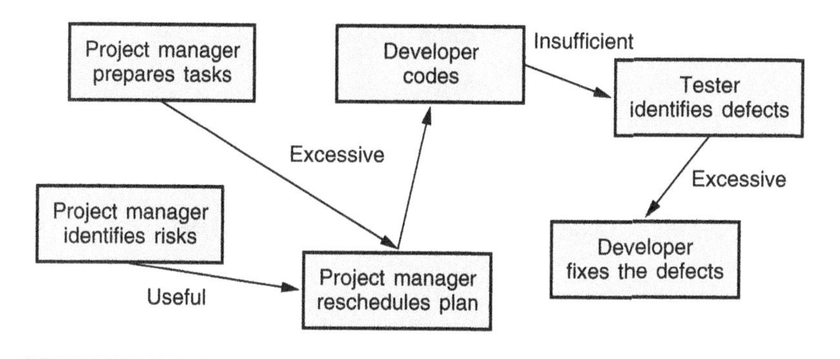

Figure 9.2 Graphical description of subject, action, and object flow.

3. A component can be trimmed if a new component can perform its function in the system. If the project manager can directly hire resources, there is no need for HR, and the entire component of HR can be removed.

Activity: *Draw the system design for all the activities that you or your team performs throughout the week. Classify the actions into useful, harmful, insufficient, and excessive. Improve the process, calculate the benefits, and report.*

SUBSTANCE FIELD MODEL

Altshuller found some limitations with the contradiction matrix in identifying the right contradiction for any given problem and wanted to replace the contradiction matrix with a more effective method of problem solving. That is when he came up with the *substance field model*, popularly called the *su-field model*. Altshuller's main proposition was that every technical system could be thought of as a network of subsystems, each of which performs some specific function. Thus, every system has subsystems, and every subsystem is said to belong to a supersystem. It is exactly like a process, where every process has process steps and an upstream process. A technical system can be described as a su-field, and the most simple su-field model is shown in Figure 9.3.

It consists of S2, the *object* or *substance*, S1, the *subject* or the *tool*, and F, the *field*. The tool is also called the *function provider* and the subject the *function receiver*. For the tool to interact with the object, a field or some form of energy is required. Depending on the type of interaction, this energy can be:

- *Mechanical—F* (Mec). Friction, pressure, manual typing
- *Gravitational—F* (Gr). Gravity
- *Acoustic—F* (Ac). Sound waves

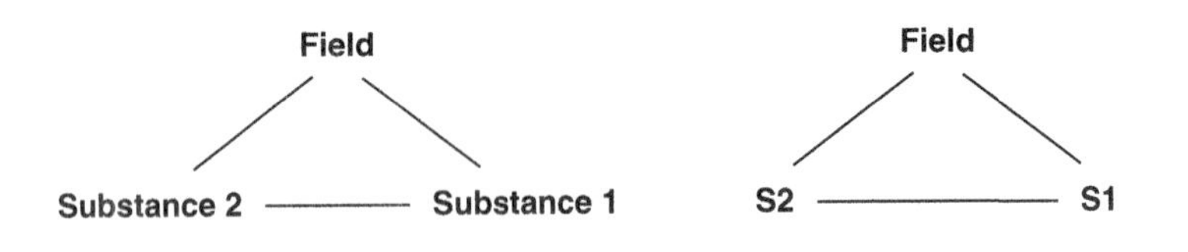

Figure 9.3 Substance field (su-field) diagram.

- *Thermal—F* (Th). Heat exchange between substances
- *Chemical—F* (Ch). Oxidation and combustion, interaction of caffeine and immune system
- *Electrical—F* (El). Lightning, battery in use, audio speakers, doorbells
- *Magnetic—F* (M). Earth's magnetic poles, solenoid to start a car
- *Electromagnetic—F* (EM). Gamma rays, X-rays, UV
- *Biological—F* (B). Fermentation, decomposition
- *Nuclear—F* (N). Nuclear fission and fusion reaction

When we are trying to apply these concepts in business, Belski (2007) proposes human fields based on human perceptions, which are organized into five classes:

1. Senses
2. Verbal communication
3. Nonverbal communication
4. Real material possession
5. Non-real material possession

Figure 9.4 shows two examples of su-field models of business systems.

As explained before, irrespective of the complexity of the system, it is important to have all three elements for any kind of system to exist. A function is characterized by a tool, an action, and an object receiving the action. A well-defined action will contain verbs like *increase*, *decrease*, or *change*, to name a few, and a property of the object, like shape, size, pressure, length, speed, or color, changed from its initial values. If the modified property of the object is desired, we call it a *useful* action; if it is undesired, we call it a *harmful* action. If it is short, then the action is *insufficient*. Figure 9.5 depicts some of the action forms and their symbolic representation.

Figure 9.4 Su-field of a business process.

Harmful	◄∿∿∿∿∿∿∿∿
Insufficient useful	◄- - - - - - - - -
Missing	- - - - - - - - - - -
Excessive	◄═══════
Useful	◄────────

Figure 9.5 Symbols used for su-field models.

EXAMPLE 1

Bob is head of sales for a factory and has a customer who is in immediate need of the product he sells. Unfortunately, the warehouse is empty and all the products are yet to be manufactured in the factory. He places the order immediately and informs the factory to manufacture the product, but the process is quite slow as the product is manufactured mechanically; after half a day the product is not even half complete.

Let's organize the interaction of this example:

- The interacting substances are the factory and the order, tool, and products, respectively.
- Factory and product interact through a mechanical field.
- The parameter of the product impacted by the factory (tool) through the mechanical field is *speed*: the factory "decreases" the speed of the product delivery.
- The impact of the factory on manufacturing speed is desired (it is desired that the factory manufactures the product and delivers it to the customer), but less than expected (the speed of manufacture is too slow), thus, the field determines an insufficient useful interaction (see Figure 9.6).

EXAMPLE 2

January to April has very low sales volume. During this period the project budget is frozen and the project does not have sufficient resources to operate. This exerts pressure on the project manager and the team, and they quit the project before completion.

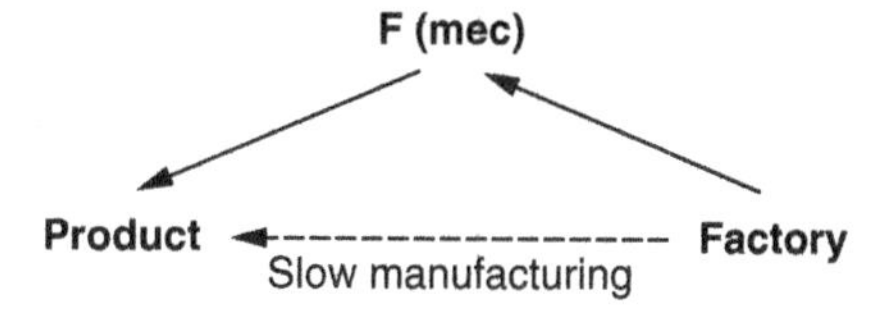

Figure 9.6 Su-field for warehouse inventory example.

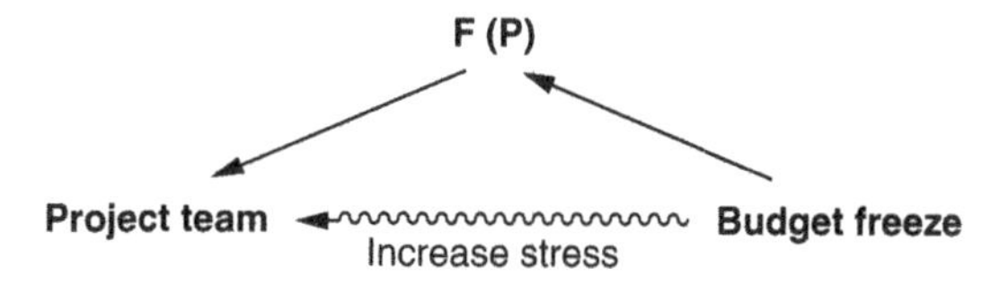

Figure 9.7 Su-field for project budget freeze example.

Let's organize the interaction of this example:

- The interacting substances are the budget and the project team, tool, and products, respectively.
- Budget and project team interact through a process field (the process where reduction in budget leads to a reduction in resources, which will exert pressure on the project).
- The parameter of the project team impacted by the budget freeze throughout the process is the *resource crunch*, that is, the budget freeze "increases" the stress on the project team.
- The impact of the budget freeze in building pressure on the team is undesired, and hence it is a harmful interaction (see Figure 9.7).

EXAMPLE 3

While making the payment for an invoice on the supplier's payment portal, Tony made a slight mistake while typing and overpaid the supplier.

Let's build a su-field model for this:

- Here we have three main substances: S1, invoice, S2, Tony's finger, S3, payment portal of the supplier.

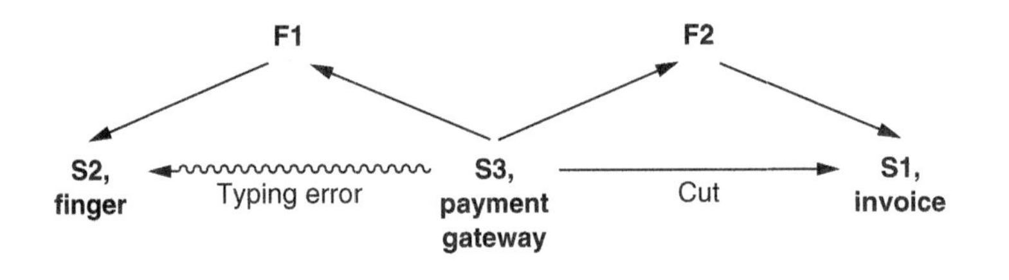

Figure 9.8 Double su-field diagram for payment issue.

- The field F1 between the payment gateway and Tony's finger is clearly mechanical.
- Since the impact of the payment gateway on the parameter of the product (number of mistakes due to incorrect typing) is undesired, the interaction between the payment gateway and Tony's finger is *harmful.*
- The field F2 between the payment gateway and the invoice is electronic, as the payment is processed electronically over the Internet: the payment gateway pays the amount that is on the invoice. Since the impact of the payment gateway on the parameter of the product (number of payments to be made) is desired, the interaction between S3 and S1 is *useful* (see Figure 9.8).

THE 76 STANDARD SOLUTIONS

Between 1975 and 1985, with the aim of providing a structured approach to the solution of a technical problem with the help of su-field analysis, Altshuller developed the 76 standard solutions. Every standard solution transforms the initial su-field model into a different model, eliminating the undesired effects in the initial model.

The 76 standard solutions are grouped into five classes:

- *Class 1* has 13 standard solutions that help in improving the system with little or no change, improving the interactions and eliminating the harmful effects. If a function is missing, or a useful collaboration between two elements of a technical system should be enhanced, relevant standards can be found here.
- *Class 2* has 23 standard solutions that help in improving the system by changing the system. If a problem is regarded as a

harmful interaction between two substances of a technical system, appropriate standards can be found here.

- *Class 3* has six standard solutions that help in transitioning to micro and macro levels. More serious problems require more radical changes to the technical system, by integration at supersystem level.
- *Class 4* has 17 standard solutions that help in improving detection and measurement problems. Detection and measurement problems can be eliminated by eliminating the need for measurement, building a new interface for information delivery, and further evolving existing measurement elements.
- *Class 5* has 17 standard solutions that help in simplifying and improving the system. Whatever standard is to be applied, some special precautions can be adopted to prevent drawbacks while introducing a new substance, a field, a phase transition, or physical and chemical effects.

We will look at each standard solution in detail, with some examples.

IMPROVEMENTS WITH MINIMAL CHANGES TO THE SYSTEM

We modify a system in order to produce a desired outcome or to eliminate an undesired outcome. It would be wonderful to be given an opportunity to completely break the product/process and implement as many changes as we need. But it happens only in the utopian world. In practice, managers and business professionals have very limited freedom to implement and drive changes. The group of solutions shown in Figure 9.9 help in improving the system with minimal changes to the existing system.

We first need to understand the problem that we are trying to solve; are we trying to improve an incomplete system or eliminate harmful effects from a system?

If the system is incomplete, then you can improve it by trying the following approaches

- If the system does not have all the required elements (S1, S2, and a field), try to complete the system by introducing the missing element. Many budget travelers were looking for a host who could provide a couch to sleep on, an experience staying with the

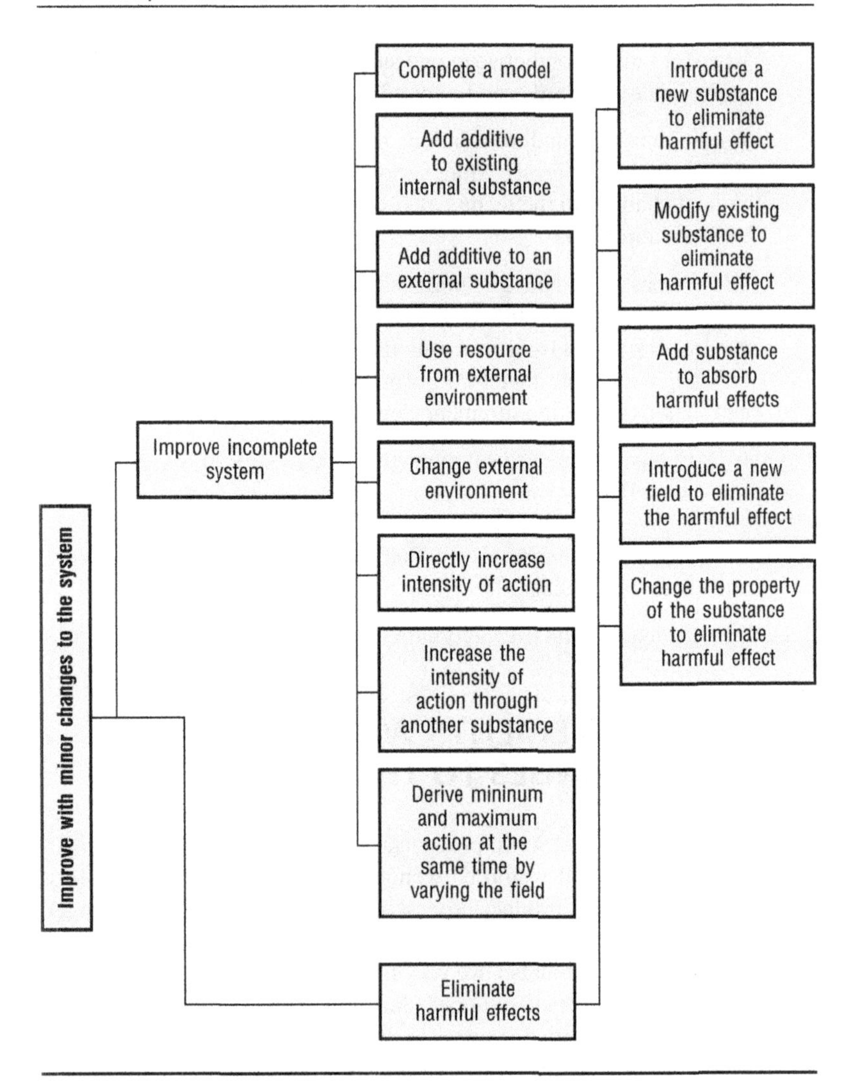

Figure 9.9 Standard solutions with minimal changes to the system.

locals, and saving money by avoiding staying at hostels and hotels. Similarly, many people wanted to host foreigners to get to know a different culture, but could not find foreigners who were looking for a host (see Figure 9.10). A company connected them electronically through a web application. This company now has 10 million members in 200,000 cities, and close to 16 million travelers have

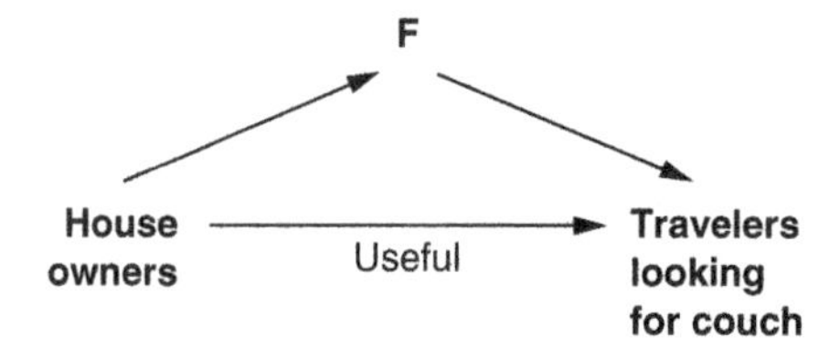

Figure 9.10 Su-field diagram for Couchsurfing example.

so far been hosted. In just 2011 and 2012 the company raised $22 million. The name of the company is Couchsurfing.

- *If the system has all the necessary substances, then try to introduce an additive for the time being.* This way you do not make a major change to the system, but temporarily or permanently introduce an additive. Netflix, the top on-demand Internet streaming company has 100 million subscribers, and one of the key factors contributing to this number is an additive, the original TV show *House of Cards.*

- *Try to solve the problem by introducing a new substance temporarily.* The difference between an external substance and an additive is that an additive changes the property of an existing substance, but this principle adds a new substance in itself. A simple example is a software program that has too many bugs. It can be improved by either training the developer to test the output (an additive) or hire a tester to test the software (external substance).

- *Try solving the problem by using a resource from an external environment.* Once in my startup, there was a need of a client for all their employees to get trained in basic French, but at that point in time we did not have the budget. We found a nonprofit society for linguistics who agreed to provide the necessary training for free.

- *Try solving the problem by making changes to the external environment.* One project team has a problem adhering to complex project guidelines, with the reason being resistance from the team members. The problem was resolved by getting help from Human Resources and adding accuracy of project guidelines to the employee incentives and promotions. H&M has been changing a brand that was viewed as cheap fashion into an ethical brand by negotiating with the prime minister of Bangladesh to raise the wages of the workers in the cotton fields and factories from which the materials are procured.

All the changes that we have spoken of so far deal with substances. We can also try to change actions to solve the problem.

If a precise amount of action or force is required, but you are unable to deliver it accurately, then increase the intensity of force/action and remove the surplus later. Every time a new product is launched, there is uncertainty about how customers will react. It is better to over-allocate resources to the customer service team, as there is a lot of uncertainty initially, and then transfer the excess resources to other departments once things settle down.

If maximum action is needed, but unfortunately you cannot take the action, then use a third party in between. This is the technique used by organizations during mass layoffs. A third party is hired to do the process of laying off in large organizations.

Try to selectively take maximum action in certain areas and shield other areas where the maximum action has a negative impact by shielding them. A social media marketing company wanted to launch a media campaign for a folding bike company. The target group on social media for folding bikes was very small; hence, they decided to launch the campaign throughout the country, which meant most of the audience who would be seeing the advertisement do not need a folding bike, which means a non-value-added investment. The social media manager came up with an idea. He chose the target group by age, those who are interested in other similar bicycle brands, who have read books related to biking, who love parks, who talk about environmental conservation, who commute to work in public transportation, and so on. Now the campaign was targeted toward the right audience and had a higher conversion ratio.

If the system is causing one or more harmful effects, then you can try the following approaches to resolve them by making minimal changes to the system:

- *Try to introduce a new substance to eliminate the harmful effect caused by one substance on another.* Involve a neutral third party to resolve conflicts.
- *Try to make changes to the subject and object to eliminate a harmful effect caused by one substance on another.* Include some flexibility or add clauses in the contract to minimize conflicts between the supplier and buyer.
- *Try to add a substance that can absorb the harmful effects of the subject or object or the field.* The difference between this and the previous solution is that here the new substance absorbs the

harmful effect, whereas in the other approach the effect is eliminated by the new substance. There was continuous difference and friction between two project teams from rival organizations working on the same program that was affecting the program. A project co-coordinator was introduced who stopped direct communication between the two teams, continuously absorbed the differences, insecurity, ego, and so on, and just delivered the required inputs and direction that was needed from one team to the other.

- *Try to bring in a new field to nullify the harmful effect of an existing field.* Completely relying on forecasting was leading to excess inventory or shortages. Introducing another input through market intelligence eliminated the forecasting error, so customer orders and inventory were better managed.
- *Try to change some of the properties of the substance or field.* The key requirements for automating a process and having a positive ROI are that the process must be repeatable, have a high volume, be low in complexity, and lastly, have a standard input format. When an insurance organization decided to move from paper-based applications to electronic applications, the automatable processes increased by 75%, and so did the bottom-line cost savings.

IMPROVEMENTS WITH MAJOR CHANGES TO THE SYSTEM

The above techniques can be used to drive incremental changes to the system, but what about radical changes, or what the Japanese call *kaikaku*, or evolutionary change. The following techniques can be used to make major changes to the system to solve problems and improve the system (see Figure 9.11).

One way of improving the system is by making the system more complex by connecting a chain of substances and fields:

- *Try introducing a substance S3 into the su-field model where field F1 acts on S2 applied to S3. S3 creates a new field F2 applied to S1, and field F2 acts on chain su-field model.* Involve a subject matter expert from the development team to explain the product to a challenging customer along with the sales team (see Figure 9.12).
- *Try taking better control over the system by moving to a double su-field model, that is, applying a second field to the system.* Split the orders between two suppliers in different proportions to reduce

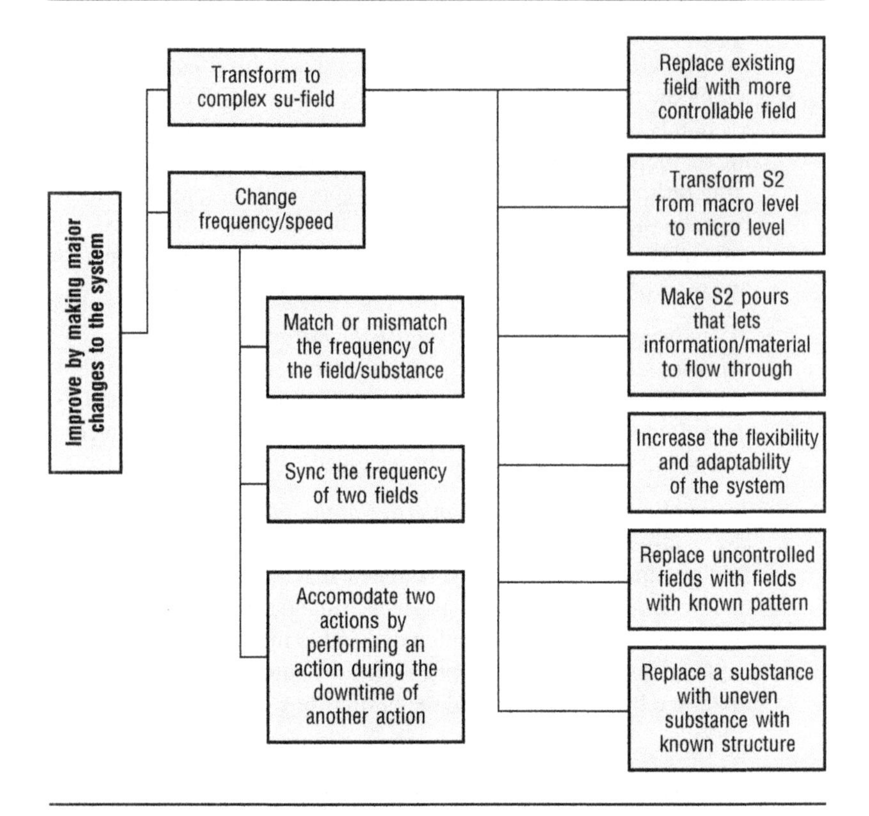

Figure 9.11 Standard solutions by making major system changes.

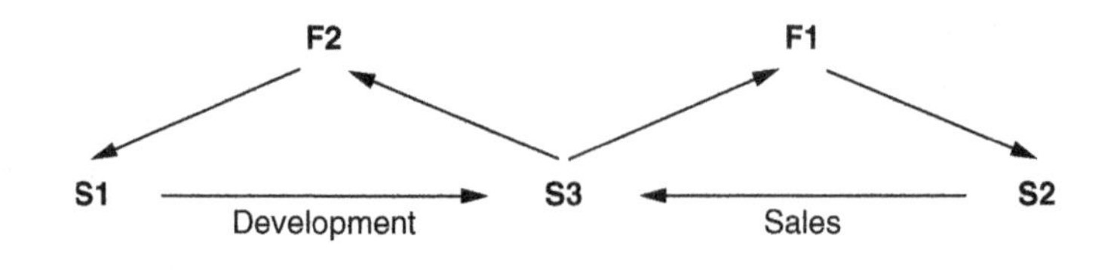

Figure 9.12 Chain su-field model for development and sales team.

the risk of stock-out and reduction in effective lead time (see Figure 9.13).

- *Remove fields with less control and replace them with fields with more control.* Example: The model of customer feedback flowing from retailer to distributor to factory is replaced by end customer to production floor through mobile and web applications.

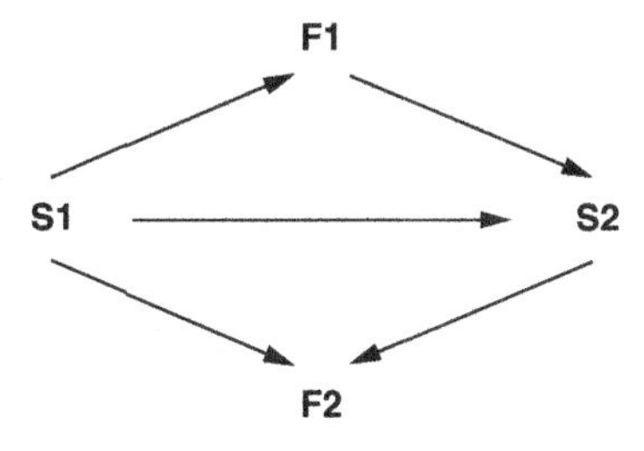

Figure 9.13 Su-field model for stock-out problem.

- *Try to reduce S2 from a macro level to a micro level.* Against the traditional design of having furniture with large pieces of wood or plastic, a bean bag is filled with minute particles of polystyrene. Similarly, a human's thought process and actions can be broken into minute logical process steps and automated through machine learning and artificial intelligence.
- *Change S2 to a porous material that will allow material and information to pass through.* Increase communication between different levels of the organization, and also make information easily available across the project as needed.
- *Try making the system more agile and adaptable.* Who would have thought in the early '90s that the biggest threat to the camera industry would be mobile phone companies? But when they saw it coming in the late '90s the camera companies could do nothing and sank. Measure the agility and adaptability of the business through metrics like *velocity* (the average amount of work a team can deliver in a limited time), collaboration within the team, percentage of the team that is informed and has a clear understanding of the organization's goal, and so on.
- *Try replacing an uncontrolled field with a field with predetermined patterns that may be permanent or temporary.* A commodity market trader who used to trade purely on historical data changed his strategy. He went on a tour, interviewing farmers on the anticipated yield for the upcoming harvest, created a predictive model with the data that he collected on the farms, and refined his trades with better accuracy.
- *Try to change a uniform or unrestrained substance into a nonuniform substance with a predetermined spatial structure that*

may be permanent or temporary. Heijunka is a strategy for level loading the production floor by scheduling tasks of uneven lead time, mixing different models, and breaking time unevenly.

We have seen the improvements that can be made through integration of su-fields. Similarly, a lot of improvements can be achieved through synchronization of activities. Effective coordination demands the right people doing the right job so the business can thrive. Changing the speed and coordination of a process helps in increasing the efficiency of the process; following are some helpful techniques:

- *Matching or mismatching the regularity of F and S1 or S2.* This principle is key if social media content has to go viral. A Facebook post reaches 70% of its engagement in four hours, so how to make sure it has maximum engagement? We need to know when our audience will be online and synchronize the posts accordingly, in short, feed the right content to the right audience at the right time.
- *Matching the beats of F1 and F2.* Another way of getting higher engagement for social media content is to post content that is currently trending at the moment, or a topic that the audience is discussing at the moment.
- *Two incompatible or independent actions can be accomplished by running each during the downtime of the other.* Carpenters, plumbers, electricians, and building maintenance contractors successfully promote their businesses during the summers in Europe when people are traveling for vacation.

Integrating ferromagnetic material and magnetic fields is an effective way to improve the performance of a system. In su-field models, the magnetic field due to a ferromagnetic material is given the special designation *fe-field*, or FFe. Ferromagnetism is the property of a material being strongly attracted to a magnetic field and becoming a powerful magnet. In business there are a lot of fields that have attractive properties (discounts—customer, incentives—employee) and repulsive properties (dip in sales numbers, fall in share price). These properties can be used instead of ferromagnetic material and magnetic substances; following are some examples:

- *Add ferromagnetic material and/or a magnetic field to the system.* Examples: Traveling magnetic field for propulsion on a railed vehicle; levitation of a monorail train.
- *Using more controlled fields, ferromagnetic materials, and magnetic fields in combination.* Examples: A team resistant to

change (uncontrolled field) can be improved by converting the fear of change to fear of competition (controlled field) by introducing incentives (magnetic material that attracts or motivates); the rigidity of a rubber mold can be controlled by adding ferromagnetic material and then applying a magnetic field; an atomic force microscope is used to deposit molecules (metal and semiconductor) on a gold surface, like ink on paper.

- *Use a magnetic liquid.* Magnetic liquids are colloidal ferromagnetic particles suspended in kerosene, silicone, or water. Ferrofluidic seals are used for doors, zero gravity applications, rotating shafts inside computer drives, and so on. A magnetic door jamb is used in conjunction with a door with a seal filled with ferrofluidic material with a given Curie point. When the temperature is lowered below the Curie point, the door is sealed, and can be opened by raising the temperature above the Curie temperature. Example: Introduce and remove performance incentives based on business performance and keep them very flexible and fluid from department to department.
- *Use capillary structures that contain magnetic particles or liquid.* Example: Construct a filter of ferromagnetic material between magnets. The alignment is controlled by the magnetic fields.
- *Use additives (such as a coating) to give a nonmagnetic object magnetic properties.* May be temporary or permanent. Examples: In order to direct molecules of medication to the exact location where they are needed in the body, attach a magnetic molecule to the drug molecule and use an external array of magnets around the patient to guide the medication to where it is needed; replace individual performance incentives with team performance incentives where the team members who are not motivated are forced to perform along with the motivated team members.
- *Introduce ferromagnetic materials into the environment, if it is not possible to make the object magnetic.* Example: Place a rubberized mat with magnetic material encapsulated in it on a car to keep tools handy while working, without having to magnetize the car! A similar device is used for surgical instruments.
- *Use natural phenomena (such as alignment of objects with the field, or loss of ferromagnetism above the Curie point.)* Examples: *Magnetic resonance imaging* (called MRI in medicine and *nuclear magnetic resonance*, or NMR, in physics) uses a tuned

oscillating magnetic field to detect the resonance of particular nuclei. An image is then developed to show the concentration of those nuclei as colored areas. Use statistical tools such as clustering to study and understand the problem better.

- *Use a dynamic, variable, or self-adjusting magnetic field.* Examples: The thickness of the wall of an irregularly shaped hollow object can be measured using an inductive transducer on the outside and a ferromagnet on the inside of the object. To increase accuracy, make the ferromagnet in the shape of an inflatable elastic balloon coated with magnetic particles so it will exactly fit the inside of the object being measured. Monitor the sales and keep adjusting the price dynamically across geographies on a need basis.
- *Modify the structure of a material by introducing ferromagnetic particles, then apply a magnetic field to move the particles.* More generally, transition from an unstructured system to a structured one, or vice versa, depending on the situation. Examples: The conductivity of a polymer can be improved by doping with conductive material. If the material is ferromagnetic, then a magnetic field can align the material to create a more effective conductor requiring less doping. Attract more customers by adding additives to the service that contribute more value to the product, like free pickup or delivery.
- *Matching the rhythms in the fe-field models.* In macro systems this is the use of mechanical vibration to enhance the motion of ferromagnetic particles. Examples: Material composition can be identified by the spectrum of the resonance frequency of electrons in response to changing frequencies of a magnetic field. The technique is called ESR, electron-spin resonance. Microwave ovens heat food because they cause the water molecules to vibrate at their resonant frequency. Include the latest trending topics in the marketing content that appeal to the customer.
- *Use electric current to create magnetic fields, instead of using magnetic particles.* Example: Electromagnets of all shapes and sizes. They can be used in temperature ranges beyond the Curie point of magnetic materials and in areas where permanent magnets cannot be secured. They have the further advantage that they can be turned off when not in use, and they can be finely tuned to an exact magnetic field by varying the current. Change

the price, quantity, quality, and other factors that are in your control to increase sales and attract more customers.

- *Rheological liquids have viscosity controlled by an electric field.* They can be used in combination with any of the methods here. They can mimic liquid/solid phase transitions. Examples: A "universal chuck" secures any shape part to a milling machine. The part is placed in a pool of rheological liquid and positioned properly, then an electric field is applied to solidify the liquid and secure the part. In a dynamic shock absorber, the system is controlled using an electric field to allow or inhibit the flow of a rheological liquid. Control the product's supply chain by varying the price of the product.

IMPROVEMENTS BY TRANSITIONING THE SYSTEM TO MICRO OR MACRO LEVEL

As I stated earlier, an *ideal* process or product will perform a required function without existing as an individual entity. Now visualize any system in the center of a nine windows and ask how to make the system disappear. The answer would be either to move the functionality to be part of the supersystem, which is called a *macro level* transition, or make it part of a component, which is called a *micro level* transition (see Figure 9.14).

First, let us see the improvements that can be made by making the system transition to a macro level:

- *Try to create a bi- or poly-system, that is, merge two or more systems together.* System efficiency at any stage of its evolution can be improved by combining the system with another system (or systems) to form a bi- or poly-system. For a simple formation of bi- and poly-systems, two or more components are combined. Components to be combined may be substances, fields, substance–field pairs and whole substance–field systems. Examples: To transport thin sheets of glass, form a block by stacking several sheets of glass, using oil as a temporary adhesive; instead of collecting and reporting data from one system, collecting a larger set of data from different systems can be more informative; instead of having status reviews with each team separately, a cross-functional review will provide more insights.

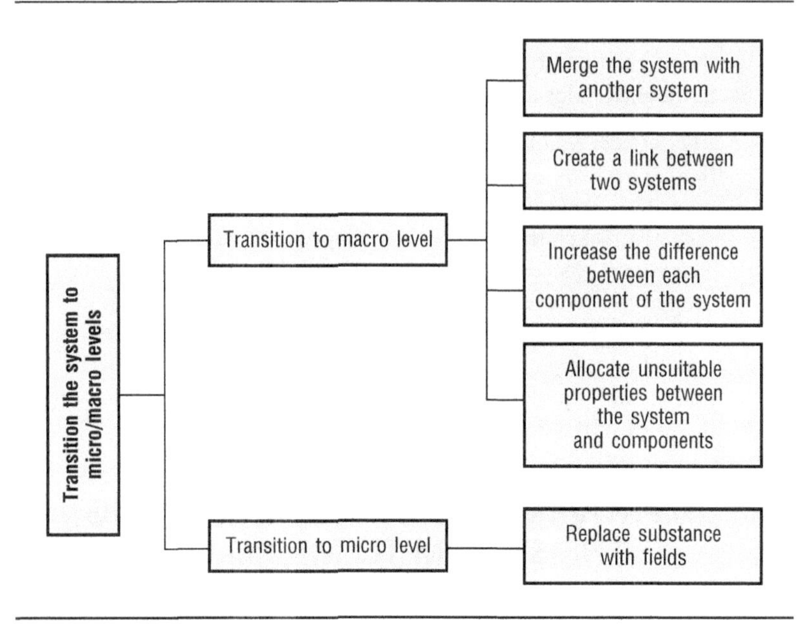

Figure 9.14 Improving the system by transitioning to micro/macro levels.

- *Efficiency of bi- and poly-systems can be improved by connecting different system components.* Improving the real-time visibility of customer demand, manufacturing, supply chain, and procurement will increase the efficiency of operations.
- *Efficiency of bi- and poly-systems can be improved by increasing the difference between the components.* This is similar to a pencil with lead on one end and an eraser on the other end. Examples: A project team's capability can be increased by hiring resources with large differences in skills; creating a service or product that provides a function as well as the opposite function, like a software company that specializes in implementing new software for small, medium, and large organizations but also helps to customize existing software rather than implement the new software.
- *Try improving the system through convolution, that is, by integrating many components into a single component, especially by removing supplementary components.* An organization's functions of serving the customer, being compliant, and upholding the organization's culture have been combined into every mono-system (a system with a single function or component) in today's

project teams. We do not need a separate department or team to do so. For smaller projects, hire developers with good testing and project management skills to eliminate the supplementary testing and project management components.

- *Try improving the efficiency of the system by leveling unharmonious properties among the system and its parts.* That is, construct a two-level structure in such a way that the whole system has a particular property while its components have an anti-property. The most common example is a bicycle chain, which has rigid components that create a flexible system when linked. An extremely customizable user-friendly product can be developed by combining multiple rigid products, functionalities, or services.

Following are some techniques for improving the system by transitioning it to a micro level:

- *Try to improve the efficiency of a system by transitioning it from a macro level to a micro level.* This can be done by replacing the existing components of the system with fields or making the components interact with fields to deliver the function. Many mundane managerial decision-making activities can be automated by combining machine learning, analytics, and robotic process automation tools and making the managerial system an efficient component of a larger umbrella. Similarly, the hiring function of an HR department involves manually looking into hundreds of resumes each day. A word cloud can be used to short- or long-list candidates faster using keywords, and hence the function can be a small automated component of the system.

IMPROVE THE DETECTABILITY AND MEASUREMENT ACCURACY OF THE SYSTEM

As Robert Heinlein wrote, "If it can't be expressed in figures, it is not science; it is opinion." Measurement is the first step toward improvement, and many problems remain unsolved not because the solutions are hard, but purely because there is difficulty in measuring the parameters or the wrong metrics are measured. Many organizations, governments, and start-ups have gone bankrupt due to lack of an efficient measurement system. On the contrary, General Electric started to encourage employees to measure everything and embrace a data-based problem-solving approach.

They asked employees to invest 100 hours in getting trained in Six Sigma, and the results GE saw are why Jack Welch is considered one of the best CEOs the world has ever seen. A better detection and measurement system gives better control over the system. Broadly, there are three ways TRIZ can improve detection and measurement effectiveness (see Figure 9.15).

The first one is the indirect method, and you can use the following technique if you are unable to measure the system and its outcomes directly:

- *Try to improve the measurement system by modifying the system instead of trying to detect or measure something.* This way we completely eliminate the need for measurement. Examples: Reengineer business processes to perform at set levels by default rather than measuring their performance through KPIs, which need constant corrective and preventive action. The lean tool mistake-proofing helps in eliminating the defects. Some online applications must go through an audit to make sure the customer has entered all the required information. This measurement process can be eliminated by making the required fields mandatory, and the system not allowing the customer to submit the application without filling them in.
- *Try to measure a copy or an image of the output rather than directly measuring it from the system.* Example: Measure the number of views received by a video or each page of a website to understand more about customer requirements rather than doing a survey or interviews to understand customer needs.
- *Try using two measurement points instead of continuous measurements.* Examples: Instead of sending continual customer satisfaction surveys, measure the total customer base and the number of customers acquired through existing-customer referrals. This provides a lot of information regarding customer satisfaction. Instead of continuously monitoring improvement benefits, track the opening and closing benefit over a time period.

The second method is to create a new measurement system by adding some elements or fields to the existing system:

- *Try to complete an incomplete su-field system to create a single or double su-field system by creating a field as an output and then measuring the output characteristics.* Example: If you are unable to measure the true employee satisfaction, measure some of the visible

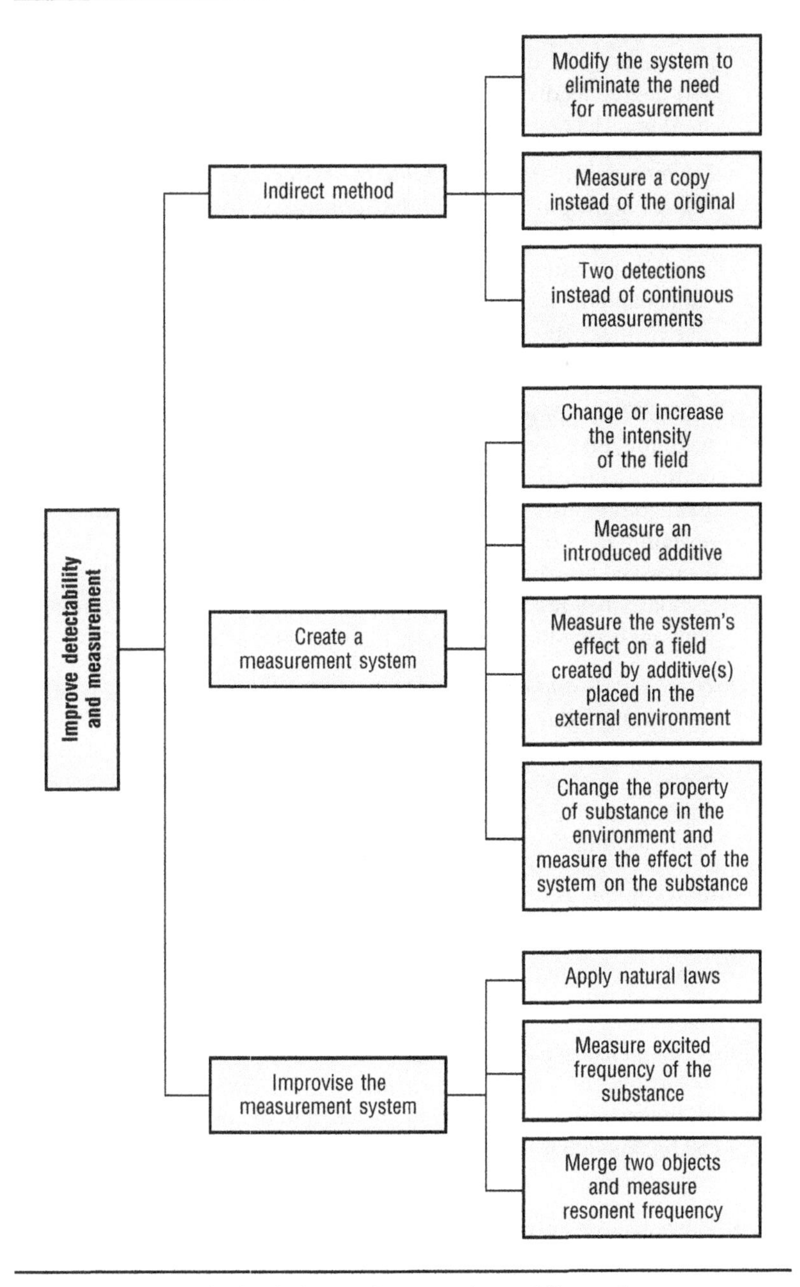

Figure 9.15 Standard solutions to improve detectability and measurement.

parameters, like the number of trainings taken by an employee, 360-degree feedback, project involvement, accountability, and so on, that reflect employee happiness.

- *Try introducing an additive into the system and measure the change in the parameters of the additive.* As soon as a change is planned, place a suggestion box where the stakeholders can anonymously share their opinions. Study the opinions to understand the level of resistance to change, and based on that take further necessary actions.
- *Try to detect or measure the system's effect on a field created by additive(s) placed in the external environment.* Example: A folding bike company wanted to understand the market for folding electric bikes. They went to different online bicycle forums and anonymously posted about the idea of building one, without revealing their brand name. The reception was very good. They even asked how much the customer was willing to pay, and the response they received was very helpful in setting the price along with analyzing the market size in different countries.
- *Try to create additives by decomposing or changing the state of something that is already in the environment, and measure the effect of the system on these created additives.* Example: If there is no group on social media for a product, then create a group or join a group for a similar category of products, post questions and opinions, and see how the group reacts.

The third technique is by enhancing the measurement system:

- *Try to apply natural phenomena.* Example: Use motivation theories and Maslow's hierarchy of needs to measure the motivation and satisfaction level of the employees in the organization.
- *Try to measure the excited resonant frequency of the system or an element in order to measure changes.* Example: Share all the proposed features to be included in the product on social media, and identify the features that have maximum customer engagement.
- *Try to measure the resonant frequency of an object joined to another of known properties.* Example: Analyze similar products on social media and study the posts with maximum engagement.

SIMPLIFY THE SYSTEM

The last way to improve the system would be to remove complexities from the system. A less complex system adds more value for the customer than a more complex system. There are numerous techniques from TRIZ standard solutions for removing complexity from a system. These techniques can be broadly classified into four categories: techniques that can simplify the system by introducing a substance into the system, using fields, using phase transition, and lastly by generating a new substance (see Figure 9.16). One or more techniques can be used to make the process/product/service simple and less complicated.

Let us look at the techniques for simplifying the system by introducing a new substance into the system:

- *Try to use "nothing" in the system.* Technically, *nothing* means air, vacuum, bubbles, foam, voids, hollows, clearances, pores, holes, voids, and so on. In short, remove components from the system. Removing an approval step in the hierarchy reduces the cycle time of the process. Even auto-approvals can be considered as adding nothing in the process. One company paid higher incentives to the maintenance team member who did nothing; the more maintenance work they did, the less they were paid. Hence, the team started working on preventive actions rather than corrective actions.
- *Try to replace substances with a field.* Hiring managers can use a word cloud and look for keywords in all the résumés to short- or long-list potential candidates rather than mechanically going through thousands of resumes. Replace scanned image documents with a system-readable database.
- *Try to make use of an external additive instead of an internal one.* Train suppliers on the applications and tools that are used to forecast demand, and provide market intelligence information to help them manage inventory better. A gaming company from Singapore announced incentives to customers who could find bugs in the game, which eliminated the testers from the process of game development and also shifted the customer's expectation from experiencing a bug-free game to identifying bugs in the game.
- *Try to use a small amount of a very active additive.* Frank Abagnale is a former confidence trickster, check forger, and impostor who now works as a security consultant with banks to

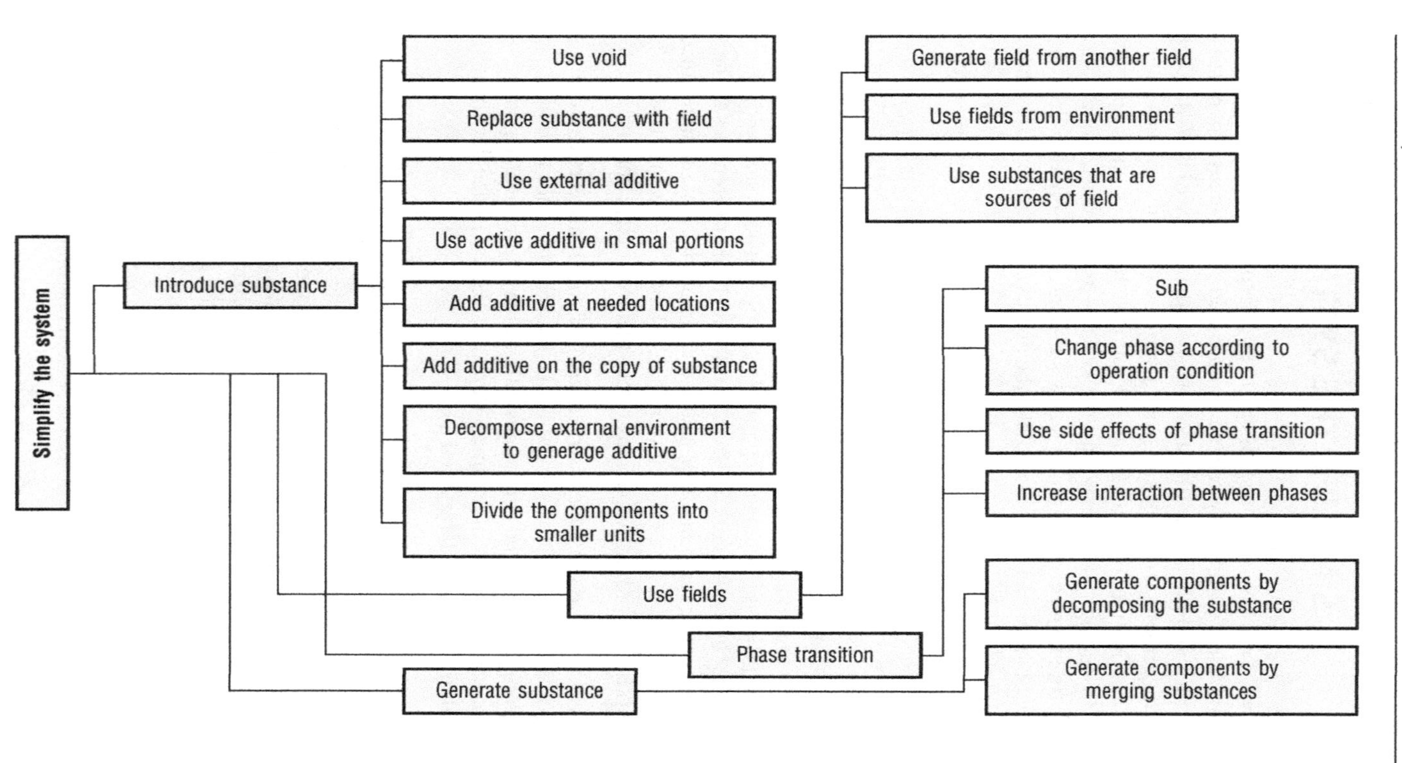

Figure 9.16 Standard solutions to simplify the system.

identify and mitigate the chances of forgery. So far, more than 14,000 institutions have adopted his fraud prevention programs, which simplify the fraud identification process for banks.

- *Try to concentrate the additive at a specific location.* Provide custom upgrade offers to high-value, loyal, or repeat unhappy customers.
- *Try to add an additive temporarily.* Bring in a temporary new supplier during high-demand seasons. Hire temporary contractors to accomplish irregular or high-skilled niche tasks instead of adding more resources to the project.
- *Try to add additives on a copy or model of the object instead of the original object.* Use simulations, test environments, test databases, and so on. Most of the popular celebrities have a stand-in who is used during photo shoots to save the time of the celebrity.
- *Try to add a compound that reacts, yielding the desired elements.* To avoid human sentiments, feed the algorithm into the system where the algorithm interacts with historical data and produces decisions.
- *Try to get the required additive by decomposing either the environment or the object itself.* One of the key additives for improvement is past experiences. Continuously gather lessons learned and best practices from external as well as internal projects and implement them in the business; continuously gather data from different sources for forecasting.
- *Apply the principle of* segmentation *to the components.* Break larger showrooms into smaller franchises, staging areas, warehouses, and so on. Fragment a large market into smaller segments to understand the customers better.
- *Try to implement the self-service principle where the additive eliminates itself after use.* Monitoring the customer's psychology and needs is a difficult task in today's fast-paced global market. Making the customer interact with artificial intelligence will capture the actions taken by the customer and also change the algorithm, and hence the decisions based on the recent and past actions taken by the customer. Cookies are another example where the customer's log-in credentials are stored in the system temporarily and are automatically deleted once the customer logs off.

- *Try to use "nothing" if circumstances do not permit the use of large quantities of material.* Encourage employees to take leave without pay to travel or attend university when there are fewer projects and the company is overstaffed. Use a blank purchase order agreement with a supplier when the quantities are unknown.

The following set of techniques can be applied to simplify the system primarily by using fields:

- *Try to use one field to cause the creation of another field.* A startup in Italy created a portal where unhappy customers could complain about an existing service provider. This information was shared with other competitors, who would contact the customer with a better deal. Rather than reacting to a customer's problem escalation, create a statistical predictive model that will indicate the probability of customer dissatisfaction based on historical data and KPIs at the process level so you can take action accordingly.
- *Try to use the fields that are present in the environment.* Social media influencers use the latest trending topics in their posts and tweets to get more subscribers. Use standard processes and methodologies if the processes and methods followed within the organization are unable to solve the problem. Use market benchmark data for improvement. Use ready-to-use plug-and-play robots for process improvements.
- *Try to use substances that can generate the fields.* If historical data are not available within the organization or in the market for understanding a problem, hire a consultant who was knowingly or unknowingly generating the data that you are looking for and can provide insight into the problem. Use a statistical simulator that generates data similar to the market demand.

Another way of simplifying the system is through phase transition, where we can play around with the different phases of the system in different space and time combinations:

- *Try substituting the phases.* The schedule can be broken into three phases: the first is a solid phase where no changes can be implemented as the activities are already in progress and close to the date of delivery, then a liquid state, where activities are planned but not started yet, which is ahead in time of the solid state and the deliverable date, and where minimal changes are acceptable, and finally the gaseous state, which is far from the delivery date, and any amount of change is welcome. In call centers the supervisors motivate the team when there is a higher call rate that takes the agents to the phase of peak performance, and on low volume days the supervisors are in a relaxed phase and so are the agents.

- *Try to use a dual-phase state.* That is, change the phase according to the operating conditions. Encourage changes and new ideas until the end of the planning phase of the project.
- *Try to use the complementary phenomena of the phase change.* As the phenomena are already taking place within the system, the associated resources are freely available. Using such free internal resources can increase the ideality of the system. When the project moves from planning to execution phase, the team needs to be more aggressive. This aggression can be used to drive process improvement projects. When the project is near the closure stage, the team has more bandwidth and can invest this time in training.
- *Try to transition to the two-phase state,* that is, by substituting the substances of a single-phase state with substances of a dual-phase state. Try to design products that have needs even during off seasons. Sunblock and decorative umbrellas are sold even during rainy and non-rainy seasons, respectively. Build a team that is capable of managing services when there are projects, and use the low-demand time to design new products and services.
- *Make use of the interaction of the phases.* Increase the effectiveness of the system by inducing an interaction between the elements of the system or the phases of the system. While hiring a sales manager, ask the supply chain and production managers to conduct a round of interviews as they will be working very closely. Supply chain performance can be increased by making the sales team interact more with the production team. Make brandy with double distillation and age it in wooden casks.

Systems can be simplified by applying the natural phenomena of nature using the following techniques:

- *Try using self-controlled transitions.* That is, transition the object from one state to the other by itself. If customers are excited about your new product, create a public forum in which the customers can talk about it and increase sales. If the customers are unhappy with the product, create a private forum to register complaints and fix the issues. Create a self-troubleshooting application that will help the customer resolve most problems themselves.

- *Try to amplify the output field when there is a weak input field.* Startups can invest a small amount in building a high-quality prototype or beta version of a product and aggressive marketing to attract investors to scale the business. If the input demand is fixed, try to increase the profits by reducing or eliminating the number of stakeholders in the value chain.

Finally, a system can be simplified by generating higher or lower forms of substances:

- *Try to generate substance particles through decomposition of existing components or elements.* Decompose the project scope to generate a list of deliverables, decompose the deliverables to generate activities, decompose activities to get a clear time and cost estimate. If there is not enough material to fulfill the customer orders for warranty, disassemble the materials from the newly built product or work in progress inventory to avoid causing further pain to the customer who is already frustrated.
- *Try to generate substance particles by merging components of lower levels.* Use parametric estimation techniques to estimate cost or schedule. When I consult with many startups on innovation, the most common problem they have is that they cannot afford to have a project manager due to budget constraints. We then assign an additional responsibility to each team member and train them to manage and track cost, schedule, risk, or scope through standard operating procedures and templates. That way the project stays on track, and any threat or issue gets flagged immediately.
- *Try to generate substance particles by using the nearest-level elements.* If a bicycle manufacturer is unable to get historical data on the number of bikes sold in his country, it is better to look for the number of bicycle frames manufactured—which is a level below a complete bicycle—rather than looking for the number of nuts and bolts manufactured.

(Terninko et al. n.d.) (Mishra 2013)

UZBEKISTAN: IN THE LAND OF TIMUR

From Samarkand we traveled to Bukhara, Uzbekistan's fifth-largest city. The bazaar was so gorgeous; it had beautiful carpets, clothes, and ceramics. Sunil had to literally cover my eyes. But he spotted a man selling samosas. Sunil had been eating samosas wherever he went, so he needed to try these too. "This is the best one so far," he said as soon as he had a bite of it. It was very different from Indian samosas and had a good amount of cheese in it; it was more like a puff. Sunil bought one every day that we were in Bukhara.

One day he asked the samosa man for the best place for Uzbek pilau.

"My place. Come back here tomorrow at lunch time and I will take you home. My wife makes the best pilau."

When we returned the next day, the samosa man's son took us home as he was busy. At his house, the low table was already set in the courtyard. Samosa man's wife was still cooking; she was heaping the pilau like a mountain and made some holes. Just then, a man arrived with a guitar; samosa man had sent him for our entertainment. He sang Jimi Hendrix, The Beatles, Bryan Adams, Elvis Presley; he even took requests.

The lunch was delicious too, and we were in no doubt that samosa man's wife makes the best pilau in all of Bukhara.

10

Motivation Strategies for TRIZ beyond the Carrot and Stick

I have been part of many innovation and improvement projects and worked with several cross-cultural teams. If I were asked about which was the best work environment, I wouldn't hesitate to reply, "results-only work environment (ROWE)."

For one project, I was contracted to improve a hospital's efficiency, which included huge changes to existing processes. The entire project needed to be done in a virtual setting because team members were situated in different geographical locations. Surprisingly, this turned out to be the most efficient project I've ever been involved in because there was no policing or tracking, and none of the team members were mandated to have log-in times or face time.

The project's final result was the only thing that was measured. It turned out to be the most effective and creative self-directed team I had worked on. In addition, we completed the project in less than half of the time and effort than it would have taken in a normal work environment.

The reason? Team members and stakeholders were not asked to perform a set of tasks. Instead, they were asked to deliver clear, measurable end results without missing the deadline. Hence, they were part of the change transformation rather than the victims of change.

I thought this would be a one-time experience. But I have worked on 13 more virtual change transformation projects, mostly related to TRIZ, while on the road. All of them have been great experiences because the teams were not asked to simply perform tasks but rather charged to deliver clear results.

What motivates this behavioral shift from a task-driven environment to a results-oriented environment?

CARROT AND STICK

In business terms, *motivation* is defined as internal and external factors that stimulate desire and energy in people to be continually interested in and committed to a task or job. As change acceleration professionals, most of us are aware of the importance of change and transformation. The hardest part is getting stakeholder buy-in to embrace the change. This calls for behavioral change, and it is important to identify what motivates stakeholders to accept and proactively implement change in a system.

The traditional method of motivation has been the carrot-and-stick method, in which an employee is either rewarded for embracing change or punished for failing to do so. This method works wonders if there is no creativity or serious cognition involved. It works on two basic human emotions—desire and fear—and acts as a good incentive under three conditions:

1. The carrot is sweet enough.
2. The work doesn't involve too much effort.
3. The employee is hungry.

Even if it works well the first time, the same carrot might not be as attractive the second or third time, and hence sustainability can drop. Similarly, the stick can produce instantaneous results, but can be used only for a short duration because it can put great stress on employees. The stick should be the last resort because this type of motivation will work only during the time the motivator is present. The most commonly used incentives are money, promotion, or both.

Hence, the carrot-and-stick model of motivation, which is also an extrinsic motivation, works well for change acceleration only when:

- The change to be implemented or embraced needs few skills and a set of rule-based, left-brain work such as simple accounting, or data entry and analysis, that can be done with software.
- Monetary need is the employee's strongest desire.
- Fear doesn't lead to any type of employee revolt.
- Instantaneous change must be embraced.

The problem is that change transformation requires stakeholders with high cognitive skills to understand the current state and have a vision for the future. To visualize the future, you must free yourself from past limitations and practices to envision a future that has never existed, and embrace new practices. This entire cycle involves much right-brain thinking, and creativity is at its core. Therefore, the carrot and stick may not be the best incentives for this model. So, what will motivate an organization's employees to proactively welcome complex change and embrace it faster?

AUTONOMY, MASTERY, AND PURPOSE

I came across a TED talk called *The Puzzle of Motivation* in which Daniel Pink, a career analyst, talks about experiments funded by the Federal Reserve Bank of the United States and conducted by economists from MIT, Carnegie Mellon University, the London School of Economics, and the University of Chicago (Pink 2009).

Pink proves that the classical motivators, such as the "if-then rewards," are not effective for simple tasks involving rudimentary cognitive skills. Larger rewards actually can lead to poorer performance. The best rewards for actions involving cognitive skills are:

- *Autonomy.* The desire to do what we like. The best example of this is Wikipedia, an encyclopedia developed by people who do not earn anything for contributing, and the reward is doing something for fun. Another example is W. Edwards Deming, a statistician sent to Japan as a census consultant. He was not shown a carrot or a stick by his then boss, General Douglas MacArthur, to work on statistical process control. It was purely for fun and out of personal interest that he developed the plan–do–study–act cycle by studying the work of Walter Shewhart. Hence, autonomy is an intrinsic motivator that will change employee behavior to drive and accept change.
- *Mastery.* What makes people who work on complex projects also want to work on sophisticated open-source projects without any monetary benefit? Why do some quality experts publish and review research papers when they do not get paid for it? This is what mastery is all about. Mastery is a type of motivation in which the reward is going deeper and mastering a particular subject or sharpening a particular skill. Employees must be given an environment where they encounter challenges that will sharpen the skills they intend to master.
- *Purpose.* The most important intrinsic motivator is purpose, that is, "Why am I driving change as a change manager?" or "Why should

I embrace change?" Author and motivational speaker Simon Sinek proposes, "People don't buy what you do, they buy why you do it" (Sinek 2011).

For example, Virgin America airline's answer to why it does what it does is "To make flying good again." Apple? "We believe in thinking differently." Similarly, every employee should have their own purpose to accept or resist change. It is the change owner's responsibility to create an environment in which the organization's purpose for driving change is clear so that it can be in sync with its actual purpose.

ROWE MODEL

Having covered the three types of intrinsic motivators, what kind of work environment is the best fit for an autonomy–mastery–purpose model? What kind of work environment will help employees to be independent, master a subject, and embrace change with a purpose?

The answer is the results-only work environment (ROWE). Essentially, its mantra is "Work whenever you want, wherever you want, however you want, as long as the work gets done" (Mather 2015). This way, if change has a direct impact on the result, surely it will be embraced. In addition, stakeholders are not asked to buy into the change, but instead are made part of the change by creating the expected results.

Google has a "20% time" philosophy in which one day each week employees can work on any project they wish that they feel is helpful to Google. Some of the outcomes from this 20% are Gmail, Google Transit, Google Talk, Google News, and AdSense, which alone contributes 25% of the company's annual revenue (Gersch 2013).

That 20% time philosophy gave Google employees enough space to do something they loved (autonomy), attempt to innovate something new with all the cognitive skills they had (mastery), and, in the end, contribute something to their employer (purpose).

It could be a bit frightening for an organization to let go of 20% of employees' time and productivity like Google did, but maybe 5% for a small group could be a start in implementing this model over a short period. It can then be stretched as needed.

The first step would be to identify departments or processes where change is needed, and identify employees who will be part of the program. Next, provide these employees with a purpose, and have informal weekly status meetings to understand what they've been creating. If it works well, the organization can opt to extend the duration from 5% to 10% of the employees' time, or more. If it fails, root cause analysis is needed.

The ROWE model has been adopted by many organizations, and this has great potential to be the future of motivation to bring rapid change acceleration into a business.

In an organization or system, if tasks don't need cognitive skills, a carrot-and-stick method might work as a good motivator. If the tasks need cognitive and creative skills, and you're trying to create a culture that openly embraces and initiates change transformation, the best motivators are autonomy, mastery, and purpose. ROWE is the best environment for providing such motivations, and TRIZ works best in such environments.

JOURNEY THROUGH TURKEY

We were cycling through Turkey when all the major incidents happened. While in Cappadocia, there was blast in Istanbul airport, but our host made sure we were safe and secure. We were being hosted by two young religious Muslim girls in a small town near the Black Sea region when the coup happened. Part of the army captured the city of Istanbul. We were scared that the army might come and arrest religious people, and started hiding the Quran and other religious texts under our cots and in our bicycle bags. Things settled down in a few days and life got back to normal. We were hosted in a small town close to the Georgian border where three policemen were killed in front of our house by a Kurdish terror group. Six terrorists were on the loose, and I encountered a terrorist just 10 meters away from me.

In spite of all these incidents, we were going to the Syrian refugee camps and training them on lean and Six Sigma through origami, consulting on managing the camps more efficiently, teaching in universities, and writing this book.

Our humble gratitude goes out to all the hosts who made sure we were safe and secure.

11

ARIZ: Algorithm for Inventive Problem Solving

At some point, you might have wondered whether there is a systematic way to apply all these principles to solve a problem, and the answer lies in *algorithm for inventive problem solving*, or ARIZ, which was also developed by Genrich Altshuller. ARIZ is a set of sequential, logical procedures for analyzing the initial problem situation in order to create the most effective solutions using fundamental concepts and methods of TRIZ. There were several version of ARIZ, and the first one was developed in 1956. As the standard solutions evolved, so did the ARIZ versions. The name ARIZ was first introduced in the autumn of 1965. Subsequent modifications to ARIZ are named ARIZ-68, ARIZ-71, ARIZ-77, ARIZ-82, and the last modification of ARIZ, ARIZ-85C, which we will look at in this chapter. ARIZ 85C helps us to use the individual TRIZ tools in a structured manner to achieve the best possible solutions to a problem. ARIZ-85C performs TRIZ management duties and guides us with a step-by-step approach in analyzing the problem and choosing the best solution. ARIZ is a multi-step process asking the user a series of questions, integrating different tools of TRIZ.

The entire algorithm consists of eight parts, and I will explain the flow with a real-time example. One of my clients in Georgia had a very popular winery that produced high-quality red and white wine. They approached me for help and said the problem was to bring more customers to their website, or in short, increase their web traffic. When I started working toward the root of the problem, I understood their ambition more clearly. The goal was not just to increase web traffic but to increase sales with much less marketing cost. They had a very good reputation and market in Georgia, and they saw a huge market potential in Russia. With their quality standard they were confident they could be easily be among the top 20 wines that are imported into Russia. They started exporting through some distributors, but the marketing was not sufficient and hence sales were very low compared to the total market potential. Their goal was to attract more customers online rather than customers who choose their wine from a retail store. Fortunately, my client was fine with me sharing this case study without revealing their brand name. Hence, let's call my client's brand Zura's wine company. I used ARIZ to solve their problem.

The first two parts of ARIZ are the analytical stages:

Part 1—Analyzing the problem. The objective is to transform the indefinite initial problem into a simplified problem or model.

Step 1.1 Formulate the mini problem. The system contains Zura's website, customers, and the need or motivation for the customer to visit the website.

> Technical conflict 1 (TC#1): More customers visiting the website will increase sales but will also increase the marketing cost.

> Technical conflict 2 (TC#2): Fewer customers visiting the website will mean fewer sales but will not cause additional marketing cost.

The desired result: *It is necessary, with minimum changes to the system, to provide the required engagement level with Zura's website while keeping the campaign and marketing costs low or nil.*

Step 1.2 Define conflicting elements. Conflicting pair:

> Marketing—sales

> Tool—Customers visiting the website

Step 1.3 Describe graphic models.

TC#1 (more marketing)

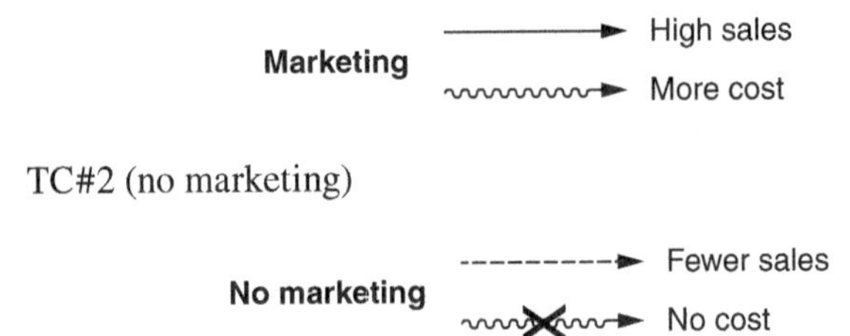

Step 1.4 Select one graphic model. From the two models we need to choose the one that provides the best performance for the main function. The main useful function is to increase the sales, but the marketing cost is high. Hence I will choose TC#1.

Step 1.5 Intensify the conflict by indicating the extreme state of the elements. Extremely aggressive marketing will bring a lot of customers to the website and this will increase the sales of wine.

Step 1.6 Describe the problem model. Define the problem model that indicates:

a. *The conflicting pair.* Marketing cost and sales.

b. *Intensified conflict definition.* Investing profits back into marketing will bring a lot of customers to the website from the competitors, and sales will be very high.

c. What the new element "X" introduced into the system should do to solve the problem (what X must keep, eliminate, improve, provide, and so on). In our example, the X element must reduce marketing cost and increase sales.

Step 1.7 Try to apply some of the techniques from the standard solutions. I first looked at the class one standard solution techniques to improve sales by making very minimal changes to the system. In this case I want to eliminate the harmful effect of a potential customer in need approaching a different brand instead of Zura's website, and the techniques that I can apply are:

- Introduce a new substance that would attract potential customers to Zura's website.
- Modify an existing substance that would attract potential customers to Zura's website.
- Lastly, introduce a field that would attract potential customers to Zura's website.

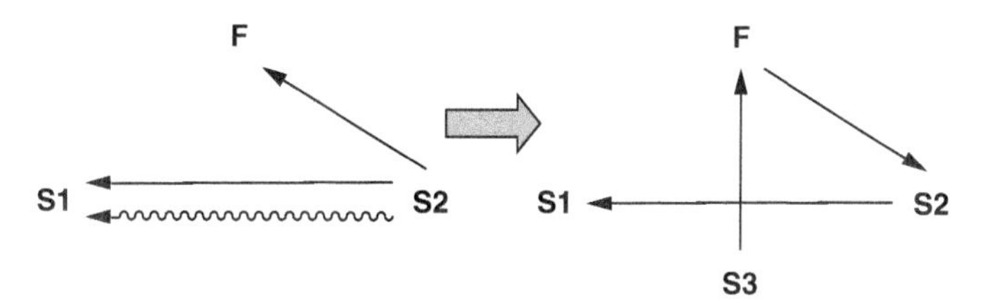

S1—Sales

S2—Marketing

F—Marketing cost

S3 = ? F2 = ?

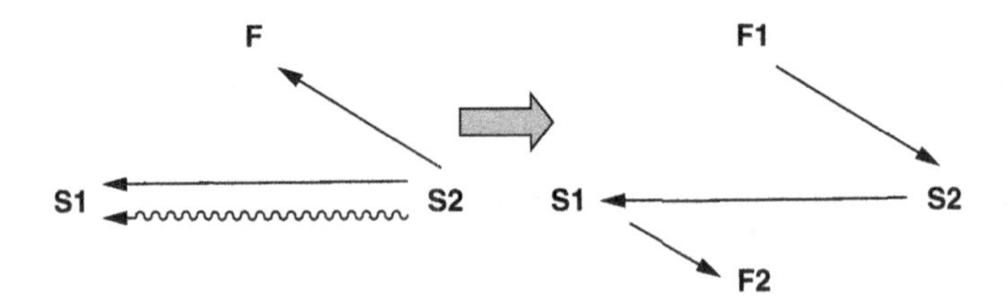

Part 2 Analyzing the problem model. The objective is to identify available resources like space, time, substances, and fields that could be used to solve the problem.

Step 2.1 Define the operational zone. Analyze and describe the zone in which the entire product operates.

> Definition of the operational zone: Customers who are aware of Zura's website and are in need of wine, on the Internet, and order wine online.

Step 2.2 Define the operational time. Defined as the time before the conflict (T1) and after the conflict (T2).

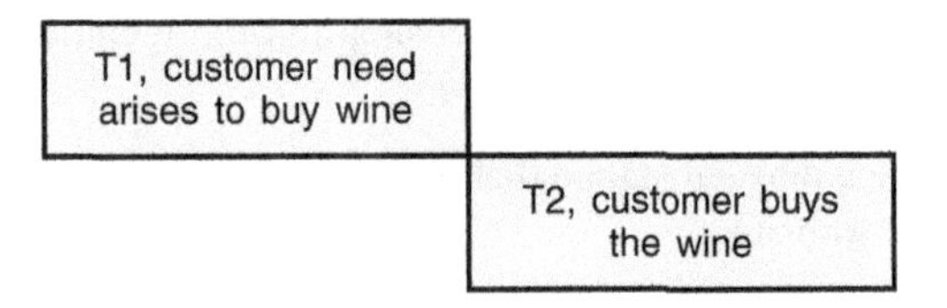

Hence, here T1: Customer need arises to buy wine; T2: Customer buys wine from Zura's website.

Step 2.3 Define substance field resources (SFRs). SFRs are the existing available resources within the system, and should be utilized first:

a. *System's internal resources.* Sales team, distributors, website traffic, demand, and so on.

b. *External resources.* Sales revenue, target sales, target revenue, target market and brand awareness, social media, and so on.

c. *SFRs of the supersystem.* Winemasters, chefs, housewives, family, Internet, market demand, competition, restaurants, and so on.

Part 3 Defining the ideal final result and physical contradiction. The objective is to formulate the *ideal final result* (IFR) and identify the physical contradictions that act as a hurdle in achieving the IFR.

Step 3.1 Defining the ideal final result (IFR). Without adding any complexity to the system, the X element eliminates all *harmful actions* within the *operational time*, inside the *operational zone*, and retains the tool's ability to provide the *needed useful action*. So, in our example the IFR would be:

> *Without adding any complexity to the system, the X element eliminates the need for marketing or creating brand awareness whenever the customers have a need to buy wine, and brings them to Zura's wine website and keeps sales very high.*

Step 3.2 Intensify the definition of the IFR, which we call the IFR-1. Here we will be introducing additional requirements, but we cannot introduce a new substance or field and must use only the available SFRs:

a. High website traffic *eliminates the need for marketing or creating brand awareness* whenever the *customers have a need*, and *brings them to Zura's website* and keeps *sales very high*.

b. High market demand *eliminates the need for marketing or creating brand awareness* whenever the *customers have a need*, and *brings them to Zura's website* and keeps *sales very high*.

Step 3.3 Identify the physical contradiction at the macro level. The identified contradiction has to be defined in the following pattern:

> *The resources in the operational zone* within the *operational time* have to *define the physical macro-state* in order to perform *insert one of the conflicting actions* and have to *define the opposite physical state* to perform *define another conflicting action or requirement*.

Let us use this in our example:

> *Customers with an immediate need at any given time* have to *automatically reach Zura's website* in order to *buy their wine without any marketing and increase sales for Zura's wine company*.

Step 3.4 Identify the physical contradiction for the micro level. The identified contradiction has to be defined in the following pattern:

> There should be particles of a substance *define their physical state or action* in the *operational zone* within the *operational time* in order to provide *include the macro state as per step 3.3*, and there should be no particles or particles should have the opposite state or action in order to provide *indicate another macro state according to step 3.3*.

Using this in our example:

> *There must be* ***force to attract every single customer with an immediate need*** *to buy wine at any given* ***time*** and have them *automatically reach Zura's website* in order to *buy their needs* ***with or without any brand awareness*** *and* ***increase sales for Zura's wine company****.*

Step 3.5 Formulate IFR-2. Identify and define the IFR-2 using the following pattern:

> The operational zone *indicate* has to provide *the opposite macro or micro states* itself within the *operational time.*

Using this in our example:

> The operational zone *customers have to get pulled* to *Zura's website* and *buy without any marketing* whenever *there is a need.*

Step 3.6 Apply inventive standards to resolve the physical contradiction.

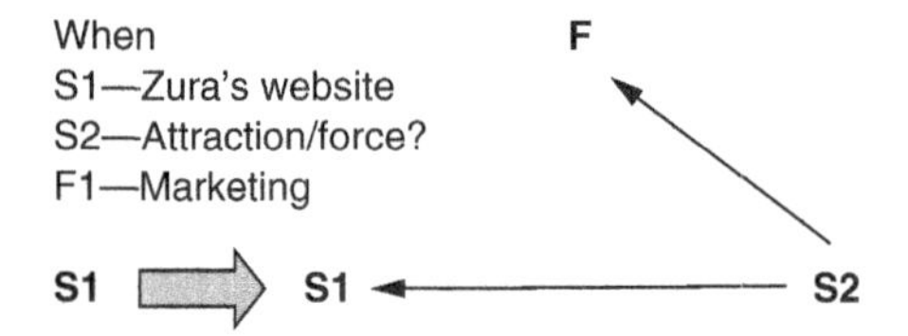

Part 4 Mobilizing and using substance field resources (SFR). This consists of systematic procedures for increasing the availability of resources. It helps in modifying already existing resources and obtaining new resources for free. At step 2.3 we identified the resources that are available for free. In part 4 we will use a systematic approach to increase the availability of resources through slight modification of already available resources.

Step 4.1 Simulation with little creatures. Here we describe a graphic model of the conflict using the *simulation with little creatures* (SLC) and change the graphic model in such a way that the little creatures act without conflict.

Corollary:

1. There should be a substance in the operational zone within the operational time T1 that will detect the customer's need.
2. There should be a substance that will bring the customer with the need to Zura's website.

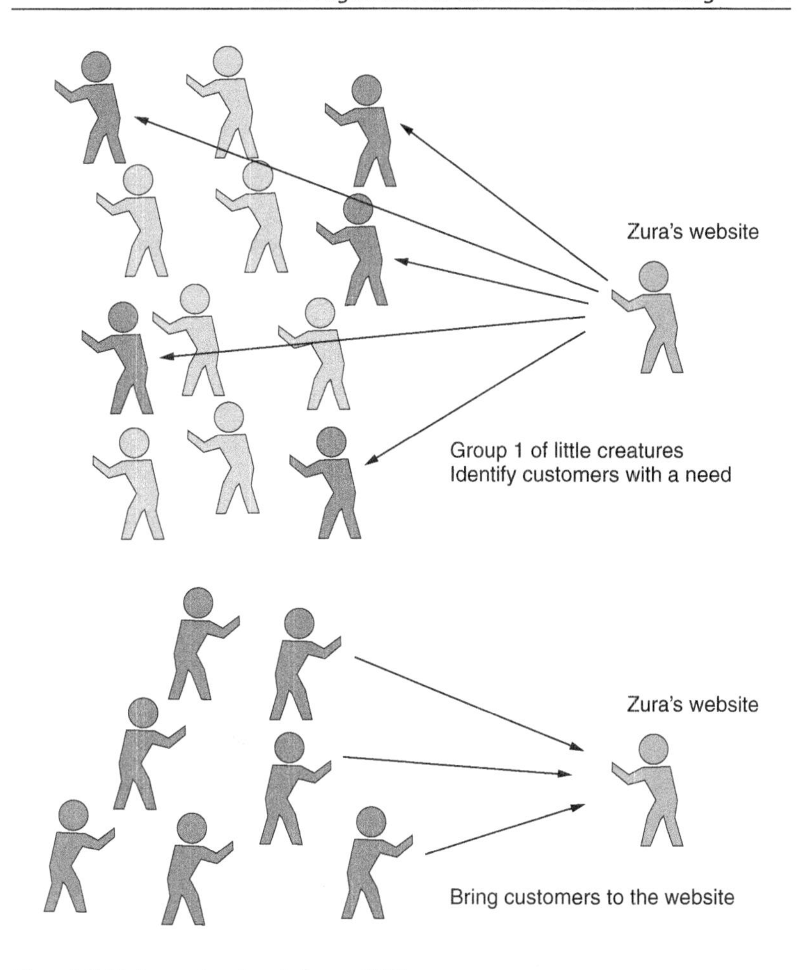

Step 4.2 Take a step back from IFR.

1. IFR: The customers come to Zura's website every time there is a need to order.
2. A step back from IFR: One customer had a need but was not aware of Zura's website and hence did not order from Zura's website.
3. Micro problem: How to get this lost customer to the website.
4. Solution for the micro problem: An external force/substance or field has to direct the customer to the website.
5. Intensification of the micro problem: How to bring back a lot of lost customers to Zura's website who went to shop in different directions.

6. Solution to the intensified micro problem: An external force/substance or field will bring all the customers to the website the moment they realize their need.
7. Transition from the micro problem to the real one: In the operational zone the forces must arise that would take the customer to the website at time T1, the moment the need arises.

Step 4.3 Using a combination of substance resources. Can we generate the force that will bring the customers to the website by mixing the resources of the substance? *Think*!

Step 4.4 Using "voids." Can we generate the force that will get the customers to the website by replacing the existing substance resources with an empty space or a mixture of substance resources and empty space? *Think*!

Step 4.5 Using derived resources. Derived substance resources can be obtained by changing the phase of the existing substance resources. Can we generate the force that will get the customers to the website using derived substance resources or a mixture of derived substances and empty space? *Think*!

Step 4.6 Using a field and field-sensitive substances. Consider the possibility of solving the problem using a pair of fields and a substance additive that is responsive to the field.

I discovered that many customers visit popular winemasters' websites, copy the names of recommended wines, and buy them from different sources. We exploited this opportunity and introduced a substance additive to the popular winemasters' websites in Russia, which had very high web traffic, in the form of an API (application programming interface) where, once the customer reads the review of a wine, with a click of a button he or she can place an order for Zura's wine and get it delivered to their doorstep. The winemasters get a share in the total revenue. This way the sales for Zura's went up by 71% with zero spending on marketing.

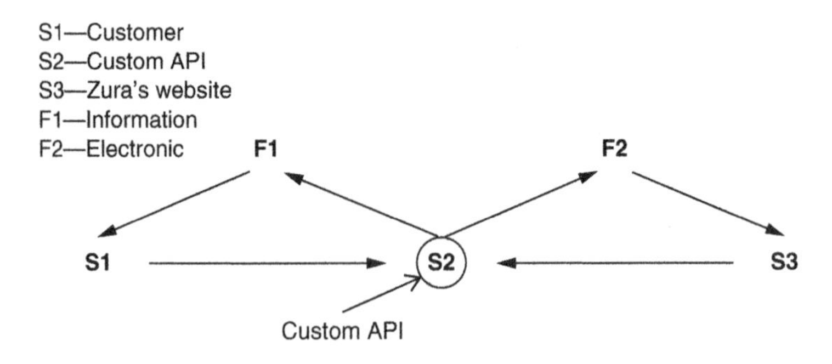

Part 5 Applying the knowledge base. Most of the time we arrive at a solution in Part 4 as we saw above, but sometimes we need to dig further, and Part 5 helps to assemble the past experiences of the TRIZ knowledge database. At a quality conference in Greece I met Costas, the cofounder of innovation company Happen.com, and he shared a lot of business innovation success stories. One such scenario was during early 2000 when Happen.com discovered that the next wave in the coffee vending machine industry would be a vending machine that could produce both hot and cold coffee.

Step 5.1 Applying the system of standard solution to IFR-2. Consider the possibility of solving the problem by applying the inventive standards and using external additives to the SFRs. The initial approach was to produce cold coffee by modifying the existing hot coffee vending machine by integrating a freezer that would produce ice, a crusher to crush the ice, and a mixer. The problem was that this made the machine three times bigger than a normal vending machine.

Step 5.2 Applying previous solutions. Solve the problem by applying the solution concepts to nonstandard problems that have already been solved using ARIZ. Costas and his team started to dig and research through the patent database and found a very simple solution. How is snow produced? By forcing water and pressurized air to pass through cold air. They did the same with the hot coffee and produced "snow coffee," or cold coffee, and eliminated the need for crusher, mixer, and freezer.

Part 6 Changing or substituting the problem. Most problems are solved by resolving the contradiction, but some complex problems demand changing the problem statement that was created with mental inertia.

Part 7 Analyzing the method of resolving the physical contradiction. The objective is to check the quality of the solution obtained. A good solution is one where the physical contradiction is removed without anything, or *ideally*.

Step 7.1 Control the solution concept. Here we question whether it is possible to apply the available or derived SFRs instead of introducing new substances or fields. In the Zura's example, the APIs on the review website are the introduced substances. Is there a way to eliminate them?

Step 7.2 Evaluate concept. Here we evaluate whether the solution for the Zura's example has met all the requirements:

a. Have we met the main requirements of IFR-1? *Yes*

b. Which physical contradiction have we resolved in the solution concept? *Increase the sales and revenue without any cost for marketing.*

c. Does the system contain any easily controllable element? *The wine that is ordered can be controlled through the APIs.*

Part 8 Applying obtained results. It is not where we take it from, but where we take it to. The objective of this step is to enable the innovator to leverage the ideas for other similar problems and make sure there is a maximum utilization of the idea. We can estimate the changes at the supersystem level to find out if the solutions can be applied elsewhere, and apply the solutions to other applications.

Part 9 Analyzing the problem-solving process. The objective of this part is to analyze the solution process and increase the creative potential of the inventor. We identify the gaps between the real process used to solve the problem and the process described in ARIZ, and contribute to the evolution of ARIZ by sharing the approaches that were taken to arrive at the final intended result.

ARIZ is a very powerful tool for systematic problem solving. The art of problem solving can be improved and brought close to perfection by solving more problems using the ARIZ methodology. A complete structured flow for using ARIZ is in Appendix B.

CYCLING THROUGH THE NORTH KOREA OF ASIA: TURKMENISTAN

"From which border will you exit Turkmenistan," the officer asked me. I fumbled, but Sunil quickly answered his question. The officer then had some more queries. Our grilling went on for about 30 minutes and finally we were allowed to enter Turkmenistan. But there was a catch: we had to exit the country in four days. We decided to quicken our pace, but the road was muddy and it was very difficult to cycle. It had rained the previous night, and there was slush all around. We flagged a truck down, hoping to hitchhike. But the Turkish driver gave us water and apologized.

"Police are very strict, and we aren't allowed to give foreigners a ride in this country. If you cycle on for another 10 km, you will find a shop." So we struggled through the muddy road for 10 km. Men with donkeys waved at us as we passed them by. People were friendlier than we thought.

ONE NIGHT IN A TRUCK STOP

"This must be it," Sunil said when we saw the "shop." Some ladies were sitting having tea; they gestured to us to join them and gave us sweets, bread, and tea.

The oldest lady was the owner of the shop. We asked her if we could pitch our tent for the night, and she readily said yes. Truckers stopped by for dinner or a night's rest. I turned in early but Sunil decided to chat up some truck drivers and even had dinner with them. We woke up early in the morning, and the lady asked us to come inside for breakfast. There was bread, salad, omelets, cheese, and juice on the table. She sat next to us and spoke to us for some time; I think she was talking about her family and grandchildren. She didn't let us pay for breakfast, so we bought a few things for our trip. She gave us a big hug and packed lunch for us.

Appendix A

The TRIZ Contradiction Matrix

Table A.1 TRIZ contradiction matrix.

Parameters/features/ characteristics	**40 inventive principles**
1. Weight of moving object	1. Segmentation
2. Weight of stationary object	2. Extraction, Separation, Removal, Segregation
3. Length of moving object	3. Local quality
4. Length of stationary object	4. Asymmetry
5. Area of moving object	5. Combining, Integration, Merging
6. Area of stationary object	6. Universality, Multi-functionality
7. Volume of moving object	7. Nesting
8. Volume of stationary object	8. Counterweight, Levitation
9. Speed	9. Preliminary anti-action, Prior counteraction
10. Force (Intensity)	10. Prior action
11. Stress or pressure	11. Cushion in advance, compensate before
12. Shape	12. Equipotentiality, remove stress
13. Stability of the object's composition	13. Inversion, The other way around
14. Strength	14. Spheroidality, Curvilinearity
15. Duration of action of moving object	15. Dynamicity, Optimization
16. Duration of action of stationary object	16. Partial or excessive action
17. Temperature	17. Moving to a new dimension
18. Illumination intensity	18. Mechanical vibration/ oscillation
19. Use of energy by moving object	19. Periodic action
20. Use of energy by stationary object	20. Continuity of a useful action
21. Power	21. Rushing through

Continued

Table A.1 *Continued.*

Parameters/features/ characteristics	40 inventive principles
22. Loss of energy	22. Convert harm into benefit, "Blessing in disguise"
23. Loss of substance	23. Feedback
24. Loss of information	24. Mediator, intermediary
25. Loss of time	25. Self-service, self-organization
26. Quantity of substance	26. Copying
27. Reliability	27. Cheap, disposable objects
28. Measurement accuracy	28. Replacement of a mechanical system with "fields"
29. Manufacturing precision	29. Pneumatics or hydraulics
30. Object-affected harmful factors	30. Flexible membranes or thin film
31. Object-generated harmful factors	31. Use of porous materials
32. Ease of manufacture	32. Changing color or optical properties
33. Ease of operation	33. Homogeneity
34. Ease of repair	34. Rejection and regeneration, Discarding and recovering
35. Adaptability or versatility	35. Transformation of the physical and chemical states of an object, Parameter change, Changing properties
36. Device complexity	36. Phase transformation
37. Difficulty of detecting and measuring	37. Thermal expansion
38. Extent of automation	38. Use strong oxidizers, Enriched atmospheres, Accelerated oxidation
39. Productivity	39. Inert environment or atmosphere
	40. Composite materials

Table A.2 TRIZ contradiction matrix.

	Working feature ⇒ Improving feature ⇓	Weight of moving object	Weight of stationary object	Length of moving object	Length of stationary object	Area of moving object	Area of stationary object	Volume of moving object	Volume of stationary object	Speed	Force (intensity)	Stress or pressure	Shape	Stability of the object's composition
		1	2	3	4	5	6	7	8	9	10	11	12	13
1	Weight of moving object	+		15, 8, 29, 34		29, 17, 38, 34		29, 2, 40, 28		2, 8, 15, 38	8, 10, 18, 37	10, 36, 37, 40	10, 14, 35, 40	1, 35, 19, 39
2	Weight of stationary object		+		10, 1, 29, 35		35, 30, 13, 2		5, 35, 14, 2		8, 10, 19, 35	13, 29, 10, 18	13, 10, 29, 14	26, 39, 1, 40
3	Length of moving object	8, 15, 29, 34		+		15, 17, 4		7, 17, 4, 35		13, 4, 8	17, 10, 4	1, 8, 35	1, 8, 10, 29	1, 8, 15, 34
4	Length of stationary object		35, 28, 40, 29		+		17, 7, 10, 40		35, 8, 2, 14		28, 10	1, 14, 35	13, 14, 15, 7	39, 37, 35
5	Area of moving object	2, 17, 29, 4		14, 15, 18, 4		+		7, 14, 17, 4		29, 30, 4, 34	19, 30, 35, 2	10, 15, 36, 28	5, 34, 29, 4	11, 2, 13, 39
6	Area of stationary object		30, 2, 14, 18		26, 7, 9, 39		+				1, 18, 35, 36	10, 15, 36, 37		2, 38
7	Volume of moving object	2, 26, 29, 40		1, 7, 4, 35		1, 7, 4, 17		+		29, 4, 38, 34	15, 35, 36, 37	6, 35, 36, 37	1, 15, 29, 4	28, 10, 1, 39
8	Volume of stationary object		35, 10, 19, 14	19, 14	35, 8, 2, 14				+		2, 18, 37	24, 35	7, 2, 35	34, 28, 35, 40

Table A.2 *Continued.*

	Working feature ⇒	Strength	Duration of action of moving object	Duration of action of stationary object	Temperature	Illumination intensity	Use of energy by moving object	Use of energy by stationary object	Power	Loss of energy	Loss of substance	Loss of information	Loss of time	Quantity of substance
	Improving feature ⇓	**14**	**15**	**16**	**17**	**18**	**19**	**20**	**21**	**22**	**23**	**24**	**25**	**26**
1	Weight of moving object	28, 27, 18, 40	5, 34, 31, 35		6, 29, 4, 38	19, 1, 32	35, 12, 34, 31		12, 36, 18, 31	6, 2, 34, 19	5, 35, 3, 31	10, 24, 35	10, 35, 20, 28	3, 26, 18, 31
2	Weight of stationary object	28, 2, 10, 27		2, 27, 19, 6	28, 19, 32, 22	19, 32, 35		18, 19, 28, 1	15, 19, 18, 22	18, 19, 28, 15	5, 8, 13, 30	10, 15, 35	10, 20, 35, 26	19, 6, 18, 26
3	Length of moving object	8, 35, 29, 34	19		10, 15, 19	32	8, 35, 24		1, 35	7, 2, 35, 39	4, 29, 23, 10	1, 24	15, 2, 29	29, 35
4	Length of stationary object	15, 14, 28, 26		1, 10, 35	3, 35, 38, 18	3, 25			12, 8	6, 28	10, 28, 24, 35	24, 26,	30, 29, 14	
5	Area of moving object	3, 15, 40, 14	6, 3		2, 15, 16	15, 32, 19, 13	19, 32		19, 10, 32, 18	15, 17, 30, 26	10, 35, 2, 39	30, 26	26, 4	29, 30, 6, 13
6	Area of stationary object	40		2, 10, 19, 30	35, 39, 38				17, 32	17, 7, 30	10, 14, 18, 39	30, 16	10, 35, 4, 18	2, 18, 40, 4
7	Volume of moving object	9, 14, 15, 7	6, 35, 4		34, 39, 10, 18	2, 13, 10	35		35, 6, 13, 18	7, 15, 13, 16	36, 39, 34, 10	2, 22	2, 6, 34, 10	29, 30, 7
8	Volume of stationary object	9, 14, 17, 15		35, 34, 38	35, 6, 4				30, 6		10, 39, 35, 34		35, 16, 32 18	35, 3

Table A.2 *Continued.*

	Working feature ⇒ Improving feature ⇓	Reliability 27	Measurement accuracy 28	Manufacturing precision 29	Object-affected harmful factors 30	Object-generated harmful factors 31	Ease of manufacture 32	Ease of operation 33	Ease of repair 34	Adaptability or versatility 35	Device complexity 36	Difficulty of detecting and measuring 37	Extent of automation 38	Productivity 39
1	Weight of moving object	1, 3, 11, 27	28, 27, 35, 26	28, 35, 26, 18	22, 21, 18, 27	22, 35, 31, 39	27, 28, 1, 36	35, 3, 2, 24	2, 27, 28, 11	29, 5, 15, 8	26, 30, 36, 34	28, 29, 26, 32	26, 35 18, 19	35, 3, 24, 37
2	Weight of stationary object	10, 28, 8, 3	18, 26, 28	10, 1, 35, 17	2, 19, 22, 37	35, 22, 1, 39	28, 1, 9	6, 13, 1, 32	2, 27, 28, 11	19, 15, 29	1, 10, 26, 39	25, 28, 17, 15	2, 26, 35	1, 28, 15, 35
3	Length of moving object	10, 14, 29, 40	28, 32, 4	10, 28, 29, 37	1, 15, 17, 24	17, 15	1, 29, 17	15, 29, 35, 4	1, 28, 10	14, 15, 1, 16	1, 19, 26, 24	35, 1, 26, 24	17, 24, 26, 16	14, 4, 28, 29
4	Length of stationary object	15, 29, 28	32, 28, 3	2, 32, 10	1, 18		15, 17, 27	2, 25	3	1, 35	1, 26	26		30, 14, 7, 26
5	Area of moving object	29, 9	26, 28, 32, 3	2, 32	22, 33, 28, 1	17, 2, 18, 39	13, 1, 26, 24	15, 17, 13, 16	15, 13, 10, 1	15, 30	14, 1, 13	2, 36, 26, 18	14, 30, 28, 23	10, 26, 34, 2
6	Area of stationary object	32, 35, 40, 4	26, 28, 32, 3	2, 29, 18, 36	27, 2, 39, 35	22, 1, 40	40, 16	16, 4	16	15, 16	1, 18, 36	2, 35, 30, 18	23	10, 15, 17, 7
7	Volume of moving object	14, 1, 40, 11	25, 26, 28	25, 28, 2, 16	22, 21, 27, 35	17, 2, 40, 1	29, 1, 40	15, 13, 30, 12	10	15, 29	26, 1	29, 26, 4	35, 34, 16, 24	10, 6, 2, 34
8	Volume of stationary object	2, 35, 16		35, 10, 25	34, 39, 19, 27	30, 18, 35, 4	35		1		1, 31	2, 17, 26		35, 37, 10, 2

Table A.2 *Continued.*

	Working feature ⇒ / Improving feature ⇓	Weight of moving object 1	Weight of stationary object 2	Length of moving object 3	Length of stationary object 4	Area of moving object 5	Area of stationary object 6	Volume of moving object 7	Volume of stationary object 8	Speed 9	Force (intensity) 10	Stress or pressure 11	Shape 12	Stability of the object's composition 13
9	Speed	2, 28, 13, 38		13, 14, 8		29, 30, 34		7, 29, 34		+	13, 28, 15, 19	6, 18, 38, 40	35, 15, 18, 34	28, 33, 1, 18
10	Force (Intensity)	8, 1, 37, 18	18, 13, 1, 28	17, 19, 9, 36	28, 10	19, 10, 15	1, 18, 36, 37	15, 9, 12, 37	2, 36, 18, 37	13, 28, 15, 12	+	18, 21, 11	10, 35, 40, 34	35, 10, 21
11	Stress or pressure	10, 36, 37, 40	13, 29, 10, 18	35, 10, 36	35, 1, 14, 16	10, 15, 36, 28	10, 15, 36, 37	6, 35, 10	35, 24	6, 35, 36	36, 35, 21	+	35, 4, 15, 10	35, 33, 2, 40
12	Shape	8, 10, 29, 40	15, 10, 26, 3	29, 34, 5, 4	13, 14, 10, 7	5, 34, 4, 10		14, 4, 15, 22	7, 2, 35	35, 15, 34, 18	35, 10, 37, 40	34, 15, 10, 14	+	33, 1, 18, 4
13	Stability of the object's composition	21, 35, 2, 39	26, 39, 1, 40	13, 15, 1, 28	37	2, 11, 13	39	28, 10, 19, 39	34, 28, 35, 40	33, 15, 28, 18	10, 35, 21, 16	2, 35, 40	22, 1, 18, 4	+
14	Strength	1, 8, 40, 15	40, 26, 27, 1	1, 15, 8, 35	15, 14, 28, 26	3, 34, 40, 29	9, 40, 28	10, 15, 14, 7	9, 14, 17, 15	8, 13, 26, 14	10, 18, 3, 14	10, 3, 18, 40	10, 30, 35, 40	13, 17, 35
15	Duration of action of moving object	19, 5, 34, 31		2, 19, 9		3, 17, 19		10, 2, 19, 30		3, 35, 5	19, 2, 16	19, 3, 27	14, 26, 28, 25	13, 3, 35
16	Duration of action of stationary object		6, 27, 19, 16		1, 40, 35				35, 34, 38					39, 3, 35, 23

Table A.2 *Continued.*

	Working feature ⇒	Strength	Duration of action of moving object	Duration of action of stationary object	Temperature	Illumination intensity	Use of energy by moving object	Use of energy by stationary object	Power	Loss of energy	Loss of substance	Loss of information	Loss of time	Quantity of substance
	Improving feature ⇓	14	15	16	17	18	19	20	21	22	23	24	25	26
9	Speed	8, 3, 26, 14	3, 19, 35, 5		28, 30, 36, 2	10, 13, 19	8, 15, 35, 38		19, 35, 38, 2	14, 20, 19, 35	10, 13, 28, 38	13, 26		10, 19, 29, 38
10	Force (Intensity)	35, 10, 14, 27	19, 2		35, 10, 21		19, 17, 10	1, 16, 36, 37	19, 35, 18, 37	14, 15	8, 35, 40, 5		10, 37, 36	14, 29, 18, 36
11	Stress or pressure	9, 18, 3, 40	19, 3, 27		35, 39, 19, 2		14, 24, 10, 37		10, 35, 14	2, 36, 25	10, 36, 3, 37		37, 36, 4	10, 14, 36
12	Shape	30, 14, 10, 40	14, 26, 9, 25		22, 14, 19, 32	13, 15, 32	2, 6, 34, 14		4, 6, 2	14	35, 29, 3, 5		14, 10, 34, 17	36, 22
13	Stability of the object's composition	17, 9, 15	13, 27, 10, 35	39, 3, 35, 23	35, 1, 32	32, 3, 27, 16	13, 19	27, 4, 29, 18	32, 35, 27, 31	14, 2, 39, 6	2, 14, 30, 40		35, 27	15, 32, 35
14	Strength	+	27, 3, 26		30, 10, 40	35, 19	19, 35, 10	35	10, 26, 35, 28	35	35, 28, 31, 40		29, 3, 28, 10	29, 10, 27
15	Duration of action of moving object	27, 3, 10	+		19, 35, 39	2, 19, 4, 35	28, 6, 35, 18		19, 10, 35, 38		28, 27, 3, 18	10	20, 10, 28, 18	3, 35, 10, 40
16	Duration of action of stationary object			+	19, 18, 36, 40				16		27, 16, 18, 38	10	28, 20, 10, 16	3, 35, 31

Table A.2 *Continued.*

	Working feature ⇒	Reliability	Measurement accuracy	Manufacturing precision	Object-affected harmful factors	Object-generated harmful factors	Ease of manufacture	Ease of operation	Ease of repair	Adaptability or versatility	Device complexity	Difficulty of detecting and measuring	Extent of automation	Productivity
	Improving feature ⇓	**27**	**28**	**29**	**30**	**31**	**32**	**33**	**34**	**35**	**36**	**37**	**38**	**39**
9	Speed	11, 35, 27, 28	28, 32, 1, 24	10, 28, 32, 25	1, 28, 35, 23	2, 24, 35, 21	35, 13, 8, 1	32, 28, 13, 12	34, 2, 28, 27	15, 10, 26	10, 28, 4, 34	3, 34, 27, 16	10, 18	
10	Force (Intensity)	3, 35, 13, 21	35, 10, 23, 24	28, 29, 37, 36	1, 35, 40, 18	13, 3, 36, 24	15, 37, 18, 1	1, 28, 3, 25	15, 1, 11	15, 17, 18, 20	26, 35, 10, 18	36, 37, 10, 19	2, 35	3, 28, 35, 37
11	Stress or pressure	10, 13, 19, 35	6, 28, 25	3, 35	22, 2, 37	2, 33, 27, 18	1, 35, 16	11	2	35	19, 1, 35	2, 36, 37	35, 24	10, 14, 35, 37
12	Shape	10, 40, 16	28, 32, 1	32, 30, 40	22, 1, 2, 35	35, 1	1, 32, 17, 28	32, 15, 26	2, 13, 1	1, 15, 29	16, 29, 1, 28	15, 13, 39	15, 1, 32	17, 26, 34, 10
13	Stability of the object's composition		13	18	35, 24, 30, 18	35, 40, 27, 39	35, 19	32, 35, 30	2, 35, 10, 16	35, 30, 34, 2	2, 35, 22, 26	35, 22, 39, 23	1, 8, 35	23, 35, 40, 3
14	Strength	11, 3	3, 27, 16	3, 27	18, 35, 37, 1	15, 35, 22, 2	11, 3, 10, 32	32, 40, 25, 2	27, 11, 3	15, 3, 32	2, 13, 25, 28	27, 3, 15, 40	15	29, 35, 10, 14
15	Duration of action of moving object	11, 2, 13	3	3, 27, 16, 40	22, 15, 33, 28	21, 39, 16, 22	27, 1, 4	12, 27	29, 10, 27	1, 35, 13	10, 4, 29, 15	19, 29, 39, 35	6, 10	35, 17, 14, 19
16	Duration of action of stationary object	34, 27, 6, 40	10, 26, 24		17, 1, 40, 33	22	35, 10	1	1	2		25, 34, 6, 35	1	20, 10, 16, 38

Table A.2 *Continued.*

	Working feature ⇒ Improving feature ⇓	Weight of moving object 1	Weight of stationary object 2	Length of moving object 3	Length of stationary object 4	Area of moving object 5	Area of stationary object 6	Volume of moving object 7	Volume of stationary object 8	Speed 9	Force (intensity) 10	Stress or pressure 11	Shape 12	Stability of the object's composition 13
17	Temperature	36, 22, 6, 38	22, 35, 32	15, 19, 9	15, 19, 9	3, 35, 39, 18	35, 38	34, 39, 40, 18	35, 6, 4	2, 28, 36, 30	35, 10, 3, 21	35, 39, 19, 2	14, 22, 19, 32	1, 35, 32
18	Illumination intensity	19, 1, 32	2, 35, 32	19, 32, 16		19, 32, 26		2, 13, 10		10, 13, 19	26, 19, 6		32, 30	32, 3, 27
19	Use of energy by moving object	12, 18, 28, 31		12, 28		15, 19, 25		35, 13, 18		8, 35, 35	16, 26, 21, 2	23, 14, 25	12, 2, 29	19, 13, 17, 24
20	Use of energy by stationary object		19, 9, 6, 27								36, 37			27, 4, 29, 18
21	Power	8, 36, 38, 31	19, 26, 17, 27	1, 10, 35, 37		19, 38	17, 32, 13, 38	35, 6, 38	30, 6, 25	15, 35, 2	26, 2, 36, 35	22, 10, 35	29, 14, 2, 40	35, 32, 15, 31
22	Loss of energy	15, 6, 19, 28	19, 6, 18, 9	7, 2, 6, 13	6, 38, 7	15, 26, 17, 30	17, 7, 30, 18	7, 18, 23	7	16, 35, 38	36, 38			14, 2, 39, 6
23	Loss of substance	35, 6, 23, 40	35, 6, 22, 32	14, 29, 10, 39	10, 28,24	35, 2, 10, 31	10, 18, 39, 31	1, 29, 30, 36	3, 39, 18, 31	10, 13, 28, 38	14, 15, 18, 40	3, 36, 37, 10	29, 35, 3, 5	2, 14, 30, 40
24	Loss of information	10, 24, 35	10, 35, 5	1, 26	26	30, 26	30, 16		2, 22	26, 32				

Table A.2 *Continued.*

	Working feature ⇒	Strength	Duration of action of moving object	Duration of action of stationary object	Temperature	Illumination intensity	Use of energy by moving object	Use of energy by stationary object	Power	Loss of energy	Loss of substance	Loss of information	Loss of time	Quantity of substance
	Improving feature ⇓	**14**	**15**	**16**	**17**	**18**	**19**	**20**	**21**	**22**	**23**	**24**	**25**	**26**
17	Temperature	10, 30, 22, 40	19, 13, 39	19, 18, 36, 40	+	32, 30, 21, 16	19, 15, 3, 17		2, 14, 17, 25	21, 17, 35, 38	21, 36, 29, 31		35, 28, 21, 18	3, 17, 30, 39
18	Illumination intensity	35, 19	2, 19, 6		32, 35, 19	+	32, 1, 19	32, 35, 1, 15	32	13, 16, 1, 6	13, 1	1, 6	19, 1, 26, 17	1, 19
19	Use of energy by moving object	5, 19, 9, 35	28, 35, 6, 18	–	19, 24, 3, 14	2, 15, 19	+	–	6, 19, 37, 18	12, 22, 15, 24	35, 24, 18, 5		35, 38, 19, 18	34, 23, 16, 18
20	Use of energy by stationary object	35				19, 2, 35, 32	–	+			28, 27, 18, 31			3, 35, 31
21	Power	26, 10, 28	19, 35, 10, 38	16	2, 14, 17, 25	16, 6, 19	16, 6, 19, 37		+	10, 35, 38	28, 27, 18, 38	10, 19	35, 20, 10, 6	4, 34, 19
22	Loss of energy	26			19, 38, 7	1, 13, 32, 15			3, 38	+	35, 27, 2, 37	19, 10	10, 18, 32, 7	7, 18, 25
23	Loss of substance	35, 28, 31, 40	28, 27, 3, 18	27, 16, 18, 38	21, 36, 39, 31	1, 6, 13	35, 18, 24, 5	28, 27, 12, 31	28, 27, 18, 38	35, 27, 2, 31	+		15, 18, 35, 10	6, 3, 10, 24
24	Loss of information		10	10		19			10, 19	19, 10		+	24, 26, 28, 32	24, 28, 35

Table A.2 *Continued.*

	Working feature ⇒	Reliability	Measurement accuracy	Manufacturing precision	Object-affected harmful factors	Object-generated harmful factors	Ease of manufacture	Ease of operation	Ease of repair	Adaptability or versatility	Device complexity	Difficulty of detecting and measuring	Extent of automation	Productivity
	Improving feature ⇓	**27**	**28**	**29**	**30**	**31**	**32**	**33**	**34**	**35**	**36**	**37**	**38**	**39**
17	Temperature	19, 35, 3, 10	32, 19, 24	24	22, 33, 35, 2	22, 35, 2, 24	26, 27	26, 27	4, 10, 16	2, 18, 27	2, 17, 16	3, 27, 35, 31	26, 2, 19, 16	15, 28, 35
18	Illumination intensity		11, 15, 32	3, 32	15, 19	35, 19, 32, 39	19, 35, 28, 26	28, 26, 19	15, 17, 13, 16	15, 1, 19	6, 32, 13	32, 15	2, 26, 10	2, 25, 16
19	Use of energy by moving object	19, 21, 11, 27	3, 1, 32		1, 35, 6, 27	2, 35, 6	28, 26, 30	19, 35	1, 15, 17, 28	15, 17, 13, 16	2, 29, 27, 28	35, 38	32, 2	12, 28, 35
20	Use of energy by stationary object	10, 36, 23			10, 2, 22, 37	19, 22, 18	1, 4					19, 35, 16, 25		1, 6
21	Power	19, 24, 26, 31	32, 15, 2	32, 2	19, 22, 31, 2	2, 35, 18	26, 10, 34	26, 35, 10	35, 2, 10, 34	19, 17, 34	20, 19, 30, 34	19, 35, 16	28, 2, 17	28, 35, 34
22	Loss of energy	11, 10, 35	32		21, 22, 35, 2	21, 35, 2, 22		35, 32, 1	2, 19		7, 23	35, 3, 15, 23	2	28, 10, 29, 35
23	Loss of substance	10, 29, 39, 35	16, 34, 31, 28	35, 10, 24, 31	33, 22, 30, 40	10, 1, 34, 29	15, 34, 33	32, 28, 2, 24	2, 35, 34, 27	15, 10, 2	35, 10, 28, 24	35, 18, 10, 13	35, 10, 18	28, 35, 10, 23
24	Loss of information	10, 28, 23			22, 10, 1	10, 21, 22	32	27, 22				35, 33	35	13, 23, 15

Table A.2 *Continued.*

	Working feature ⇒	Weight of moving object	Weight of stationary object	Length of moving object	Length of stationary object	Area of moving object	Area of stationary object	Volume of moving object	Volume of stationary object	Speed	Force (intensity)	Stress or pressure	Shape	Stability of the object's composition
	Improving feature ⇓	**1**	**2**	**3**	**4**	**5**	**6**	**7**	**8**	**9**	**10**	**11**	**12**	**13**
25	Loss of time	10, 20, 37, 35	10, 20, 26, 5	15, 2, 29	30, 24, 14, 5	26, 4, 5, 16	10, 35, 17, 4	2, 5, 34, 10	35, 16, 32, 18		10, 37, 36, 5	37, 36,4	4, 10, 34, 17	35, 3, 22, 5
26	Quantity of substance/ matter	35, 6, 18, 31	27, 26, 18, 35	29, 14, 35, 18		15, 14, 29	2, 18, 40, 4	15, 20, 29		35, 29, 34, 28	35, 14, 3	10, 36, 14, 3	35, 14	15, 2, 17, 40
27	Reliability	3, 8, 10, 40	3, 10, 8, 28	15, 9, 14, 4	15, 29, 28, 11	17, 10, 14, 16	32, 35, 40, 4	3, 10, 14, 24	2, 35, 24	21, 35, 11, 28	8, 28, 10, 3	10, 24, 35, 19	35, 1, 16, 11	
28	Measurement accuracy	32, 35, 26, 28	28, 35, 25, 26	28, 26, 5, 16	32, 28, 3, 16	26, 28, 32, 3	26, 28, 32, 3	32, 13, 6		28, 13, 32, 24	32, 2	6, 28, 32	6, 28, 32	32, 35, 13
29	Manufacturing precision	28, 32, 13, 18	28, 35, 27, 9	10, 28, 29, 37	2, 32, 10	28, 33, 29, 32	2, 29, 18, 36	32, 23, 2	25, 10, 35	10, 28, 32	28, 19, 34, 36	3, 35	32, 30, 40	30, 18
30	Object-affected harmful factors	22, 21, 27, 39	2, 22, 13, 24	17, 1, 39, 4	1, 18	22, 1, 33, 28	27, 2, 39, 35	22, 23, 37, 35	34, 39, 19, 27	21, 22, 35, 28	13, 35, 39, 18	22, 2, 37	22, 1, 3, 35	35, 24, 30, 18
31	Object-generated harmful factors	19, 22, 15, 39	35, 22, 1, 39	17, 15, 16, 22		17, 2, 18, 39	22, 1, 40	17, 2, 40	30, 18, 35, 4	35, 28, 3, 23	35, 28, 1, 40	2, 33, 27, 18	35, 1	35, 40, 27, 39
32	Ease of manufacture	28, 29, 15, 16	1, 27, 36, 13	1, 29, 13, 17	15, 17, 27	13, 1, 26, 12	16, 40	13, 29, 1, 40	35	35, 13, 8, 1	35, 12	35, 19, 1, 37	1, 28, 13, 27	11, 13, 1

Table A.2 *Continued.*

	Working feature ⇒ / Improving feature ⇓	Strength	Duration of action of moving object	Duration of action of stationary object	Temperature	Illuminatin intensity	Use of energy by moving object	Use of energy by stationary object	Power	Loss of energy	Loss of substance	Loss of information	Loss of time	Quantity of substance
		14	15	16	17	18	19	20	21	22	23	24	25	26
25	Loss of time	29, 3, 28, 18	20, 10, 28, 18	28, 20, 10, 16	35, 29, 21, 18	1, 19, 26, 17	35, 38, 19, 18	1	35, 20, 10, 6	10, 5, 18, 32	35, 18, 10, 39	24, 26, 28, 32	+	35, 38, 18, 16
26	Quantity of substance/ matter	14, 35, 34, 10	3, 35, 10, 40	3, 35, 31	3, 17, 39		34, 29, 16, 18	3, 35, 31	35	7, 18, 25	6, 3, 10, 24	24, 28, 35	35, 38, 18, 16	+
27	Reliability	11, 28	2, 35, 3, 25	34, 27, 6, 40	3, 35, 10	11, 32, 13	21, 11, 27, 19	36, 23	21, 11, 26, 31	10, 11, 35	10, 35, 29, 39	10, 28	10, 30, 4	21, 28, 40, 3
28	Measurement accuracy	28, 6, 32	28, 6, 32	10, 26, 24	6, 19, 28, 24	6, 1, 32	3, 6, 32		3, 6, 32	26, 32, 27	10, 16, 31, 28		24, 34, 28, 32	2, 6, 32
29	Manufacturing precision	3, 27	3, 27, 40		19, 26	3, 32	32, 2		32, 2	13, 32, 2	35, 31, 10, 24		32, 26, 28, 18	32, 30
30	Object-affected harmful factors	18, 35, 37, 1	22, 15, 33, 28	17, 1, 40, 33	22, 33, 35, 2	1, 19, 32, 13	1, 24, 6, 27	10, 2, 22, 37	19, 22, 31, 2	21, 22, 35, 2	33, 22, 19, 40	22, 10, 2	35, 18, 34	35, 33, 29, 31
31	Object-generated harmful factors	15, 35, 22, 2	15, 22, 33, 31	21, 39, 16, 22	22, 35, 2, 24	19, 24, 39, 32	2, 35, 6	19, 22, 18	2, 35, 18	21, 35, 2, 22	10, 1, 34	10, 21, 29	1, 22	3, 24, 39, 1
32	Ease of manufacture	1, 3, 10, 32	27, 1, 4	35, 16	27, 26, 18	28, 24, 27, 1	28, 26, 27, 1	1, 4	27, 1, 12, 24	19, 35	15, 34, 33	32, 24, 18, 16	35, 28, 34, 4	35, 23, 1, 24

Table A.2 *Continued.*

	Working feature ⇒	Reliability	Measurement accuracy	Manufacturing precision	Object-affected harmful factors	Object-generated harmful factors	Ease of manufacture	Ease of operation	Ease of repair	Adaptability or versatility	Device complexity	Difficulty of detecting and measuring	Extent of automation	Productivity
	Improving feature ⇓	**27**	**28**	**29**	**30**	**31**	**32**	**33**	**34**	**35**	**36**	**37**	**38**	**39**
25	Loss of time	10, 30, 4	24, 34, 28, 32	24, 26, 28, 18	35, 18, 34	35, 22, 18, 39	35, 28, 34, 4	4, 28, 10, 34	32, 1, 10	35, 28	6, 29	18, 28, 32, 10	24, 28, 35, 30	
26	Quantity of substance/ matter	18, 3, 28, 40	13, 2, 28	33, 30	35, 33, 29, 31	3, 35, 40, 39	29, 1, 35, 27	35, 29, 25, 10	2, 32, 10, 25	15, 3, 29	3, 13, 27, 10	3, 27, 29, 18	8, 35	13, 29, 3, 27
27	Reliability	+	32, 3, 11, 23	11, 32, 1	27, 35, 2, 40	35, 2, 40, 26		27, 17, 40	1, 11	13, 35, 8, 24	13, 35, 1	27, 40, 28	11, 13, 27	1, 35, 29, 38
28	Measurement accuracy	5, 11, 1, 23	+		28, 24, 22, 26	3, 33, 39, 10	6, 35, 25, 18	1, 13, 17, 34	1, 32, 13, 11	13, 35, 2	27, 35, 10, 34	26, 24, 32, 28	28, 2, 10, 34	10, 34, 28, 32
29	Manufacturing precision	11, 32, 1		+	26, 28, 10, 36	4, 17, 34, 26		1, 32, 35, 23	25, 10		26, 2, 18		26, 28, 18, 23	10, 18, 32, 39
30	Object-affected harmful factors	27, 24, 2, 40	28, 33, 23, 26	26, 28, 10, 18	+		24, 35, 2	2, 25, 28, 39	35, 10, 2	35, 11, 22, 31	22, 19, 29, 40	22, 19, 29, 40	33, 3, 34	22, 35, 13, 24
31	Object-generated harmful factors	24, 2, 40, 39	3, 33, 26	4, 17, 34, 26		+					19, 1, 31	2, 21, 27, 1	2	22, 35, 18, 39
32	Ease of manufacture		1, 35, 12, 18		24, 2		+	2, 5, 13, 16	35, 1, 11, 9	2, 13, 15	27, 26, 1	6, 28, 11, 1	8, 28, 1	35, 1, 10, 28

Table A.2 *Continued.*

	Working feature ⇒	Weight of moving object	Weight of stationary object	Length of moving object	Length of stationary object	Area of moving object	Area of stationary object	Volume of moving object	Volume of stationary object	Speed	Force (intensity)	Stress or pressure	Shape	Stability of the object's composition
	Improving feature ⇓	1	2	3	4	5	6	7	8	9	10	11	12	13
33	Ease of operation	25, 2, 13, 15	6, 13, 1, 25	1, 17, 13, 12		1, 17, 13, 16	18, 16, 15, 39	1, 16, 35, 15	4, 18, 39, 31	18, 13, 34	28, 13 35	2, 32, 12	15, 34, 29, 28	32, 35, 30
34	Ease of repair	2, 27 35, 11	2, 27, 35, 11	1, 28, 10, 25	3, 18, 31	15, 13, 32	16, 25	25, 2, 35, 11	1	34, 9	1, 11, 10	13	1, 13, 2, 4	2, 35
35	Adaptability or versatility	1, 6, 15, 8	19, 15, 29, 16	35, 1, 29, 2	1, 35, 16	35, 30, 29, 7	15, 16	15, 35, 29		35, 10, 14	15, 17, 20	35, 16	15, 37, 1, 8	35, 30, 14
36	Device complexity	26, 30, 34, 36	2, 26, 35, 39	1, 19, 26, 24	26	14, 1, 13, 16	6, 36	34, 26, 6	1, 16	34, 10, 28	26, 16	19, 1, 35	29, 13, 28, 15	2, 22, 17, 19
37	Difficulty of detecting and measuring	27, 26, 28, 13	6, 13, 28, 1	16, 17, 26, 24	26	2, 13, 18, 17	2, 39, 30, 16	29, 1, 4, 16	2, 18, 26, 31	3, 4, 16, 35	30, 28, 40, 19	35, 36, 37, 32	27, 13, 1, 39	11, 22, 39, 30
38	Extent of automation	28, 26, 18, 35	28, 26, 35, 10	14, 13, 17, 28	23	17, 14, 13		35, 13, 16		28, 10	2, 35	13, 35	15, 32, 1, 13	18, 1
39	Productivity	35, 26, 24, 37	28, 27, 15, 3	18, 4, 28, 38	30, 7, 14, 26	10, 26, 34, 31	10, 35, 17, 7	2, 6, 34, 10	35, 37, 10, 2		28, 15, 10, 36	10, 37, 14	14, 10, 34, 40	35, 3, 22, 39

Table A.2 *Continued.*

	Working feature ⇒	Strength	Duration of action of moving object	Duration of action of stationary object	Temperature	Illumination intensity	Use of energy by moving object	Use of energy by stationary object	Power	Loss of energy	Loss of substance	Loss of information	Loss of time	Quantity of substance
	Improving feature ⇓	**14**	**15**	**16**	**17**	**18**	**19**	**20**	**21**	**22**	**23**	**24**	**25**	**26**
33	Ease of operation	32, 40, 3, 28	29, 3, 8, 25	1, 16, 25	26, 27, 13	13, 17, 1, 24	1, 13, 24		35, 34, 2, 10	2, 19, 13	28, 32, 2, 24	4, 10, 27, 22	4, 28, 10, 34	12, 35
34	Ease of repair	11, 1, 2, 9	11, 29, 28, 27	1	4, 10	15, 1, 13	15, 1, 28, 16		15, 10, 32, 2	15, 1, 32, 19	2, 35, 34, 27		32, 1, 10, 25	2, 28, 10, 25
35	Adaptability or versatility	35, 3, 32, 6	13, 1, 35	2, 16	27, 2, 3, 35	6, 22, 26, 1	19, 35, 29, 13		19, 1, 29	18, 15, 1	15, 10, 2, 13		35, 28	3, 35, 15
36	Device complexity	2, 13, 28	10, 4, 28, 15		2, 17, 13	24, 17, 13	27, 2, 29, 28		20, 19, 30, 34	10, 35, 13, 2	35, 10, 28, 29		6, 29	13, 3, 27, 10
37	Difficulty of detecting and measuring	27, 3, 15, 28	19, 29, 39, 25	25, 34, 6, 35	3, 27, 35, 16	2, 24, 26	35, 38	19, 35, 16	18, 1, 16, 10	35, 3, 15, 19	1, 18, 10, 24	35, 33, 27, 22	18, 28, 32, 9	3, 27, 29, 18
38	Extent of automation	25, 13	6, 9		26, 2, 19	8, 32, 19	2, 32, 13		28, 2, 27	23, 28	35, 10, 18, 5	35, 33	24, 28, 35, 30	35, 13
39	Productivity	29, 28, 10, 18	35, 10, 2, 18	20, 10, 16, 38	35, 21, 28, 10	26, 17, 19, 1	35, 10, 38, 19	1	35, 20, 10	28, 10, 29, 35	28, 10, 35, 23	13, 15, 23		35, 38

Table A.2 *Continued.*

	Working feature ⇒ Improving feature ⇓	27 Reliability	28 Measurement accuracy	29 Manufacturing precision	30 Object-affected harmful factors	31 Object-generated harmful factors	32 Ease of manufacture	33 Ease of operation	34 Ease of repair	35 Adaptability or versatility	36 Device complexity	37 Difficulty of detecting and measuring	38 Extent of automation	39 Productivity
33	Ease of operation	17, 27, 8, 40	25, 13, 2, 34	1, 32, 35, 23	2, 25, 28, 39		2, 5, 12	+	12, 26, 1, 32	15, 34, 1, 16	32, 26, 12, 17		1, 34, 12, 3	15, 1, 28
34	Ease of repair	11, 10, 1, 16	10, 2, 13	25, 10	35, 10, 2, 16		1, 35, 11, 10	1, 12, 26, 15	+	7, 1, 4, 16	35, 1, 13, 11		34, 35, 7, 13	1, 32, 10
35	Adaptability or versatility	35, 13, 8, 24	35, 5, 1, 10		35, 11, 32, 31		1, 13, 31	15, 34, 1, 16	1, 16, 7, 4	+	15, 29, 37, 28	1	27, 34, 35	35, 28, 6, 37
36	Device complexity	13, 35, 1	2, 26, 10, 34	26, 24, 32	22, 19, 29, 40	19, 1	27, 26, 1, 13	27, 9, 26, 24	1, 13	29, 15, 28, 37	+	15, 10, 37, 28	15, 1, 24	12, 17, 28
37	Difficulty of detecting and measuring	27, 40, 28, 8	26, 24, 32, 28		22, 19, 29, 28	2, 21	5, 28, 11, 29	2, 5	12, 26	1, 15	15, 10, 37, 28	+	34, 21	35, 18
38	Extent of automation	11, 27, 32	28, 26, 10, 34	28, 26, 18, 23	2, 33	2	1, 26, 13	1, 12, 34, 3	1, 35, 13	27, 4, 1, 35	15, 24, 10	34, 27, 25	+	5, 12, 35, 26
39	Productivity	1, 35, 10, 38	1, 10, 34, 28	18, 10, 32, 1	22, 35, 13, 24	35, 22, 18, 39	35, 28, 2, 24	1, 28, 7, 10	1, 32, 10, 25	1, 35, 28, 37	12, 17, 28, 24	35, 18, 27, 2	5, 12, 35, 26	+

SHOWER OF KINDNESS AND IRANIAN HOSPITALITY

Iranian hospitality had continued endlessly since we entered Iran. Sunil went to buy headache tablets, and they didn't take any money as he was a guest from another country. Sometimes, the café owner didn't let us pay, saying that we were their guests. If we asked for directions from someone, they invited us to stay in their home. People's generosity and hospitality came from every angle in Iran.

We stayed with Couchsurfing hosts in big cities, but if we needed to find a place to stay on the way, we always found people who let us stay somehow. Once, a truck driver told us that we could stay in a mosque and dropped us near the mosque, but we wanted to see if we could pitch our tent in someone's garden. When we saw a family with babies (they were beautiful triplets) standing in front of their house, we asked them if we could pitch our tent in their garage or garden. They not only said yes but they invited us to come to their summer house and fruit orchards. It was Friday evening and the family called every relative to spend the evening with the two foreigners, and everyone came to the summer house with lots of food. We were about 30 of us. It is guaranteed that many people sing really well in Iran. As this family was a very strict Muslim family, the women didn't take off their scarves, and didn't sing or dance in front of Sunil, but they showed me their beautiful wedding video. While I was busy watching the wedding video, Sunil carried on eating and eventually joined in the singing. We went back home late and slept well in the tent.

In the morning they invited us for breakfast. The young house owner trained in zurkhaneh, *which is known as* kusthi *in India. Zurkaneh is a traditional sport in Iran that involves martial arts, calisthenics, strength, and music. He first played the video of his team, then later on he showed us some movements using heavy wooden bats in both hands. Apparently some people use a 50 kg bat. Sunil tried to use bats like him but could only manage to lift them. We left there promising that Sunil would work out harder and come back with his six-pack next time. As of today I just see one big travel pack.*

The other memorable stay happened on the way to Shahrekord. We stopped cycling and were having lunch at a small kebab shop. A man wearing Baluch trousers ordered a plate of food for takeout. We casually asked him where he was going, and as it happened to be close to Sanandaj, we asked him if he could drop us somewhere on the way. We were expecting to be on the truck bed with our bicycles, but he insisted that we sit in front with his heavily pregnant wife and small son. We were completely squashed, and I was very worried that I would push his wife's tummy. We kept asking if we could sit in the back, but he wouldn't let us as we were his guests.

Instead dropping us, he took us to his house first and then took us to a beautiful waterfall. Just to get some ice cream for them was very tough, and we needed to act very quickly, otherwise he paid for us. Sunil saw him borrow money from the neighbors. (Silly me didn't know about it when I was in Iran.) In the evening, his wife cooked chicken and some rice. We could see they were not wealthy, but the husband wanted us to eat well. We pretended we were full so that the pregnant lady could eat, and their family pretended they were full. We were in a very uncomfortable situation. I could see that the wife wanted to feed her small son and her baby in her tummy. We felt very guilty eating, and we could hardly eat. It was the same the next morning; the husband asked his wife to cook eggs for us, but we wanted her to eat. Staying with them made us think a lot, and we often talked about them. This incident made us think that we would like to host and help people whenever we can, and we were careful to make sure we did not become a burden for someone who was helping us, but we accepted their hospitality.

Appendix B
Project Improvement Ideas Using the TRIZ Contradiction Matrix

CUSTOMER TIMELINE CONFLICTS (250)

Problem

Sarah works for a manufacturing firm as a customer relationship manager. In the past six months there have been numerous complaints from the customer's end about not meeting the deliverables on time as committed to in the contract, and the company has lost a few important customers and huge revenue. To fix the issues right away she starts doing a root cause analysis by interviewing the stakeholders within the organization. Stakeholders from every department justify the delay by blaming the upstream or downstream processes. Sarah is unable to nail it down to a few causes and fix it immediately, but she hasn't the luxury of collecting data and doing a detailed analysis. Instead of trying to identify the root causes, Sarah can identify the conflicts and use these ideas to resolve most of the speed issues and improve the timeliness of the deliverables more effectively. Table B.1 shows some of the conflicts Sarah received from the stakeholders and the innovative solutions she used to resolve them.

A. Increasing the project execution speed requires extensive supervision to control the fast-paced environment. (9/10)

    1. Train the process step owners to be accountable for the deliverable timelines, and report the status to the supervisor regularly rather than the supervisor having to manage every activity.

    2. Replace effort-consuming steps like report generation with something much simpler, or automate the process.

Table B.1 Nine windows for project schedule management.

	Past	Present	Future (Execution)
Supersystem	Project charter, contract	Project plan, contract	Contract, project plan
System	Milestone	Project schedule	Deliverable date
Components	Risks, milestones, deliverable date, lead time, estimation technique, tools and techniques, scope	Activities, process steps, skills, knowledge, tools and techniques	Reschedules

3. Create an environment with open, continuous, and interactive communication across the hierarchy.
4. Deploy resources into the process steps where they have proven optimal performance.
5. Periodically consolidate the deliverable status information and take necessary actions.

B. Increasing the processing speed creates a lot of pressure on the stakeholders. (9/11)

1. Create or choose components/tools/processes/resources that can be used for multiple process steps. This will avoid dependency and motion.
2. Decrease the lead time of the process steps by providing necessary training.
3. Create an environment that encourages faster performance through rewards and recognition.
4. Drive team-building initiatives.
5. Form a team comprising resources with multiple skills, processing speed, personalities, and stress-handling levels.

C. Increasing the processing speed will disturb the activities, resources, cost, sequence, and so on. (9/12)

1. Replace or retrain resources on critical process steps.
2. Make identical processes/resources work or interact together.
3. Break the entire process into segments and increase the processing speed just on the most feasible segments that do not impact the components of the project.
4. Replace the resource with a faster-performing resource or automation.

D. Increasing the project execution speed consumes a lot of resource effort. (9/19)

1. Add buffer resources wherever there is a higher-effort utilization in the process.
2. Establish flow by removing bottlenecks, wait times, defects, and rework from the project. Perform a value stream mapping workout.
3. Based on the expertise of the resources, broaden or shorten the process steps and process complexity so that the lead time of the process step is reduced.
4. Implement automation for mundane process steps.
5. Create an environment that encourages faster processing through rewards and recognition.

E. Increasing the processing speed exhausts the resources. (9/22)

1. Increase the duration or the number of breaks.
2. Remove non-value-added steps that consume resources or energy, like unnecessary motion.
3. Train resources on faster processing tips from experts.
4. Implement 5S.

F. Increased execution speed was not sustained for more than a week. (9/27)

1. Anticipate delay and add buffer time in advance.
2. Have necessary backups in case of delay in the schedule to mitigate the risk.
3. Use buffer resources when the process speed drops.

4. Let the resources use their own procedure to accomplish the task with the intended speed, or provide a standard procedure to be followed.
5. Automate process steps that involve manual intervention.
6. Constantly monitor performance and take necessary actions on the resources (replace or retrain).

G. Increase in project execution speed leads to a drop in output quality. (9/29)

1. Identify process steps with a high probability of defects and implement mistake-proofing.
2. Define a standard operating procedure.
3. Replace or retrain resources with higher defect rates.
4. Increase visibility in areas where the probability of committing an error is high, for example, by implementing KPIs at process steps, dashboards, control charts, color coding, status reports, and so on.
5. Minimize manual processing steps and let the system automatically pick the required information based on the information available, for example, auto-fill, guided workflow.
6. Create a checklist based on the most common defects and implement these checks at the respective process steps.
7. Determine whether the transaction can identify its own defect itself, for example, the system does not let the user move to the next field if the previous field is blank.
8. Collect the errors, document the learning, and take preventive actions.

H. Increase in processing speed makes the resources less adaptable to different scenarios. (9/35)

1. Anticipate the skills that might be required in future.
2. Train all of the key resources on the different skills that might be required.
3. Move or shuffle the roles and responsibilities of the resources based on skills and process changes.

4. Train the resources on dummy future-state processes; for example, create a test environment in which to practice.

IMPROVE PRODUCTIVITY

Insurance Example

Bob works as head of operations for an insurance company. Due to the economic crisis, the company decided to downsize operations resources and increase the resources in the sales team. Even before the downsizing was done, Bob had difficulty and issues with productivity as the team was unable to process all the applications submitted by the insured on time. Now, after downsizing, Bob and his team are under huge pressure to increase the productivity of the team. Table B.2 shows options Bob can implement to increase productivity using the TRIZ contradiction matrix.

A. To increase productivity, higher supervision and micro-management is needed. (39/10)

    1. Replace or retrain resources who do not meet the process objective consistently, leading to constant supervision.

    2. Change the inputs, tools, process, and resources at every process step for optimal productivity and minimum management.

Table B.2 Nine windows for improving productivity .

	Past	**Present**	**Future (Execution)**
Supersystem	Upstream processes, customer	Process performance, turnaround time (TAT),	Customer satisfaction, sales, marketing
System	Process inputs	Productivity	Process output
Components	Input availability, input quality, resources, capacity, and so on	Process to convert input to output, capacity, resources, skills, output quality, and so on	Quality, defects, TAT

3. Implement a pull system and create continuous flow for all the processes involved, from past/system to future/supersystem.

4. Make the input reach the processor/supervisor rather than the processor/supervisor manually picking each transaction.

5. Create a free flow where the supervisor is updated on all required information, challenges, and status without any delay or effort.

6. Identify the input requirements at the system level for optimal performance and implement the changes at the *past/system* level in the nine windows. For example, move from paper-based application to electronic application, which removes many possible errors, enables automation, and hence reduces supervision.

7. Based on volume, complexity, skill, past performance, risk, and so on, identify how much supervision or management is required (high, low, medium) and identify the sample size to be monitored/controlled/tested.

B. Increase in productivity leads to increase in stress on the stakeholders. (39/11)

1. Set the productivity increase expectation with the stakeholders across all the levels of the organization well in advance, and provide sufficient time to meet the productivity target.

2. Test productivity performance before going live.

3. Perform 5S activity and remove all the bottlenecks from the process.

4. Implement motivation strategies like carrot and stick, rewards and recognition, growth, incentives, and so on, that motivate the resources to meet the productivity targets.

5. Bring all the stakeholders closer and increase the interaction and information exchange. Kill bureaucracy and multiple handoffs.

C. Increase in productivity requires increase in process changes, reengineering, resource allocation, and so on.

1. Create communication, flow, and interaction between all the process steps. Implement U-shaped cells.

2. Make changes to the inputs to meet the optimal performance of the existing process.
3. Provide standard operating procedures and a clear workflow guide to the resources.
4. Move resources to the next process/project once their task is accomplished.
5. Bring a resource into the process only when all the required inputs are ready.
6. Use experienced resources with multiple skill sets who can easily adapt to process changes.
7. Form a team with a good mix of process knowledge, versatile skills, experience, and so on.

D. Increase in productivity leads to team members moving to teams with lesser productivity targets, internally or outside the organization. (39/13)

1. Provide flexibility at work, like flexible work hours, flexible work environment (work from home), flexible workdays, and so on.
2. Remove work pressure that is not directly related to the process, for example, some of the mandatory training that is not required at the moment can be pushed back.
3. Schedule the workload unevenly, for example, a high-volume day followed by a low-volume day.
4. Instead of having a standard work environment, modify it based on each resource's convenience. For example, provide work-from-home if you have a pregnant woman on the team.
5. Based on their skills, have each resource perform what they enjoy and are good at.
6. Highlight the new skills resources are gaining by achieving higher productivity levels, and how it is improving their market value.
7. Use attrition as an opportunity to replace underperforming resources, hire new resources with desired skills, implement new policies, and so on.

8. Have policies that mitigate the risk of attrition by having a clear estimate of the notice period to be served for each role, depending on the time required to hire and train a new resource, and the penalties levied if the employee quits before this period, rather than having a generic policy for all the employees.

E. Increase in productivity consumes a lot of effort of the resources. (39/19)

1. Automate mundane manual process steps.
2. Provide necessary training, standard operating procedures, workflows, and so on, before the resources perform the activity.
3. Perform 5S and make sure all the required inputs are present before the work is performed.
4. Remove toxic energy from the environment, and keep resources motivated to perform at their full potential.
5. Instead of long breaks, split the break to help resources relieve stress.

F. Increase in productivity leads to the resources getting exhausted mentally and physically. (39/22)

1. Train resources who get exhausted easily on best practices from other resources.
2. Replace resources who get exhausted quickly and cannot be trained.
3. Make all the inputs available in order before processing, and remove the lean waste motion from the process.
4. Break longer lead times or complex process steps into simpler process steps.
5. Change the input and output formats (for example .pdf to Excel) to reduce manual effort and enable automation.

G. Increase in productivity leads to increase in inventory at one or more process steps. (39/26)

1. Implement pull to avoid inventory piling up at a high-lead-time process step.

2. Provide the necessary inputs in the required order or format to the bottleneck process steps.
3. Reduce the processing time of the bottleneck process step through automation.
4. Match the processing speed of other processes to keep up with the bottleneck process.
5. Add more resources to the bottleneck process.
6. Break complex process steps into simpler process steps.

H. Increase in productivity leads to inconsistency of performance. (39/27)

1. Study the process steps and identify the steps that show a significant trend in performance through root cause analysis, and take corrective and preventive actions.
2. Group the resources based on performance, and increase the supervision and training for the resources with higher inconsistency.
3. Make changes to the inputs, process, resources, outputs at process steps with performance inconsistency.
4. Change the input and output formats to reduce manual intervention and leverage automation.
5. Set key performance indicators at every process step and take necessary actions immediately whenever there is a dip.
6. Measure the consistency of the resources' performance and tie it to appraisals, growth, incentives, and other motivations.
7. Keep motivating the team and create an encouraging environment.

I. Increase in productivity leads to decrease in processing accuracy. (39/29)

1. Automate the processes that are mundane and consume manual effort.
2. Implement mistake-proofing at process steps that have a higher inaccuracy rate.

3. Reduce overlooked errors by using a guided workflow technique.
4. Identify methods to make the errors visible and easily detectable.
5. Identify the process steps, resources, and causes that impact processing accuracy and group them into high, medium, and low based on their impact, and take corrective or preventive actions against each group like training, process reengineering, and so on.

J. Increase in productivity increases the complexity of the process. (39/36)

1. Remove multiple handoffs from the process.
2. Create different custom inputs (applications) and teams to handle different scenarios.
3. Fetch information from other sources automatically through integration, which will eliminate a few process steps.
4. Outsource part of a complex process to a third party.

K. Increase in productivity makes the process less adaptable to changes. (39/35)

1. Make changes to the input that serves in the completion of a particular scenario. For example, have different loan applications for different coverages requested. This way, process changes are minimal.
2. Create an environment that embraces change and is flexible in managing multiple scenarios.
3. Increase the concentration of expert resources when a change is implemented.
4. Provide change acceleration process training.
5. Replace or train resources who are resistant to changes or change management.
6. Increase the capacity of the team during the period when a change is implemented.

L. Increase in productivity leads to a decrease in detectability of defects. (39/37)

1. Hire low-cost resources to perform quality control, or outsource the process.
2. Constantly measure key process indicators (KPIs) (preferably, automate the process) and make defects visible.
3. Automate the critical process steps to remove manual or overlooked errors.
4. Isolate a process that has a higher probability of defects, and perform quality control.

M. Increase in productivity makes the process less automatable. (39/38)

1. Integrate the automatable and non-automatable processes in a logical sequence.
2. Send duplicate information in the desired format to multiple process steps rather than segregating the information and sending it multiple times.
3. Reuse information or components multiple times by making it available to many instead of recreating or requesting it multiple times.

CUSTOMER RELATIONSHIP AND REDUCE MURI

Joanna is a customer relationship manager for a Fortune 100 company, and her job is to make sure the customers are happy with her organization's service and products. She works at an account level and hence interacts with the top leaders of the customer's organization. If they have any problem, she has to immediately work with the stakeholders within her organization and bring it to closure as soon as possible. She is accountable for customer retention and identifying new business opportunities. Everything was going well until last year when the organization took on a new project worth 25 million. The customer's requirements kept changing frequently, and the organization was unable to accommodate many of the requirements. Joanna's organization missed the deadlines many times, had many defects in the output, and the project cost went much higher than estimated, and so forth. Joanna had to come up with clear action items to gain the customer's confidence back and reassure the unhappy stakeholders on her own project team, and she had one week to do this before her next meeting with the client. She had to both manage the stakeholders and bring the project to successful closure. All she had to do was choose Stress/Pressure as the improving parameter from the contradiction matrix and choose every worsening parameter, apply the principles, and resolve the contradictions, as shown below:

A. Frequent changes to project scope put a lot of pressure on the project team. (11/7)

   1. Design requirements in such a way that one requirement is able to perform multiple functions and hence eliminate the possibility of a scope change.

   2. Define all the clauses for scope changes in the Statement of Work, such as timelines for making scope changes, cost to implement or include the change, and so on.

   3. Identify the root cause of frequent scope changes (often, the process used for requirements gathering) and take corrective action.

   4. Anticipate scope change at every stage and have an alternate plan handy.

B. Improving project execution speed puts a lot of pressure on the project team. (11/9)

   1. Use multiskilled resources and inputs at processes that can be used in numerous ways and scenarios. For example, developer is also a tester, business analyst is also a project manager.

   2. Create outputs that can be reused for multiple process steps in multiple ways rather than recreating them again and again. For example, make changes to the parameters of the code to perform different functions in an application.

   3. Remove manual intervention through automation at mundane process steps.

   4. Slow down the speed at complex process steps, and increase the speed at simpler process steps.

   5. Increase the concentration of skilled resources at critical process steps.

   6. Conduct stress management training for the project team to help handle pressure.

C. Reducing stress in the process demands changing the entire organization structure, team structure, and process structure. (11/12)

1. Make changes to the roles, responsibilities, and accountability of the resources.
2. Make changes to the reporting structures. Change the project team's structure rather than changing the organization's hierarchical structure: flat, projectized, matrix, balanced matrix, and so on.
3. Help the team members and stakeholders break the hierarchy and discuss challenges and issues at any level.
4. Organize skip-level meetings across levels regularly.
5. Implement frequent leadership floor walks and customer visits to the workplace to understand the issues and challenges.
6. Deploy skilled resources at crucial points in the hierarchy (especially in the leadership level) who can handle stress and not let it pass down to the team members.

D. Increase in project stress is leading to shortening of the duration of stakeholders sticking with the project. (11/15)

1. Periodically replace or reassign the resources to different roles and responsibilities.
2. Stop micromanaging the stakeholders, and conduct periodic reviews to release the pressure.
3. Provide as much flexibility as possible to the stakeholders to perform the tasks under their preferred conditions and using their preferred methods.
4. Respect each stakeholder's inputs and views irrespective of the hierarchy, and challenge ideas through confrontation with authority.
5. Outsource the entire project or a portion of the project to a third party to diffuse the pressure.
6. Hire low-cost temporary resources for noncognitive high-volume activities.
7. Have high-performance/experienced/expert resources for critical process steps.

E. Working in a highly stressful environment makes the stakeholders consume more effort or capacity than required. (11/19)

1. Bring all the stakeholders, both internal and from the customer's end, together. Increase the communication channels between the stakeholders by skipping the hierarchy. This will remove the effort required to pass the information down the hierarchy.

2. Avoid surprises that cause stress, and plan for unexpected events well in advance with a mitigation plan to act on. Perform what-if analysis while planning the activities for the project.

3. Deploy buffer resources from other projects or use internal resources who have the ability to increase capacity during a crisis.

4. Have a mediator to coordinate between stakeholders (project expeditor) and provide the right direction to all the stakeholders during a crisis situation. This will help in eliminating confusion and uncertainty.

F. Working in a highly stressful environment leads to an increase in non-value-added waiting, causing delay in the project deliverables. (11/25)

1. Increase the capacity through overtime or hiring additional resources.

2. Perform the activities independently based on available resources and information, and integrate them later.

3. Reengineer the process to remove waiting times in between process steps.

4. Rather than progressing from one stage to another in a single series of steps, skip the sequence and accomplish as many tasks as possible with the available resources.

G. Working in a highly stressful environment leads to a decrease in the throughput yield. (11/26)

1. Sort and organize all the required inputs in order before starting processing.

2. Have a free flow of communication, information, and material to eliminate bottlenecks.

3. Identify defects as early as possible and take preventive actions to avoid rework.
4. Allocate all tasks and make sure every stakeholder is aware of what to do, how to do it, and what to do in advance.
5. Mix single-piece flow and batch processing at different stages depending on the circumstances.

H. Working in a highly stressful environment leads to inconsistency in meeting the objectives. (11/27)

1. Asses all risks in advance and have a mitigation plan.
2. Define performance standards for each stakeholder in advance.
3. Rather than allocating tasks, let the stakeholders pick the activities or process steps to perform to meet the deliverables.
4. Periodically monitor and control the deliverables and performance.
5. Asses the stakeholder's interests, concerns, and challenges periodically, and have an action plan to resolve them within a defined timeline.
6. Move from a subjective approach to a statistical and data-driven approach to measure reliability and convince the stakeholders.

I. Working in s highly stressful environment leads to an increase in defects in the deliverables. (11/29)

1. Change an action or an external environment (or external influence) at the process steps where defects occur.
2. Asses the skills of the stakeholders and deploy them in roles that are most suitable for his or her operation.
3. Train, motivate, and rate the resources constantly to improve on defect reduction.
4. Identify the top causes for defects (use a Pareto chart) and make necessary changes to the parameters.

J. Working in a highly stressful environment leads to difficulty in delivering the desired business outcomes. (11/32)

1. Divide the entire process into stages/departments/groups/teams. Involve the group only when they can add value to the process. For example, involve the procurement team only when there are procurement-related activities. That way, they stay out of the stressful environment.
2. Continuously plan, execute, monitor, and control activities to make sure the activities meet the business goals. If they are already doing so, decrease the frequency of monitoring.
3. Continuously perform workouts and activities to remove stress, such as team dinners, picnics, and so on.

K. Working in a highly stressful environment leads to a drop in productivity. (11/39)

1. Perform 5S and make sure all the required inputs are present before initiating the activity.
2. Perform a kaizen workout to remove bottlenecks and non-value-added activities.
3. Motivate the resources to increase their productivity through incentives, rewards, and recognition.
4. Bring all the stakeholders, both internal and external, closer to confront productivity-related issues and concerns.

COST SAVING

Who doesn't like to save on cost? This is one parameter that can put a big smile on the face of the top stakeholders of an organization provided the approach taken to save costs does not have any conflict with their objectives. Cost saving will have a direct impact on the bottom line of an organization. If such a contradiction exists in your process or project, all you need to do to run a cost saving initiative is choose *Use of energy by moving object* as the improving parameter and choose one worsening parameter at a time and apply the principles. Here are some potential contradictions in the project and the resolution technique:

A. Reducing the operating cost demands shrinking the project scope. (19/7)

1. Change the payment agreement type. For example, move from fixed billing to time-and-material or outcome-based costing models.
2. Use team members who cost nothing or less. (Hire an intern who is looking for experience.)
3. Train the resources to increase the processing speed. Make quick decisions.
4. Automate manual, noncognitive activities.
5. Outsource part of the job to an outside organization that is willing to provide credit.
6. Decrease the concentration of high-cost resources and replace them with low-cost resources.
7. Outsource the job to low-cost countries or bid the contract to the vendor with the lowest price and better quality.
8. Conduct a kaizen workout and make the process lean by removing all the non-value-added process steps.

B. Reducing the operating cost decreases the speed of the project execution. (19/9)

1. Link the speed of accomplishing activities or tasks to promotions and incentives.
2. Provide nonmonetary incentives to the stakeholders, such as days off, training, mastering a skill, and so on, as a reward for faster accomplishment of activities.

C. Reducing the operating cost creates a lot of stress on the stakeholders. (19/11)

1. Create cost pressure by providing operating cost targets to the stakeholders at the top level of the hierarchy. This pressure will flow down to the senior management, management, and project team levels to ensure that operating cost is low.
2. Increase the communication between stakeholders to understand the challenges and concerns.

3. Provide regular feedback on the rationale behind reducing the operating cost.
4. Understand the concerns of the stakeholders, take necessary corrective and preventive action, and thank the stakeholders for their cooperation and be appreciative of their effort.

D. Reduction in operating cost has led to a decrease in the durability of the outputs and deliverables. (19/15)

1. If there are a few resources who are unable to accomplish the tasks, replace or retrain these resources.
2. Increase the manpower and capacity of the team.
3. Decrease the concentration of resources with lower performance in terms of quality delivered.
4. Reengineer the process.
5. Train or hire resources that can perform multiple process steps and activities with multiple skill sets.
6. Increase the performance speed and automate the process steps as much as possible.

E. A cost-cutting initiative has discouraged the stakeholders and has made them feel they are not important to the organization, and they have started to look for new jobs. (19/13)

1. Provide confidence and hope and let the stakeholders know how it will help the future good.
2. Move the stakeholders to a different role or team or provide new responsibility to keep them challenged and excited.
3. Periodically recognize individuals for the work they have been accomplishing through rewards, recognition, or even a simple e-mail.
4. Create a culture where resources at any level of the organization's hierarchy are approachable to anyone.
5. Have regular meetings with individuals and the team (increase the frequency if already doing it) to understand their issues and concerns.
6. Conduct team-building activities regularly.

F. Reducing the operating cost has led to a decrease in the reliability of the project deliverables. (19/26)

1. Monitor and control the status and the baselines (schedule, cost, scope, and quality) periodically, and take necessary actions (preventive and corrective).
2. Perform the process steps with a huge variation in the baselines at high speed.
3. Have a mitigation action plan if reliability goes down, such as including a clause in the agreement anticipating a decline in reliability.
4. Use risk buffers like schedule buffers, buffer cost, buffer resources, and so on.

G. As part of the operating cost reduction, the role of the quality control analysts was eliminated, and the resources that perform the activities are responsible for quality. This has led to a huge difference in the quality standard reported by the team and customer complaints. (19/28)

1. Identify the key process steps where there is a huge difference in the measurements and take necessary corrective and preventive action.
2. Train or retrain the resources on what to measure, how to measure, and when to measure.
3. Use the measurement technique that is most suitable for the process and the resources rather than having a standard method across processes.
4. Use visual communication tools like dashboards, control charts, and run charts to track performance and measurements.

H. The operating cost reduction initiative will have many harmful effects and risks to the organization and affect the brand image of the organization. (19/31)

1. Break down the affected departments based on the function performed/resources/skills/impact created, and so on, and assess the risk.

2. Modify the parameters like skill, expert resource levels, paid resources levels, procurement costs, and so on, to mitigate the harmful effects.
3. Make one department/team/function/resource perform multiple functions.
4. Eliminate all non-value-added processes/resources/tools/costs and just retain high-performing and value-adding resources.
5. Hire low-cost resources temporarily.

I. As part of the operating cost cutting initiative, expert resources were moved to different roles outside the project team. This has led to an increase in the difficulty of delivering the outcomes. (19/32)

1. Replace or retrain the existing resources on the project needs and the process.
2. Make the entire project history available to the resources, including the risks and lessons learned documents.
3. Create documents like standard operating procedures, issue resolution tracker, training videos, reference documents, and so on, that help the existing resources to work independently.
4. Invite the older resources to provide complete knowledge transfer through mandatory training.
5. Keep the expert resources close to the team so that they are easily approachable when required.

J. The organization in the past had invested in software to automate many process steps, but as part of the cost-cutting initiative they want to reduce software license cost, and removed all the existing paid licensed software. (19/38)

1. Make changes to the input formats of data to make use of free automation software. For example, moving from PDF to Excel will enable the user to use free excel macros.
2. Use visual management to link the process of communication and decision making.
3. Retain the license on the process steps where the risk, lead time, effort, or complexity are very high.

4. Remove software from the process steps where it does not provide significant savings of effort.

K. A decrease in the operating cost leads to a decline in productivity. (19/39)

1. Perform a kaizen/value stream mapping workshop to remove lean wastes from the process.
2. Replace or retrain resources that are in the bottom quartile of performance.
3. Provide productivity targets and tie them to the employee's growth, incentives, bonuses, or anything that motivates the employee.
4. Automate manual, mundane process steps.

EXTENT OF AUTOMATION

As *automation* is the current mantra in business management processes, these contradictions and solutions will help in automating some of the business processes in your project:

A. The scope is too large to automate the process.

1. Change the parameters that affect automation capability, such as input formats, tools, software, and so on.
2. Instead of identifying the process steps that can be automated, identify the process steps that cannot be automated, change the parameters, and make them automatable.
3. If automating the entire process is hard, try to automate the 20 percent of the process that contributes 80 percent of the total effort.

B. The extent of automation has started to put pressure on stakeholders from operations. who are insecure and scared that they might lose their jobs due to automation. Without the support of the stakeholders it is impossible to automate the processes.

1. Let the stakeholders from operations drive the automation initiative.
2. Reward the resources who identify opportunities to automate.

3. Help the team understand that if not them, someone else will automate the process.
4. Train the team on the automation tools and techniques.
5. Move the resources who are good with automation skills from operations to a role on the automation team.

C. Automating a process requires process reengineering to be done at process, resource, system, and organization levels.

1. Identify the resources who are quick learners and can be moved across the process.
2. Automate one process or activity at a time.
3. Split the process into parts, automate the small process steps, and integrate the output.
4. Make changes to the output generated by the manual process steps that are feasible for automation.
5. If the process is still not automatable, break down the process steps further.
6. Change the input formats. Use color coding to make the automation process simpler.
7. Ask every resource to design the solution or ideas to automate the process steps that he or she is responsible for.

D. Though automation has increased the durability of the outputs and deliverables the scope for automation is decreasing.

1. Anticipate all the process changes that might occur in the near future and make the automation capable of adapting to such changes.
2. Identify the possible changes that will affect the automation, and set budget aside to implement the changes in future.

5. Though automation saves cost in the long run, the initial investment of effort and money is high.

   1. Automate only the processes and process steps that require automation, that is, the process step is complex, has a long lead time, and provides return on investment more quickly.

2. Identify similar processes or process steps where one solution can be replicated.
3. Modify the process inputs and outputs to use an automated solution that is already available.
4. Can a change to the sequence of the process steps make the process automatable?

E. Though automation has helped in increasing productivity, there is a lot of manual effort wasted.

1. Implement *pull* in the process.
2. Stop batch processing and implement single-piece flow.
3. Make sure the resources in the downstream process are ready to process the outputs coming from the automated system.
4. Create a feedback loop between the manual process steps and automated process steps.
5. Remove the process steps where information or a substance has to be manually moved.
6. Remove the automation from the process steps if it is causing more troube than gains.

F. Though automation has helped in increasing productivity, it has made the resources unable to use their skills and expertise. If there is a need to perform the work manually in future, the resources might not be able to do so.

1. Find a different role for the expert skilled resources where they can enhance or learn new skills before automating the process. (Prior action)
2. Periodically (say, once a week) have a non-automation day where everything is done manually. (Vibration)
3. Document all the process steps in the form of standard operating procedures. (Property)
4. Partner with suppliers or customers where the resources and their skills can be utilized.

G. Automated process steps do not observe and capture information as a human being can. Hence, a lot of information is lost.

1. Identify the information that has to be captured and implement its collection in the automation system.

2. Is there a source where the information is already captured or can be taken from (Google) and used in the process?

H. There is a lot of wait time between the automated and manual process steps, hence there is no reduction in cycle time.

1. Have an expediter who can act like a bridge between the process steps and expedite the process.

2. Replace or retrain resources with slower processing speed.

3. Slow down the automated systems to match the speed of the manual process so that there is not much inventory accumulation between process steps.

4. Increase the number of manual resources.

5. Make the resources work very closely with the automated systems so that they are completely aware of the status of the sequence.

I. Though the first-pass yield has increased through automation, there is a lot of "work in progress inventory" between process steps.

1. Implement single-piece flow.

2. Add a delay to the lead time of faster-processing systems.

3. Program the automated systems to produce based on the inventory between the process steps.

J. Though automation has helped in reducing cost, it is not reliable.

1. Add buffer to the output (time, defects, and so on) before committing anything to the customer.

2. Hire low-cost resources who can get the service back on track manually.

3. Track the performance of each system, measure the KPIs, and identify the areas with low reliability and fix them.

4. Use control charts and run charts to find out if there is any trend.

K. Though automating the process has many advantages, it is high risk.

1. Identify the risks of automating the process steps and find a mitigation or avoidance plan.
2. Check whether the risk triggers can be automated.
3. Can automation be used to mitigate the risk?
4. Can automation be used to take action if the risk occurs?

L. It is hard to repair the outputs between the operations if the process is automated.

1. Break the automation process into stages, and provide gaps between the processes to take any corrective action.
2. Control the automation system based on the scenario, slow down the processes that are hard to fix, and check them often.
3. Automate the process of quality control and repair.

M. It is hard to automate a system that is suitable and adaptable for numerous scenarios.

1. Hire low-cost resources to manually perform the process steps where the volume or effort required is less.
2. Automate the process steps that are common and have a very high volume.
3. Break the process into scenarios and automate the longest path.
4. Make all the transactions flow through the automated system, and make changes to the output for the ones required.

JOURNEY THROUGH EUROPE

We stayed in Georgia for a month working in the vineyards, worked in the raspberry fields of Kyrgyzstan and olive fields in Greece, were invited to give a TEDx talk in Armenia, consulted many public-sector firms like the municipality of Iran and the European Union co-funding agencies' project managers, learned to make pizza in Naples, Italy, visited many universities in Europe to train students on TRIZ, and slept in churches, mosques, Buddhist temples, police stations, and even a hospital.

The 500 days on the road was all about seeking adventure by going to unknown places and solving problems many times each day. Today, standing on the shores of the Atlantic in Portugal, with America thousands of miles away, the mind again wants to return to the unknown, seek more adventure, solve more problems, and be more creative.

By the end of 500 days, we traveled more than 30,000 km through 21 countries on a budget of less than $5 a day including the visa fee and the initial flight tickets, stayed with 139 unknown families, hitchhiked with more than 200 truck drivers and strangers, met thousands of wonderful helpful souls, and created memories worth a lifetime.

Appendix C
ARIZ Flow

Use this ARIZ flowchart (starting on page 224) for problem solving. Once you have identified the problem, formulate the mini problem (step 1.1) and follow the steps shown in the flowchart. Refer to Chapter 11, ARIZ: Algorithm for Inventive Problem Solving, if you get stuck.

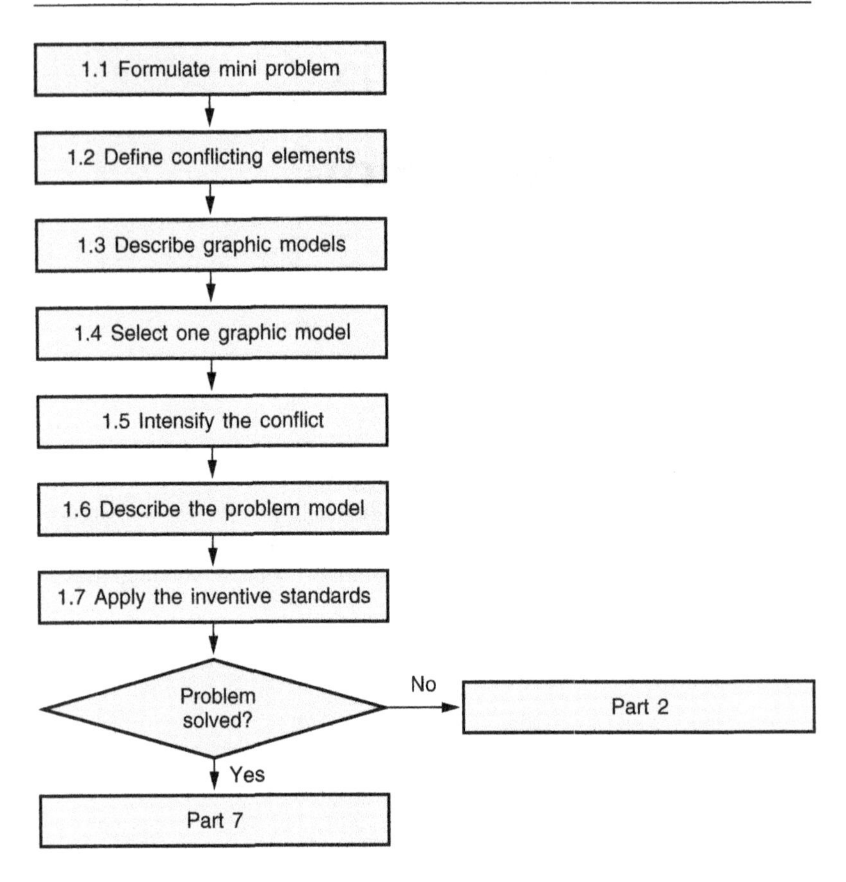
1.1 Formulate mini problem
1.2 Define conflicting elements
1.3 Describe graphic models
1.4 Select one graphic model
1.5 Intensify the conflict
1.6 Describe the problem model
1.7 Apply the inventive standards
Problem solved?
No
Part 2
Yes
Part 7

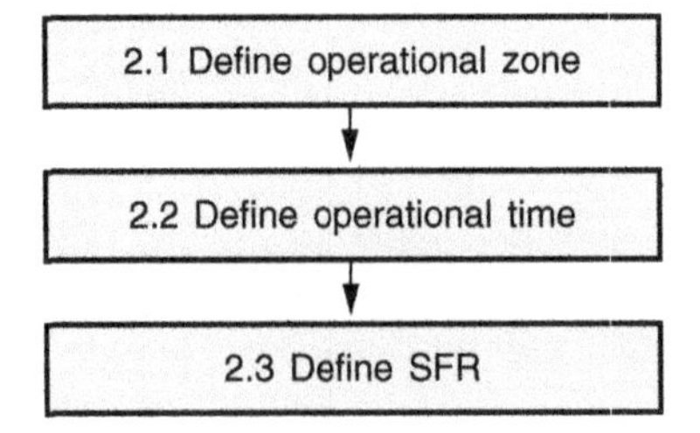
2.1 Define operational zone
2.2 Define operational time
2.3 Define SFR

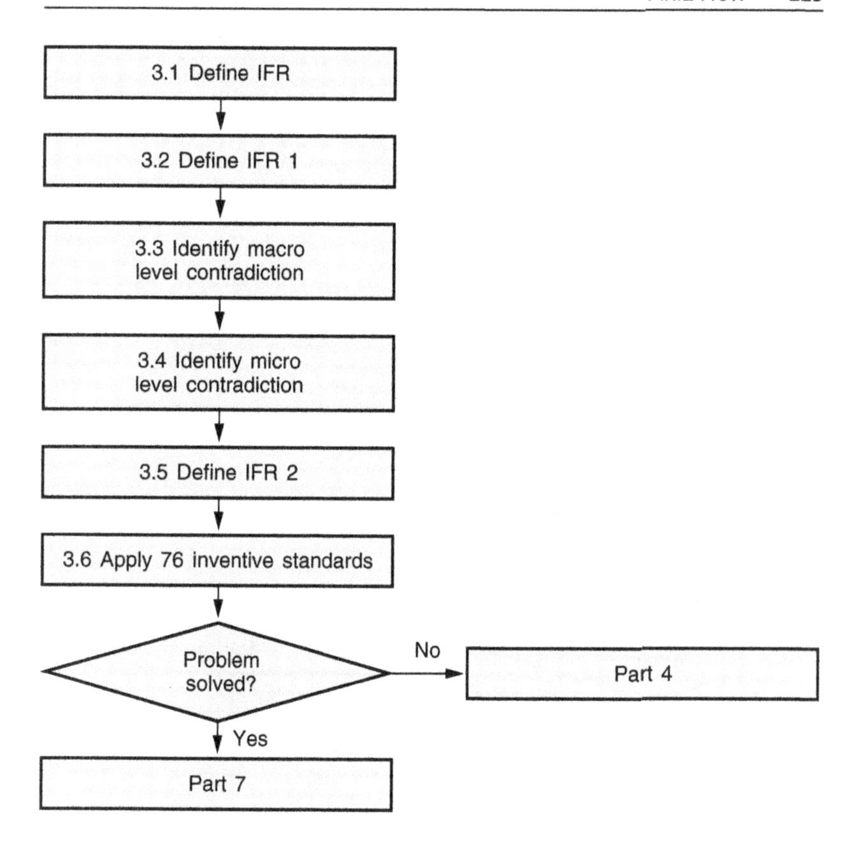
3.1 Define IFR
3.2 Define IFR 1
3.3 Identify macro level contradiction
3.4 Identify micro level contradiction
3.5 Define IFR 2
3.6 Apply 76 inventive standards
Problem solved?
No
Part 4
Yes
Part 7

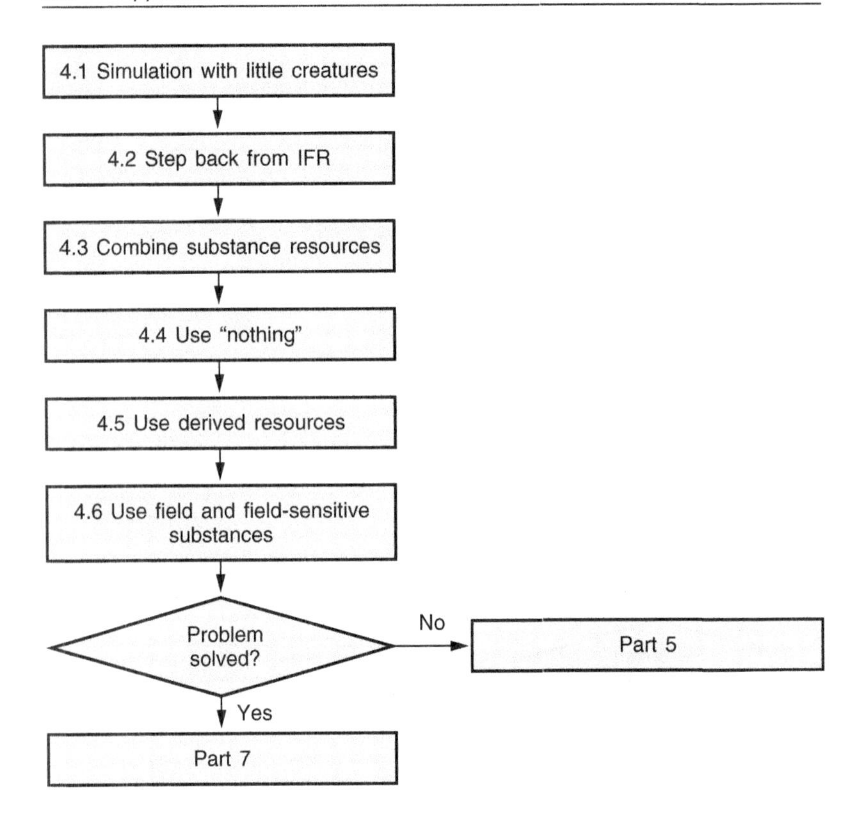
4.1 Simulation with little creatures
4.2 Step back from IFR
4.3 Combine substance resources
4.4 Use "nothing"
4.5 Use derived resources
4.6 Use field and field-sensitive substances
Problem solved?
No
Part 5
Yes
Part 7

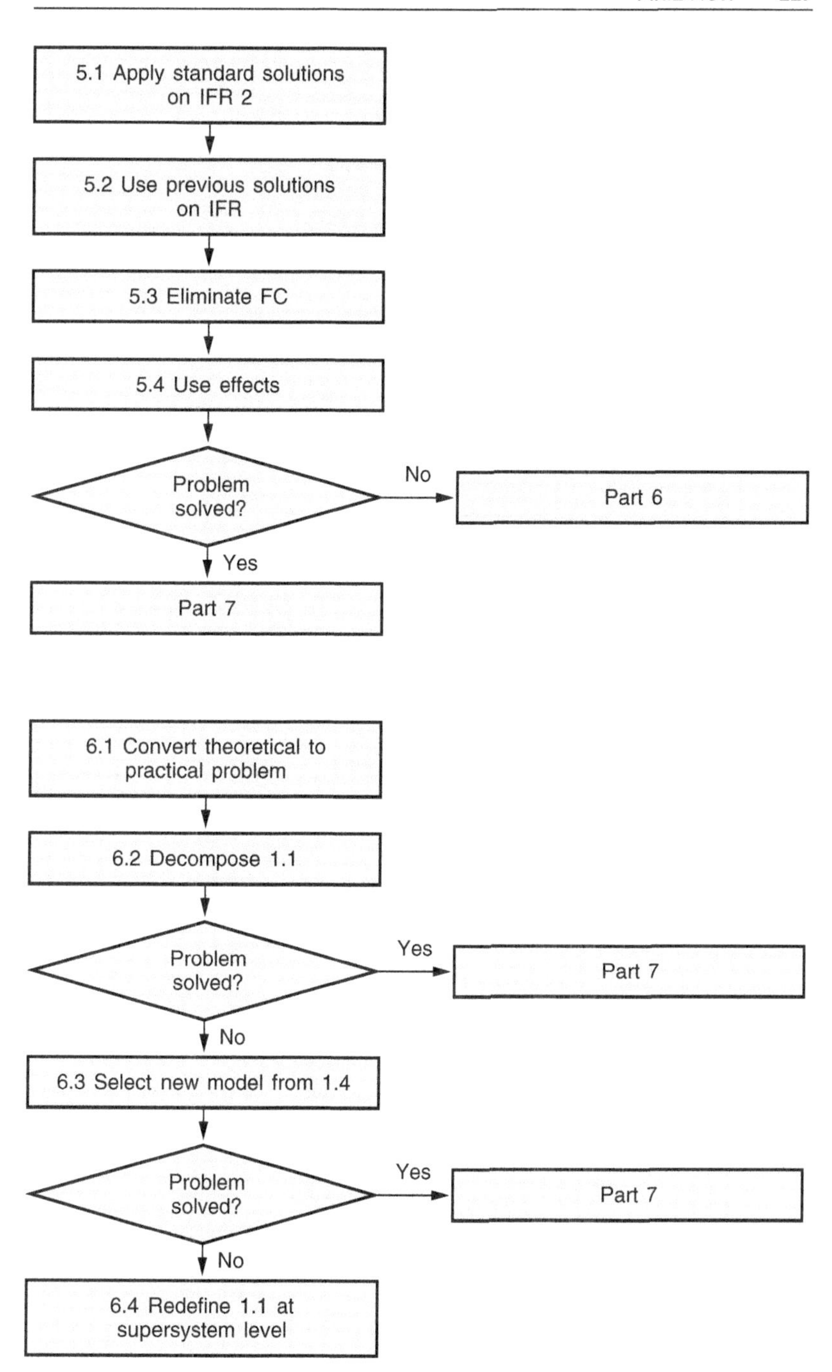
5.1 Apply standard solutions on IFR 2
5.2 Use previous solutions on IFR
5.3 Eliminate FC
5.4 Use effects
Problem solved?
No
Part 6
Yes
Part 7
6.1 Convert theoretical to practical problem
6.2 Decompose 1.1
Problem solved?
Yes
Part 7
No
6.3 Select new model from 1.4
Problem solved?
Yes
Part 7
No
6.4 Redefine 1.1 at supersystem level

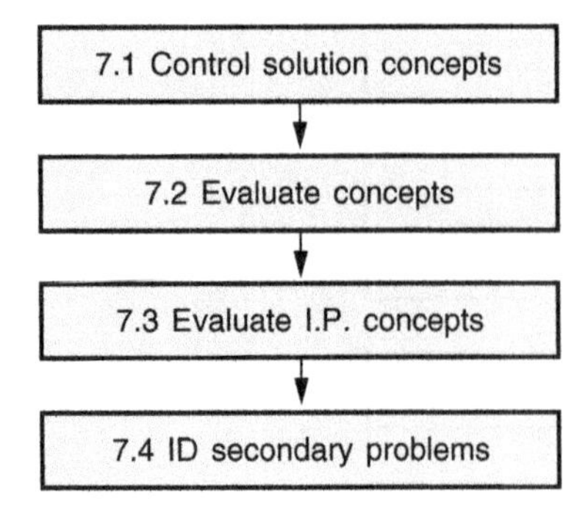
7.1 Control solution concepts
7.2 Evaluate concepts
7.3 Evaluate I.P. concepts
7.4 ID secondary problems

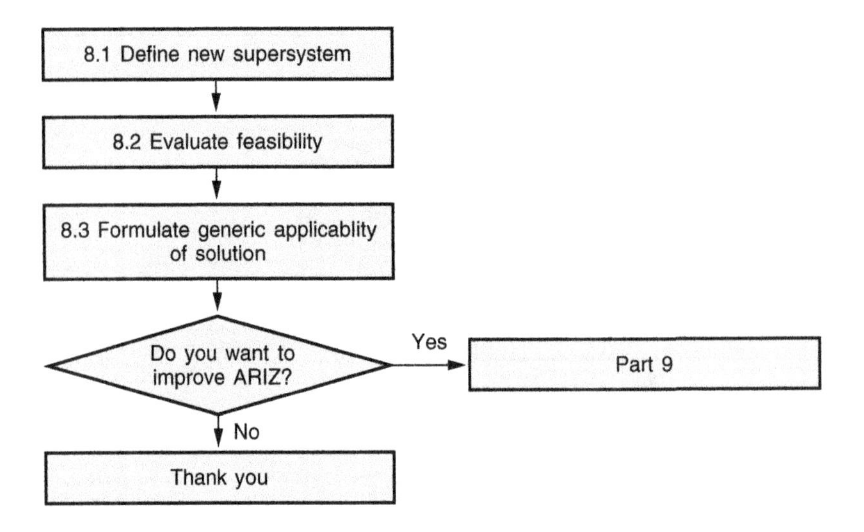
8.1 Define new supersystem
8.2 Evaluate feasibility
8.3 Formulate generic applicablity of solution
Do you want to improve ARIZ?
Yes
Part 9
No
Thank you

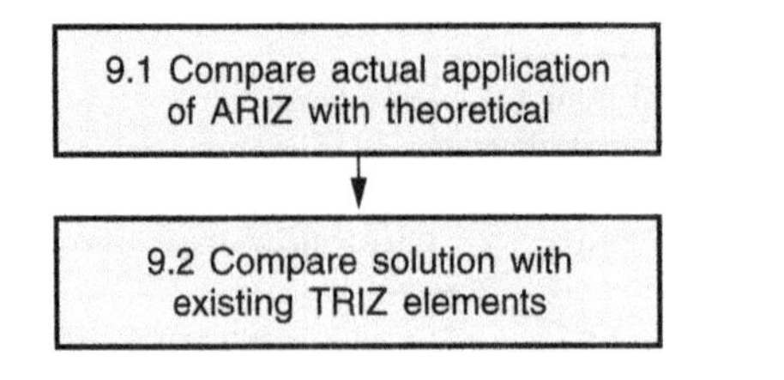
9.1 Compare actual application of ARIZ with theoretical
9.2 Compare solution with existing TRIZ elements

Bibliography

Altshuller, Genrich S. 1999. *The Innovation Algorithm: TRIZ, Systematic Innovation and Technical Creativity.* Translated, edited, and annotated by Lev Shulyak and Steven Rodman. Worcester, MA: Technical Innovation Center.

Belski, I. 2000–2006. *A Course on TRIZ.* TRIZ4U, Melbourne, Australia.

———. 2007. *Improve Your Thinking: Substance-Field Analysis.* TRIZ4U, Melbourne, Australia.

Cascini, Gaetano (University of Florence), Francesco Saverio Frillici (University of Florence), Jürgen Jantschgi (Fachhochschule Kärnten), Igor Kaikov (EIFER), and Nikolai Khomenk. 2009. "Tetris: Teaching Triz at School." TRIZ: Theory of Inventive Problem Solving—Improve Your Problem Solving Skills. European Commission, Leonardo DaVinci Programme. Available at https://issuu.com/nisargadattin/docs/tetris_-_teaching_triz_at_school.

Gersch, Kathy. 2013. "Google's Best New Innovation: Rules Around '20% Time.'" *Forbes,* August 21. Available at http://tinyurl.com/google-20-percent.

Kucharavy, Dmitry. 2006. "ARIZ: Theory and Practice." Strasbourg Cedex, France: INSA Strasbourg, Graduate School of Science and Technology. Available at http://seecore.org/d/2006m6dk.pdf.

Mather, Laura. 2015. "Four Ways of Fostering a Less-Than-Toxic Work World." *Huffington Post,* September 28. Available at http://tinyurl.com/rowe-workplace.

Miller, Joe, Ellen MacGran, and Michael Slocum. 1998. "The 39 Features of Altshuller's Contradiction Matrix." *TRIZ Journal.* November. Available at https://triz-journal.com/39-features-altshullers-contradiction-matrix/.

Mishra, Umakant. 2013. "Simplifying TRIZ Inventive Standards." Parts 1 to 5. Available at https://papers.ssrn.com/sol3/papers.cfm?abstract_id=2337692.

Pink, Daniel. 2009. "The Puzzle of Motivation" presentation. TED Talks. July. Available at http://tinyurl.com/ted-talk-dan-pink.

Scanlan, James. n.d. "TRIZ: 40 Design Principles." School of Engineering Sciences, University of Southampton. Available at https://www.southampton.ac.uk/~jps7/Lecture%20notes/TRIZ%2040%20Principles.pdf.

Sinek, Simon. 2011. *Start with Why: How Great Leaders Inspire Everyone to Take Action.* New York: Portfolio.

Souchkov, Valeri V. 2015. "Typical Patterns of Business Model Innovation." *Innovator—The Journal of the Europian TRIZ Association.* Special issue "Collection of Papers of 15th International TRIZ Future Conference—Global Structured Innovation." October 26–29.

Souchkov, Valeri, and J. P. Roxas. 2016. "A System of Standard Inventive Solution Patterns for Business and Management Problems." *Journal of the European TRIZ Association.* Special issue "Proceedings of the 12th International Conference TRIZfest 2016." Beijing, People's Republic of China, July 28–30.

Terninko, John, Ellen Domb, and Joe Miller. (n.d.). "The Seventy-Six Standard Solutions, with Examples." Section One. Accessed at http://www.metodolog.ru/triz-journal/archives/2000/02/g/article7_02-2000.PDF.

About the Author

Sunil Kumar V. Kaushik is an innovator, author, and consultant from Bangalore, India, with more than a decade of experience in TRIZ and Six Sigma. He has worked and consulted with Fortune 100 companies like IBM, GE Aviation, Emerson Electric, and Boehringer Ingelheim, and public-sector agencies like the European Union co-funding agencies, the Municipality of Iran, and many universities around the world, along with publishing numerous white papers. He holds a Master's degree in nuclear physics along with many professional certifications. An ASQ member and Influential Voice of Quality, Kaushik is also an ASQ-certified Six Sigma Black Belt and TEDx speaker. In 2016, he bicycled around the world to promote sustainable quality. He still continues to provide free custom workshops and courses on TRIZ, and can be reached at sunilkaushik15@gmail.com. You can learn more about the author's work on quality at www.Trainntrot.com, and follow his travels at www.SushiandSambar.com or on his Facebook page Sushi and Sambar.

Index

L

M

N

O

P

T

U

V

W

Z